THE CUTTING EDGE:

Women and the Pit Strike

edited by
VICKY SEDDON

LAWRENCE & WISHART
LONDON

Lawrence & Wishart Limited
39 Museum Street
London WC1A 1LQ

First published 1986

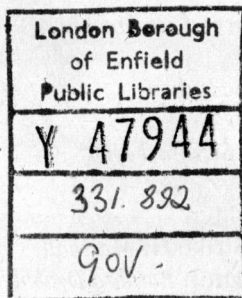

Photoset in North Wales by
Derek Doyle & Associates, Mold, Clwyd
Printed in Great Britain by
Oxford University Press

Contents

Illustrations

Acknowledgements

I talked to many women in preparing this book; all of these conversations were a pleasure, some of them deeply moving. I thank you all. Where writing contained here is the result of such a collaboration this is indicated at the end of the piece in question.

Ann Bresnihan helped me choose the photographs. My thanks also go to the people who gave me technical assistance, transcribing and typing: Jean Horton, Liz Mackey, Viv Mallinder, Duran Seddon. You made the work easier.

My colleagues and friends were very patient with me when I whittled on about producing this. They deserve my thanks.

Introduction   *Vicky Seddon*

Vicky Seddon works at Sheffield City
Polytechnic and is very active in her union,
NATFHE. A socialist and a feminist, she has
been involved particularly in women's politics
over a number of years. She has written in
Marxism Today about violence against women
and sexual harassment. She is currently
concerned with the position of women in her
own work-place, both as staff and students.

The mining industry and the organisation of its workers have a special place in labour history in Britain. 1926 is not forgotten. Neither is 1972 or 1974. But 1984-85 marks a particular watershed: a new form of organisation appeared amongst working class people. A new chapter was written in the history of struggles against industrial decisions taken without care or consideration of the people they affected: the women of the coalfields decided it was time they had a say. The threatened decisions to close pits were part of a scheme for fracturing the unity of a militant workforce. For this was no wages-and-conditions struggle, but a struggle for the existence of jobs. The women of the coalfields, noting the effect that such closures would have on *their* lives, decided to up and at 'em: they decided to get organised. They changed the nature of the conflict, and the struggle became not only of miners against the National Coal Board, union against government, but also of community against intransigence, women and men defying state power.

This book describes what women did in the strike: how they organised themselves, what activities they arranged for themselves, how they felt about it, how it affected their lives. The excitement of rallies and mass meetings, the companionship of communal meals and women's group meetings, the shouting and singing on the picket line: these are all part of women's memories of the year's struggles. But also, listening to the women, you hear the thinking, the looking beyond the slogans and the facile answers, to find an understanding of what happened. They take an 'answer', try it for size, reject it if it doesn't fit their own experience, and try the next one. Sometimes, the questions are about the tactics for challenging the state. Often, around their own unit of organisation, and its links to other bits of the organisation. Very often, it is about the men, the miners, and their relations, both as a group of women and as individual women, to the men and the NUM.

There were no questions in *their* minds about the validity of the women of their communities coming together and deciding on their own form of organisation. There were arguments about *which* activities the women should be engaged in, and how to deal with their relations with the men. Sometimes, these arguments led to highly problematic strategies, but that was only to be expected, for they were challenging communities that were very traditional in how they saw the role of women.

There have been many gains for the women: confidence in themselves, as organisers, speakers, activists. But I believe that the main gain has been that their communities have been forced to accede to them the right to gather together in public places and to organise themselves. It is a gain from which many others will flow. The fact that not all women have chosen to make use of that gain (for the women who were collectively active in supporting the miners' strike have been a minority of the women in the coalfields), does not detract from that gain: that opportunity is now available for all women to use, like the vote.

Another significant gain for some of the women in those communities, aided by the links developed with women in different types of communities or groupings, is an understanding of the network of forces that bind and constrict their lives and ideas: the Coal Board, the police, the courts, the media. Women who previously had a high regard for the fairness and objectivity of those institutions have been brought up short by their own experience of them at close quarters. They now ask questions about that 'fairness' and 'objectivity' in matters other than their own industrial dispute.

They came across the state in this 'free country' of ours in a way they had never done before. They have seen the pettiness of the social security system, and the degrading nature of the whole process of claiming. And the penalties that system puts on the wives of striking workers. They have had contact with the police and the courts, many of them for the first time, and it has been an eye-opening experience. These were not the friendly bobbies of their villages, nor the hard-but-on-the-side-of-justice coppers of the telly; they were the weapons of institutional power, playing their part in trying to break the strike. They saw the nonsense of court proceedings with a supermarket system of restrictive bail conditions and hearings where evidence that seemed to them to be clearly dishonest was used to find people guilty. It has certainly shaken their belief in 'British justice'. The women came up against state power in a very stark way; their experiences of it, and the implications, will not be forgotten.

A consideration of the case for coal as a long-term energy source has inevitably taken women into the arguments about nuclear energy, and the connections between nuclear power stations and nuclear weapons. The contact with Greenham women has helped the mining women to see those links very clearly. They have also seen the similarities between how *they* have been overpoliced, on picket lines and in their towns and villages, and how the women at Greenham are harassed by the police.

Contact with other communities has opened those women's eyes to other oppressions: of black people; of lesbians and gay men; of poverty; of the divided communities in Northern Ireland. The ideological leaps that some of the women have made are stunning: no wonder that, four months after the strike ended, many of the women feel exhausted, physically and mentally. There was no sense of relief amongst active women when the men went back to work. But they must surely need a respite, to digest what has happened, and to reflect on a changed view of the world.

A recurring joke amongst women in the coalfields is the one about the miner who says to the NUM, 'Please can I have my wife back?' Many miners have got their wives back, now that the strike is over, and the women are taking their ease a little, after the stresses and strains of the last eighteen months. The question is, are they the same wives? Certainly during the strike, the sharp differences between men and women on a variety of matters were played down, in public at least, for the sake of unity: they wanted to present a united front. But those differences cannot be shelved for ever. The woman who denounced the exposing of sexism amongst miners as alienating mining women has her head in the sand, for those struggles between women and men have surfaced, as they were bound to do once the women began to be active: they will not go away.

Many, many times I have heard women talk about their wish to be *acknowledged* for the work they did in the strike, and the role they played, not thanked. They did not do it for thanks, but they want to be recognised. The vote at the NUM national conference in July 1985 not to give associate status to the women has confirmed many of the women's suspicions: that they would be offered garlands but not the hand of partnership.

Many hundreds of thousands of women, both inside and outside the mining areas, contributed in some way to sustaining the pit strike. In this book are the stories and ideas of about thirty of them, who in one way or another played their part. Few of them are professional writers. If there are aspects of women's contributions that are not covered, it is because the variety of activities women were involved in is so great, not because I have wanted to exclude them. Not many of the women who were active in the coalfields are experienced writers, but they have all learned to talk about their activities and their involvements: many are now experienced public speakers. Much of the material in the book is the result of long conversations with mining women eager to tell their stories, to become excited again at the memories of the things they did, and how dramatic and heart-stirring and courageous it all was. And also, the bitter moments, the betrayals, the disappointments. I enjoyed talking to them immensely. The hard work came in changing those conversations into written pieces. I have tried to make a lot of space for those women to tell their stories in their own way.

This is not intended to be a complete history of the women's contribution to the strike. That would be a major task which is beyond my skills. What I have tried to do is to draw together pieces which give an indication of the variety of actions mining women were engaged in, and also the thousands and thousands of non-mining women who supported them. I have had to be firm with some of the non-mining women, to stop them using their allocated space to express their appreciation of the mining women, rather than to describe their own contribution. I told them that the book itself would be a tribute to the women of the pit villages and mining towns. So, for the women of the coalfields who might read this book, please understand that the women who have written here have done so to show their pleasure, and appreciation of your struggles. This book is for you.

Not all the women who are represented here would agree with each other, about how the strike was conducted, about the importance of the women's activities, about the future for the women's groups, about their understanding of the relations with the men. That reflects what happened in the women's groups: a cauldron of ideas, steaming and bubbling. I hope this book can be a small addition to that cooking pot.

The links, the learnings, the friendships, the excitement of organising with a sharp, urgent purpose: we have seen the flowering of the mining women. It is the fruit of the current phase of the movement for women's liberation. The message of this phase has been heard increasingly loudly over the last twenty years; it is that women are powerful, women are subversive, and that women are everywhere. In the pit strike, it was they who broke new ground, who generated an alternative welfare system, who made the ideological leaps: women were the coalfields' cutting edge.

July 1985

Women From the Valleys Turn Activist

Jane Davies and Shirley James

Jane and Shirley are miners' wives from Oakdale
in Gwent, the easternmost part of the South
Wales coalfield. They talked to me at length
about their lives before and during the strike.

Shirley has a seventeen-year-old son who is unemployed. She
described herself as having had a very humdrum life before the
strike: 'I've lived in the village all my life. My father was a
miner; he worked at Oakdale for 45 years and my grandfather
before him. My husband works there now. He did finish
working there 20 years ago, to go to the factories [local light
industry], but was made redundant twice, which is why he went
back to the pit: it was the only safe job around. So we thought,
until the strike erupted.

'I've worked most of my married life; I'm a confectioner by
trade and I work part-time in the bakery in Blackwood. I gave
up in November '84, as I was waiting to go into hospital, and
then I had more time to give to the women's group. I finished
my part-time job, but ended up with a full-time job with the
support group. I never thought about politics before the strike.
I used to go out once a week to play bingo, and we always went
out on a Saturday night, just to the local pub. Sid sings in a
choir, and sometimes I would go away with him to concerts.
Looking back, I wonder what I did to fill my time. My life
seemed full till we started the support group, and then there
weren't enough hours in every day.'

Jane is the mother of four young children. She knew Shirley
before the strike, but not particularly well. 'We would go down
the club, and meet there,' she told me. She is from Ebbw Vale
and told me jokingly that before the dispute she was a 'little
simple housewife'. Her father had encouraged her to get some
training. 'As far as he was concerned, I would get a good job. I
went to college to do a secretarial course until he found I was
spending most of the afternoons in the pub, and then I was out
of college and he took me to find a job: a secretarial job in a
solicitor's office. Most of my friends were working at Richards
Thomas and Baldwins, the steel firm, and were earning

fantastic wages. But I liked my job, though I was having £5 a week. I don't care very much how much I am paid, as long as I am happy. I worked there for seven years, both before and after I got married. Then we moved, and I was pregnant so I stopped work until the strike when I went to find another job in a factory. You would never have believed how nervous I was of that factory job, of not having the ability to do it. It was such a long time that I was stuck in the house; I could cope with the kids, great, run the house, great, but the thought of me going out to try to do a job of work petrified me. Until the first day when I saw what was involved, and then it didn't bother me. It was a twelve-week contract, initially, and they renewed it. I was laid off in April '85. I used to work shifts, so we had to find baby sitters. And not every one is happy minding four kids!'

It was the men at the lodge, the NUM branch, who first called the women together. 'In a village like this,' said Shirley 'someone has only to say there is a meeting and the word goes round. My neighbour told me the women were having a meeting about starting something to do with food distribution. It was about a fortnight into the strike. The men at the lodge had decided to start a food fund and they wanted the women to be involved, to distribute the food parcels. We didn't have to put them up, just go through the lists of names of the men entitled to it, one parcel per man, including the single men because they weren't getting anything.

'At first, because I was working, I was limited in what I could do. Anything in the afternoon, but not in the morning. At the start it was just handing out parcels. And then, when we saw it was going on, we started fund raising. We had small things like jumble sales, we had a jumble sale every fortnight. And fêtes. And we were going to rallies and meetings, and collecting money.'

Jane's involvement started a week or two later: 'I thought it was a closed shop, I didn't think just anyone could go in there. I mentioned it to my friend Brenda, and she said "Come". So I went and there were about twenty of us. Then it dropped off, for some unknown reason, and then it picked up again.' Shirley noticed something similar: 'There was a solid core, and you would get a couple who would come, then drift away, then come again. In fact, not all the women involved were miners' wives. There were some whose parents or grandparents were miners, but whose husbands weren't involved. They worked equally as hard as the miners' wives, and they weren't getting anything out of it, at least we were getting a food parcel! And if we had a jumble sale *they* could make more cakes than we could because they had more money than we had.

'To start with it didn't have a name. But we needed one, because we were doing so much fund raising that we needed a bank account so we called it the Oakdale Women's Group. We met in the Institute [Miners' Welfare Institute], where the lodge had its headquarters, and we worked hand in glove with them. We had shows there, and social evenings, anything to make money. With Sid singing we knew quite a few people who go round singing at the clubs, and they would come and do a show for expenses only. And that wasn't just local people. One singer we know lived in Cardiff, and she came down a couple of times.'

Shirley was involved from the very beginning of the dispute, though her immediate reaction on learning that the men had decided to come out was not enthusiastic: 'About two weeks before the strike they had a meeting to vote whether they were going to come out, and Sid came home and said that they had voted to come out. "What on earth do you want to strike for?" I asked. I was thinking about it from the financial point of view, though we were lucky compared to a lot of people as I had a part-time job. That was a blinkered view, and after a couple of days, after I had sat down to think about the long-term forecast for the pits, then I thought that they were right, that they should come out and everyone should stand together.

'For Sid, what was important was protecting jobs; he had been made redundant twice from the factories, and it made him think twice: if there were no pits, no one is going to have a job. He had gone back to the pit as a safe job, and then to think that that would be taken away from us as well! So we had to fight for it.'

Jane told me about her family's reaction to her being involved and how they supported her: 'My mother-in-law was very supportive, though she is not a miner's wife. She has always been involved in politics, in the Labour Party, and she thought it was great that the women were involved and active. My mother didn't pass much comment, but she had the children most of the time, she and my sister. Tony was away picketing, and every other week he was up in London, so I needed their help and they were very good to me.'

Jane told me that the men's reactions were variable. 'Some men said, "You're supporting the strike and regardless of my feelings, go and do it, at least for the duration." But other men said, "You're my wife, you should be in the house." But if the women *had* been involved, they would have found it easier to cope, instead of just being in the house and worrying about it. But you couldn't seem to get through to some of the women. Whether it was their husbands saying "No", or because it was all very different, I don't know. But if only they had come to the meetings, and just taken a small part, that would have helped.

'At first they thought we were good enough to do the food parcels, like keeping us in the kitchen. But as the women got more involved I think the men tended to look at them not just as the wife that does the cleaning and the washing, but the wife who has a brain and can use it. Which we have always had, but it hasn't been recognised.'

Shirley adds: 'The food parcels were all put up in Abertillery; we would go up there sometimes, to help put them up. They used to do approximately 5,000 a week. It was the women up there who bagged them up, and any one who would go and help. What a job going round and round putting boxes and things into bags! The lodge was very, very good. They started the group off, and they helped us with any problems.' Jane acknowledges this too: 'The lodge has been more than helpful, though there have been certain things they disapproved of. Picketing, for example. That was the only thing they said "No" to. We had decided at the beginning that we would be guided by the lodge. Not dominated, but guided: they had more experience.'

Back to Shirley: 'We did go picketing once, at the start of the strike, to the steel works at Port Talbot. That was an all-women picket. But in general we haven't been involved in that. When the strike first started the men picketed Oakdale, and then there was a token picket. But towards the end, in February and March, it was picketed when four scabs went in, and that was the first time that women had been on a picket line here. We outnumbered the men sometimes. We went down for half an hour, before they were due to come up from the day shift, or going in for the afternoon shift. You could see the taxi coming in to pick them up, and then we would watch the taxi coming out.

'We haven't had much trouble with the police here in Oakdale, because we haven't had many going back to work. They did stop one of the women: she was going on some rally. It was five o'clock in the morning and she had a pit helmet in her hand. They wanted to know where she was going. "Shopping," she said! We know that other women, especially the wives of striking miners in Nottinghamshire, had a lot of trouble, so that they couldn't go from one village to another. So we have been lucky. But the men were stopped, and of course, there was trouble on the picket lines. Towards the end we all felt, the women as well, that the more they didn't want us to do something, the more determined we were to do it. "This is our country, as well as yours, and you are not telling us what we can and what we cannot do." Especially if we were doing no wrong: like, "You cannot stand this side of the pavement, you must stand that side." It was the same when we went to London to lobby Parliament in September. I was terrified when they brought up the police horses. Everything was quiet till then. We have an Oakdale Women's Support Group banner, a white sheet and two broom handles. They wouldn't let us take it across the bridge. So we folded up the banner, one person carried one handle, another person the other, and *then* they let us across. It was very petty, because we were still carrying the broom handles!'

Both Jane and Shirley started going to London to address meetings and to argue the case for support for the miners' cause. 'We had three men stationed in Hackney Town Hall,' Shirley told me. 'Up until July they had done all the meetings, but from then on they were asking the women's support group to send women up, to do just small speeches at meetings: people in Hackney wanted to know the women and children's side of the story. They wanted to know how we were managing. I had never done any public speaking before. I had got up when Sid sang sometimes, and done a bit of singing, but it is a different thing to get up and sing, from getting up to speak. Sometimes the men would write the speech that we were going to give, and at the start of it we were so nervous that we would read what they had written. As we went along we thought, "Well, we don't like that," we would alter that and put our own little bit in. And then it became: "I don't like this at all, I'll say what *I* want to say."

'It wasn't always a public meeting, often it would be a small group meeting round a table, having a discussion, for example, a readers' and writers' group. They would ask us questions that we would never have put into a speech, because they were things that we didn't think people were interested in. I found that was much better.'

Jane found the experience very difficult: 'Terrible, terrible, I never had a night like that, the first time I ever did it. It was a meeting of about thirty, huge as far as I was concerned. It was in June. I had written down things that I wanted to say, I gave my little speech and as far as I was concerned, that was it. Someone else spoke, and then they said, "Any questions?" I thought, "I am quite safe here," they would ask the others. But I wasn't. It is not like a question and answer session round a table, it was me here and them there. I was only a little simple housewife at the time …'

Going to London, and contact with people of different backgrounds and lifestyles, and different attitudes towards family life and standards of housework has certainly made an impression on the two women. 'I learnt a lot, Shirley learnt a lot, so did Brenda, so did my kids,' said Jane. 'They have all been to London, all except the baby who was too small. For example, they met black people quite regularly: there is only one black family in our village. Shirley and I were prepared to go to London, to put up with roughing it if we had to, and to open *our* houses to other people in return. At first it was rather strange, but I found that people were no different from us.' Shirley described how she found it: 'Strange to begin with, but I am a good mixer so I didn't find it hard meeting people and making friends with people. It was an eye-opener too: *we* think more of our homes, *they* think more about having a good time. A lot of the friends we have met are never in. If you phone them, you can try a dozen times. But I think they are a lot happier for it. Mind, I don't think I could put up with the rushing around they do.

'When we have been to London, if you said you were a miner or a miner's wife you were treated like gods. That was strange too; you would think, "What's different about me?" Sometimes you would go and have three lots of accommodation offered and you would say, "I hope I am not offending you by not staying: I'll stay with you next time!" People were fantastic, opening their homes to us. We made marvellous friends, and we have still kept in contact. It is very rare, since the strike, that we don't have people down, or we go to London or Birmingham at weekends.'

These contacts have been very important to Shirley and she wants to maintain them: 'It would be terrible if we just dropped the people who helped and befriended us during the strike, now that the strike is over. It wasn't just financial help, but moral support they gave us, and sometimes that was more important than the financial help. I think a lot of barriers have been broken down, and I don't think they will ever, should ever, go back up again. We used to think that London was a long way away, but towards the end of the strike it was like going to the next town shopping: I could walk to London blindfold now.'

There had been a peace march through Oakdale early in the strike, but it was through going to Greenham that Jane and Shirley started to be interested in CND and peace issues. 'I had never been interested in CND or Greenham,' Shirley said. 'I never knew how the Hackney Greenham women got involved in supporting us, but they came down and gave us a cheque for £500. We made very good friends with Heather from that group, and we went to stay with her one day when we went to do a meeting. "Don't go back tomorrow," she said, "come to Greenham." So I phoned Sid and said, "I'm not coming home tomorrow, I'm going to Greenham."

'You hear of the Greenham women being smelly and dirty. It was a bitterly cold September day, I had my sheepskin coat on, and the first thing we saw when we got there was a woman stripped off in the bushes, washing. I thought, "Well, you are braver than me, love. There is no way I would ever wash in that cold. I would stay dirty first." So that got rid of that belief about them being dirty.

'Heather introduced us and they gave us a big box of food for the miners which we took home with us. One woman said, "This £2.31 is all I have got on me, put it into the support group fund." Whatever they had, they would share. Heather took us round the camps. They all said, "Have a cup of tea, have something to eat." We were full of tea that day. It was a nice day, cold but fine, and we walked miles round the fence. I have never seen so much barbed wire in all my life. There were soldiers on the inside walking with us. When we stopped, they stopped. There were a lot of police horses around, the police were very stand-offish.

'I think they are very dedicated women, when I think about the conditions they live under. I could go there for a visit, but I couldn't be that dedicated. They are not just doing it for themselves, they are doing it for everybody, and we are not grateful for it. Most people don't think about CND and things like that. I think it is a shame that people don't, but beforehand, I was one of those who didn't think about it.

'Heather writes to me from London. She says she is in court now for going through the fence at Greenham. They tell you incredible stories. The time we went to Greenham with her, she took this carpet. We came back that night but stayed for a long weekend. They got in that night, and then got out again. "I had to go back in," she told us, "I had left my piece of carpet. They weren't going to have my piece of carpet." So she had gone back in to get it! Another time they took a Maypole in with them, and she showed us a photograph of them dancing on top of the bunker. They were caught and she said they tried to drag them off. "We are not going without our Maypole," they said, "we have brought it in with us and we are going to take it out with us." The police treat them terribly, trying to take their fingerprints and being nasty with them.'

Shirley was very moved by the way that people who had no connection with the miners were supportive. 'People would turn round and say, "We live in a mining village, if it goes under, who the hell will worry about us?" But we have seen people who have never been to a pit village, work so hard for the NUM; to see unemployed people give you their last 10p, if that is all they had. If it came from moneyed people, they can afford it, but there is much more feeling and much more meant if it is from people who have got very little. We have been collecting outside supermarkets in London, and the kids would come and give you a tin. So it opened our eyes to the fact that there are people, in London and elsewhere, who are interested in the mining communities, who are doing their own politics, who see the importance of this struggle, because if they could break the NUM they could break any union.'

Life in the support group was not without its problems. Not everyone approved of how some women travelled, made contacts and brought new influences into the village: it was a kind of activism unknown in the community, and necessarily threatening to the established way of life and orderly existence. The community was, in many ways, very traditional. Jane in particular seemed very aware of this: 'We discuss things as a family, and decide whether we will do something or not. If I want to do something, and I think it is right, then I don't see any reason why I shouldn't do it, regardless of how disapproving other people might be. But not everyone here thinks like that: *you don't do it.* The group was like that, and there was a lot of jealousy around, as if someone was getting more praise or having more opportunities than others. But we were all in it together; any one of the women could have gone to London: they said their husbands wouldn't let them. Some wanted to go, for a bit of excitement and the glamour, but didn't like the idea of roughing it. Other people felt, "We don't want to go, we don't want to be associating with all sorts of people." Yet those people were helping us! That was what a lot of it stemmed from, that we made friends with the people we met and had them up to stay: all kinds of people, black people, gay people, people who lived together. We would open our home to anybody and everybody who supported us, and every weekend you would find god knows how many bodies in here, up from London. One night we had a group of young people up; there were some black kids with them. We went out to a pub, drinking. One of our lot, from Oakdale, started mouthing off. Tony took him on one side and said, "Don't do it. He is a friend of ours so keep your remarks to yourself." So it was a bit worrying, what people might be faced with.'

I asked Shirley what she thought about the tensions in the support group. 'A lot of the women aren't interested in anything that is happening outside Oakdale. During the strike the men would come and say they wanted someone to go and speak at a meeting somewhere or other. But only one or two of us were prepared to go. Once, because of a bus strike, it meant staying away Monday to Saturday. Quite a few of the women wouldn't go away for more than two days at a time. Perhaps they were nervous, but quite often I think it was their husbands as well. I think it is to do with not wanting to try new things. The community is very critical of things new and different. Personally, I don't give a hang; they can say what they like about me. But there are a lot of people who don't like other people watching them or saying things about them. If I want to stand on my head I will do it, and I couldn't care what other people think. But other people in the village aren't like that. Mind you, we have got good neighbours here. If my neighbour was ill I'd be in there like a shot, but in London you don't always know your neighbours. Some neighbours can get nosey, with twitching curtains. Not surprising, with the people who come and go to this house since the strike. We have had as many as 24 people staying at a time. We had a band down from Chats Palace in London. They had a barbeque till 3 o'clock, and camped out on a bitterly cold night.' Not quite what the village was used to!

Jane saw the influence of the media in shaping the opinions and attitudes of people in the village. For example, of the Greenham women she explained: 'People here weren't looking at what they were doing: they were *bound* to be dirty, *bound* to be sleeping with each other. So lacking in understanding! But most of that comes from the telly, they don't look further. When they saw the coverage of the miners' strike, they could see it [the distortion], but they just couldn't seem to understand it might be there in reporting other things. It is as if they were saying. "They are not doing justice to the miners' strike, but they *are* doing justice to the peace women, and to the situation in Belfast." Three of us would say, "The peace women are not like this," and there would be another ten on your back who would say, "They are, because we have seen it on the telly." '

The stresses in the group became so great at one point that the chair was removed and another woman, a long-standing Labour councillor, took over. Jane saw this as an attempt to control the group, linked with political status in the community, and the different ideas of different age groups. Neither she nor Shirley were attending the group at the time I talked to them (June '85); Shirley, because she wanted to get on with some personal things; for Jane, the reason was more connected with conflicts in the group. 'What we were accused of is nobody's business. It was made clear that you don't do it *that* way, it has to be done *this* way. We would have a good laugh about it, take it all in our stride. But all the "rebels" have dropped out.'

The two women had obviously been active in the strike in a way that was quite unlike anything that had happened to them before. I asked them what had happened to make that so, and the effect on themselves and their ideas. 'I think we had much more time to get organised this time,' said Shirley, 'because it has been the longest strike we have ever known. Every week we thought, "Just another fortnight," but it didn't deter us, we just kept on fund raising. Many of the women in the group you knew by sight, and to say "hello" to, but not well. They would come out with things like, "What are we going to do after the strike is finished?" This started to happen about half way through, so we were looking ahead. The suggestion was that we would all join the Labour Party. It is a very strong Labour stronghold; Neil Kinnock is the MP. He is not as well thought of as he was before. He sat on the fence; it's a wonder he didn't have splinters! My parents always voted Labour, I voted Labour as a matter of course, but I never thought about it. Round here you would think that people who are Communists had horns on their heads. We knew Allan at the lodge [a local Communist], but never personally, but we got on well with him in the strike, and when we went up to London we met many more Communists in Hackney and in Lewisham. Some of them came down to stay for the weekend.

'We were invited to go to the *Fête de l'Humanité* [festival of the French Communist newspaper] to run a stall, and we accepted. We would have gone anywhere and met anyone, as long as we could make money for the NUM. I had never been abroad before, but we had a great time. When we got to London we didn't know who we were going with, and the people on the coach [mainly Communists] were total strangers when we got on, but we knew them all when we got off. The Communist Party had a stall there, next to ours, to sell literature, peace badges and whisky. In fact, I think all the money they made came to us. We couldn't have managed without them, as a lot of them spoke French. We worked hard, and made quite a bit of money: about £3,000. So we made friends, and we could see just how much the Communist Party was helping the miners, much more than we thought the Labour Party was. So we began to think more about politics, and about Communist politics. We went to 'Left Alive', the *Marxism Today* festival, and we heard the discussion with the Communist Party about the strike. One day we talked it over with Allan, and Sid and I, Jane and Tony, said we wouldn't mind joining. He was over the moon. Because many Communists were working so hard for the miners, it made you stop and think: "Perhaps their politics *are* right." '

For Jane it seemed a natural step: 'There were four of us; we had talked about it before and not done anything about it, mainly because we didn't know anything about what it meant. We'd sit down and Tony would explain things to me, and we would go round and see Allan; it was also from the links we had with the CP in Hackney, especially Nina and John.'

However, being a Communist in Oakdale is not the same as being a Communist in Hackney, as Jane discovered. 'As far as some of the people here are concerned, you mention the word "Communist" and they don't want to know anything about it: if you were a Communist you were no good. But that was not my way of thinking. On the way back from Cardiff one day when we had been to a mass meeting of all the women's groups, one of the women was saying uncomplimentary things about Communists. "What do you think about Allan?" I asked. "Oh, a lovely man!" she replied. "He's a Communist!" I said. She didn't know what to say. Allan was someone she had known all her life, and she was shocked to discover his politics.'

Shirley found, too, that the political affiliation she had chosen was cause for comment: 'Not long after we joined, I was asked to speak to a meeting, a big party meeting, at the Friends Meeting House in London. I nearly died when I heard that Mick McGahey was going to be there. And when I saw how big the place was, I actually shook when I was making that speech. Afterwards, we had our photograph in the *Morning Star*, and someone on the picket line asked Sid, "Oh, I see you have joined the CP?" So that was people's reaction. Not that anything was said to me, but it was as if you were different, in the CP. It made us more aware of our attitude. The way we think is that I do my thing and you do yours, and if you do not like what I do, too bad. Before the strike started we were not so much inclined that way. But now, if some one told me not to do something I would be all the more determined to do it, and to hell with what they think. I wouldn't go out of my way to shock people, but the way I see it, it is my life. It is the type of thing in a village like this that people wouldn't mention, unless there was a reason. As far as religion and politics are concerned, I think it is people's own business what they want to do.'

I wondered, given their contact with different people from different life-styles, how they now felt about the village, their futures and their children's futures: 'I wouldn't like to leave the village,' said Shirley. 'I love to go to London to visit, but I wouldn't like to live away from the village. If Oakdale [pit] closed, no way would I move from Oakdale to go to another pit. I would like the pit to stay open for Nigel [her son] but he didn't want to go down anyway, he has always said he wouldn't want to go; and it is his life and choices.'

Jane, too would not like to move away, even back to Ebbw Vale where she came from, and even though, after ten years in Oakdale, she still feels a bit of a stranger. 'I don't particularly want my kids to go there, but if it is the only choice they've got and its the only job they can get, they'll have to go. Take the pit away and that's it. It is the basic employment round here. They are not closing Oakdale, but they don't seem to be taking people on. It was the best apprenticeship you could get.

'It's a queer sensation, going down: totally black, nothing in front of you. You can smell the damp: I wouldn't like the drip drip of water, and being stuck down there for god knows how many hours, coming up and no one there to meet you. In the cage you don't know if you are coming up or going down. I wouldn't like to work down there. If it meant me working or not working yes, I suppose I would go. But given a choice, no. But that is the way things are, we all do things we don't like. I would like to go back out to work, in a factory. But I would want to come home and leave it behind. I couldn't do with the pressure. I want something where I can come home and be another person.

'To a certain extent, the strike dominated our lives. We are still in dispute with the DHSS over our claim for Family Income Supplement. They took his wages from the last 18 months into account, even though he had had no money. We had the tribunal last week, now it all depends on another case that is going on. *We* will soon be on our feet. Like us, most of the people who were involved in the strike were in Coal Board houses, with just a few having mortgages. Now we pay two weeks every week instead of one, and for the central heating as well. So we are not out of it but things are a lot better. We managed, we lived through it, we would do it again.'

'The women's group is still meeting,' Shirley told me. 'They are involved in bringing the children down from London for a week's holiday, to try to repay people for what they have done for us. Life will never be the same again. We have made friends with so many people. I don't worry what people think like I used to. When I have finished some of the things I am doing at home, I might get a bit more done, be a bit more involved again.'

Jane summed up her feelings about the dispute: 'I was very, very sad to see them go back to work: I sat down and cried. But I would rather see them go back as they did than go back in dribs and drabs. They would never have lasted as long as they did without the women. Only three men went back to work early, and only for two days. But it will hang on them for ever. "It's only two days," I said to my husband. "No, they are scabs and that is it," he said.

'The strike has brought me out of my shell. I am not a quiet person, but I am not particularly outgoing. Now, if I thought something was wrong, or if someone needed my support, I would do it. I'm glad it happened, because we got up and shook ourselves.'

(*Written in collaboration with Vicky Seddon*)

Fife Women Stand Firm

*Suzanne Corrigan,
Cath Cunningham
and Margo Thorburn*

Dysart is on the north coast of the Firth of
Forth, and forms part of the Fife coalfield.
There are two pits in the area, Seafield and
Francis, with workshops at Cowdenbeath. The
strike was very solid in Fife; of 4,500 men, only
400 went back, and then only in January and
February 1985. In the strike there were ten
organising centres, for the men from the
different work-places didn't live in pit villages,
but were scattered over a wide area. The centres
had to be community-based rather than
pit-based. At each of the centres a women's
group developed, organising the women, fund
raising, attending rallies, putting on events for
the children. The central strike centre was at
Dysart, and the women had a co-ordinating
group there too. I talked with three women who
had been active in the Dysart centre, and on the
co-ordinating group: Margo, Suzanne and
Cath. Margo and Suzanne had originally been
active at the Sauchen Bush centre, but the group
had come to grief. Cath had been involved at
Cowdenbeath.

Margo: At the start of the strike soup kitchens were set up all
over. By the men. It was actually May before a women's group
was started in our centre, but it happened differently at
different centres. It was about June when we started the central
committee here at Dysart. Basically, that started with two
women from every centre coming to the meetings.

Cath: Cowdenbeath was one of the first ones, and that didn't
happen right away. The actual suggestion was brought up right
at the beginning of the strike. If you look at the background of
the women who were coming to the strike centre, they were not
very confident, or they weren't at the beginning of the strike, so
we put up a notice on the board: 'Do you think we should have
a women's action group?' They didn't have enough confidence
to put their names up; they felt they really *wanted* to do

Women working in the kitchen, Worsborough Bridge Miners' Welfare,
South Yorkshire, September 1984

something, but they just didn't think they had anything to offer. It took a lot of persuading to get them to put their names up, but of course once there were a few women who had done that, that sparked off all the action.

There were two events that helped the women to be enthusiastic about doing something together for the strike. The first was the women's demonstration in Edinburgh, early in the strike. It was organised by the Women's Advisory Committee of the Scottish TUC around the theme 'Victorian Values', and there were invitations to the women's action groups to go. A few of the Cowdenbeath women agreed to go, though they were not very enthusiastic. But when they got there there were costumes waiting, of the coal lasses in the Victorian era, so they were dressed up. They had a good time and they came back full of it; and then they had their photos in the papers.

The second was soon after, a women's rally in Lochgelly, Fife, called by the Fife NUM with Hillside Crescent [Scottish NUM Area headquarters]. The hall held four or five hundred people and was packed, mainly with women. Women were going to the rostrum to speak, about the groups they were organising, about the money they were raising, about the kitchens they were running, about the picketing they were doing. These were women who had never spoken in public before: the atmosphere was electric.

I think these two events really did have a tremendous effect on the women, and the whole thing just took off from there. Even so, though there were some women keen and enthusiastic, it was hard to get other women to come and involve themselves. Especially when not many of the men seemed to be encouraging the women's action groups at all. For whatever reason, they had the attitude that the women were alright helping in the strike, as long as it was 'in the kitchen' work and that sort of thing.

But apart from that attitude, they didn't see what the women *could* achieve. I think we proved during the strike that we have been able to do other things, and we have won a lot of men over to thinking the same way as we do. But it was a hard struggle and in every different area the women have been received with a different response.

Margo: At Sauchen Bush the men set up a kitchen with one or two women who were from the community centre where it was based. The meals were for anyone, striking miner or family. I ended up being really depressed because I wasn't able to do anything. I was working on school meals and couldn't go into the strike centre at dinner-time; I was backing my husband 100 per cent, but felt completely alienated from the strike. I wasn't doing a damn thing, I was contributing nothing. I thought, 'If I could just start something, just to give a wee bit of moral support ... I'll have to get in touch with somebody.' I just phoned round until I could get things started.

Cath: What put that spark into your mind? Was it because it had already been suggested, or because it was happening in other centres?

Margo: No, I didn't know what was happening elsewhere. We went to rallies and shortly after that we got you in, Suzanne. What we did if we went to anything that was organised, like a rally, and there were strange women in the back of the bus, I'd say to Marilyn, 'You have that one and I'll have this one.' That's what we did at the Miners' Gala: we did get a lot of women to come in. I wanted to start a group because (and I remember saying this to Alan, my husband) I was going through torment, there must have been hundreds more women going through it, feeling absolutely useless.

Suzanne: I remember the first day I was approached, it was at the Gala at the beginning of June. Then I started to go to meetings, and we were organising jumble sales. We suggested to some of the men that they ask their wives to come along, and when we got no response we would think, 'Oh, probably she doesn't want to.' But the next time we saw that woman we approached her, and she hadn't been told anything at all.

My husband quite likes it (my being involved), but he didn't like the things we were doing, a lot of new things. I wasn't there for meal times, and I wasn't there for such and such, and he would be left with the kids. I think it was just the newness that was strange.

Cath: I think what you found was that the men liked the women to be involved; it's alright for other men's wives to be involved, but not for their *own* particular wife. Not my husband, but there are men like that. When you think about it, they had never had to be in the house with the children before, and doing the domestic role. It was also strange for us. It was a step up for us, because we had been used to the domestic role and then this happened, and all the things *we* were getting into were new and exciting, whereas *they* had taken a backward step, because they didn't have their work-place involvement, and maybe they have had to take second place to some of the things that we wanted to do.

Margo: They are fairly proud of us, our own men backed us all the way. But they used to get a wee bit fed up. Because there were lots of things we went to at night: meetings and things like that.

Cath: Everybody was poor, you had nothing to hide, there were no barriers. If we had something that the others didn't have, we shared. I remember, because my neighbour was on strike too, and one night she didn't have anything in for her tea. Her husband was at his brother's. I remembered I had a packet of fish fingers, and I took in maybe four and a couple of sausages, just wee things that I had. We were all like that. If you had a pot of soup, you would send a wee pot to your neighbours, things like that.

When I was on maternity leave, and obviously, I just had my giro, yet I used to think I was better off then than I am now, because you seemed to watch what you were doing with your money. You were careful, and you did things that you needn't spend money on. We used to put the bairn in his pram at night, and we would go for walks in the summer time, and oh, it was really braw! Now, you'd take the car, because you are back to your old ways, and you miss out on a lot of things. When you looked across and saw the view across the sea, you'd say, 'It's lovely, that,' and you would feel as if you had really enjoyed yourself. Now everything is back in the fast lane, our style of life is back to what it was before, which I really regret.

Margo: What it has done is to stop me being ashamed of seeming poor. You know, friends will say, 'We're going out this Saturday, are you coming?' Before, I would either borrow it from the rent money and put it back next week or say, 'Oh, no, Alan's got such and such on.' But now, I say I cannot afford it this week. I'm not ashamed of saying I'm skint.

Suzanne: We shared things, and there was no embarrassment. Whereas before if you had £1 in your purse on Monday, and no way for more until Thursday, you would have worried, but never told anyone. But we had a laugh. You left your bag and your purse at home, I did that a hundred times, because I never had to take my purse anywhere, I didn't have any money any more.

Cath: I think it has brought out really how people actually live from day to day, people who are in poverty in this country. You are consistently having to rob Peter to pay Paul. We had resigned ourselves during the strike. But that after the strike's finished, we'd have to try to help a campaign to do away with poverty: long-term unemployment, for example.

During the strike we never bought any new clothes. Now that you are back you can, but if you were living on that all the time you'd never be able to buy yourself any new clothes, or shoes for the kids.

Suzanne: We were like that then, and you would get help from relations and parents, but there are people like that all the time, and cannot get that kind of help all the time. We got it for a short time. People were sympathetic because we were the families of miners, but if you turn round and say you are on the dole, who cares about them?

Margo: I think a lot of people knew we were really below poverty level; there were people who didn't agree with what was going on, but because they were friendly with us, gave to us. We found pensioners that used to come in and give £1 every week, I remember one or two in their seventies. I've not forgotten, we send them a wee bit of something now. You don't realise till you're on strike just what it is to be unemployed, or on a pension, because they have no light at the end of the tunnel.

Cath: I used to see the old man next door to us. When the ice cream man comes round, he goes out and asks for a scraping. He doesn't get the smallest cone, he just gets a wafer and the boy scrapes ice cream on to it, it's not even a scoop. He gets it for 5p instead of 10p or 20p. I get a lump in my throat when I think about it. People don't realise, because you are sitting at home, isolated from the rest of society, and you watch *Dallas* and you think everybody lives like that. There are very few programmes on the television that show you the poverty and degradation that people are living in. You go to your work, if you are lucky enough to have a job, and you come home and just watch the television: it takes away a lot of the community spirit.

Suzanne: During the summer we wanted to give the children something, because nobody was getting a holiday. We had a play scheme to keep the children out of the way. We had a lot of family days and some great laughs: we had a great summer. We'll never forget it, we'll never have that feeling that we had, a closeness, the men, the women and the kids. The men would come off the picket lines where they had been since the early hours of the morning, and they would come on the bus run with us. Normally, if you caught your man coming off the day shift and you were going out with the kids, he'd say, 'No, no, I'm away to my bed.' But even the men joined in with the sports. I've never had so many friends as we had then.

Cath: On a Tuesday, when we had the central meeting, the men from the strike committee used to come to the meeting to give a report. The strike committee was made up of officials from the pits and other delegates from the strike centres. They would come to the centre to meet every morning, and the information was taken back to the ten centres in the area. But we used to find that the men didn't take information back to the women, so it was important for us that they gave us their report.

Cath: We had a tremendous amount of help from the people of Dundee. In the '72 and '74 strikes the strike committee did a a lot of work, making contact with industrial workers, and a Dundee Relief Committee was set up. When this strike started the same thing happened. Jimmy Neilson was given responsibility for maintaining contacts with the labour movement. That often involved him in receiving money from work-places, but his responsibility was really to build links. He did a good job.

There are no pits north of Fife, so we had that whole area northwards that we could approach. The people of Dundee have always been supportive of the miners because they have seen hardships themselves: it's a working-class area. It was a churchman who was the chairperson, and a lawyer who was the secretary, and the trade unions, especially through Jimmy Torrance of the Trades Council Club, Labour Party, Communist Party, SNP, different political parties. They all organised themselves to raise funds. The women went and did meetings, and obviously you went to give a bit of politics, but at the same time your purpose was to get people off their backsides and to get some work done: to get some money for us because we were so desperate.

The link between the women who were involved in the Relief Committee and the women here was really strong. Right at the beginning, the Dundee women came down to meet us. They didn't organise separately from the men, they were part of the Relief Committee. They did a lot of hard work, and so did the men, but the women had a particular closeness because you can identify with other women. They came regularly to our meetings.

Margo: The worst time was watching the television if there'd been a picket. Orgreave was the worst one. I was terrified, I wasn't well until he came home.

Cath: A lot of people didn't have a television during the strike. I had one but I felt like putting my foot through it every night. You notice how the BBC are coming out with the pictures from Orgreave now, showing the bits that had been edited out at the time. Harry went down to Orgreave on our anniversary, and I was in a panic because Gordon was due to be born seven days later. We were at the Cowdenbeath strike centre, in the Miners' Welfare, and they had one of these massive great screens. They had just got it for the kids: they used to hire videos to keep the kids amused after dinner. We saw it on the television and you'd think that there had been a death in the family – everybody was just sitting there absolutely stunned, they couldn't believe the things they saw on the television. They were all so upset we couldn't wait until everybody got home. Men were coming home with cuts and bruises and bashes, some of them without their shoes because they had lost them running.

Margo: That's the way we looked at it, but the way the media put it over, other people looked at it differently. My boss is an out-and-out Tory, and she told me that I should be ashamed of my husband because he was at Orgreave. She said that miners were animals, only fit to work in the bowels of the earth.

Suzanne: Our men were at Orgreave. My husband says that the villagers were great; they were appalled and they sheltered the men, but you never saw any of the people on the telly. You would think they would have interviewed the locals, to see what they thought about it. He got separated from the crowd and ran into this field. A horse was coming up one way and a horse was coming up the other way so he stopped, because he knew he had had it anyway. He says, 'If I kept on running, they were going to club me, to knock the legs off me.' They just told him to get the other side of the fence, because if they arrested him one of them would have had to get off the horse and leave it there. So he was lucky.

Cath: My husband was faced with a choice of either getting clubbed about the brain or jumping down a bank, and it was quite high. I saw it on the telly the other night and Harry said, 'That's the bank I had to jump down.' It was 20 feet! Later on he was running away from the police, and there was a wee man painting the outside of his house white. Harry was running up the road and this police horse was chasing this man with a brush in his hand. It was anybody, indiscriminately.

Margo: You see the riots in South Africa now, they have started using horses. Looking at that I think, people are condemning South African police for what they are doing there, and the same people are now looking at these photographs and saying, 'That's what *our* police did to the miners.' People *are* thinking like that, I hope to God they are.

Cath: At the beginning of the strike many people thought that we could win with mass picketing, that that was the answer; it didn't matter about launching a public campaign as much as rallying the miners together. But after Orgreave it really did come home to us: the state machine has been well prepared against us. They have been planning that for years. The leadership thought we could have another Saltley Gate, but it was the workers inside at Saltley that shut the gate. We never had that, workers were afraid for their jobs. It is not that they didn't support us, but they were reluctant to risk their jobs.

We went picketing. I used to be annoyed because they had a patronising attitude: 'We don't advise the women to go.' But a lot of the women insisted, and I did go.

Margo: It was different at different strike centres. Our men wouldn't let us go. We *wanted* to go, *I* wanted to go and experience picketing. Though I must be quite honest, I wouldn't have liked to go to anything really violent. We asked at the centre one day, but they wouldn't let us.

Suzanne: We were advised not to go. It was getting bad. At Bilston Glen, even in Edinburgh, the women were getting shoved aside.

Cath: A lot of people would scorn men, they used to say, 'Oh, he's scared to go on a picket line.' Because they have to live up to this macho image. I would never say to a man that he was not up to it, because he couldn't go on a picket line. Because it is a frightening experience, although there's a lot of electricity running through the crowd when there is picketing. I've picketed at Tullis Russell which isn't a colliery but a paper mill. They were taking in scab coal during the strike, and I went up there. What angered me was that the men were just trying to speak to the drivers, in a proper manner, and the police were encouraging the drivers to drive through at a reckless speed.

There was a junction opposite the entrance, and some of the drivers were so pathetic. Rather than confront the pickets and say, 'Too bad, I'm going in,' they indicated left, and so we were unaware they were going in the gate, but they just charged right across as fast as they could go. One of our friends was nearly killed because of that.

The police didn't stop them. In fact the police turned a blind eye to many, many things. The law says that loads should be covered on roads, but uncovered coal was going in, and I think it was there to taunt us. Plus they were going in without any registration plates, and that's against the law.

We felt sorry one day for a man who was driving a lorry; he stopped and he was shaking, he was really nervous. The picket said to him, 'Look, we're on strike here, and we're asking you not to cross the picket line.' The boy said, 'Look, I'm going to lose my job if I don't go through.' He said, 'Well, you ken, we are in the middle of a big struggle here, and it is not just ourselves we are fighting for.' So the boy eventually turned back, he went in the gate and turned round on a wee turning point, and went out. Of course, we all cheered. Two minutes later the boss of the firm was back with it: he had sacked all the men and was driving all the coal in himself. So we were in a situation where we were fighting for jobs, but at the same time other men were losing theirs.

There was a picket at Lochgelly in the west of Fife. There was a period of a week when they tried to bring out the coal that had been building up. Of course it was Yule and Dodds that was transporting the coal, and it was really intimidating to see the lorry going in a high speed. They were going very, very fast, and they had mesh up on the windscreen. They'd never had any trouble like that in Fife, and so of course the mesh was like an incitement to the crowd: 'Well, if *they're* in for a fight, *we're* in for one too.'

The lorries going into Lochgelly, which is an open-cast mine, had to go through the village of Lochore. The children came out of school on strike, and threw things at the lorries. They even rolled a couple of bottle-bank containers across the road to stop the lorries. They knew exactly what they were doing. The police became so worried about the children running into the road that they changed the route. But the same thing happened again. People were walking backwards and forwards across zebra crossings to stop the lorries. They are totally mining villages, with a very strong socialist tradition.

The women were there on the picket line *en masse*, and we have big metal containers with sandwiches in them, and plastic bottles with orange juice: grub for the men and women that were down there. I had two big cannisters and two jugs of orange juice, and I was walking down the brae. The day before the policeman had said to me, 'Don't walk on the road, walk on the pavement.' This day I was walking on the pavement and he says, 'Don't walk on the pavement, walk on the grass or you'll be arrested.' So I turned round and said, 'What's it going to be tomorrow, don't walk on the grass, and the day after, don't breathe?' I probably called him a fascist or something. He pushed me and I remember falling my length. I was about to have Gordon at the time. I was seven months pregnant and I fell, and the sandwiches went all over the place. He just turned his back and walked away as if nothing had happened, contempt on his face. I'll never forget his face, and if I see him in the high street I'll spit on him, because that's how I feel about people like that.

Margo: We had the worst experience, in the centre of Sauchen Bush, of the whole of the ten centres. We had a terrible time and we were banned from the centre.

Suzanne: The two weeks of the Easter holiday it was pandemonium in that strike centre, because a lot of the men were taking their kids with them for their dinners (the women's group wasn't formed then), and the men were trying to get a game of pool in between picketing and whatever. They couldn't get it for the bairns running about everywhere, so they decided that something would have to be done. That's how the women's group was started. They are not daft, they knew the summer holidays were coming up. They wanted us for marches, to make up their numbers, and they wanted us for this, this and that. But … don't open your mouth!

Margo: Definitely, they wanted you there but on their terms. We didn't tell them how to wash dishes – though you should have seen some of the dishes they washed! It was the men who did the cooking. They didn't do food parcels, they didn't have the money. The way they looked at it, rather than have cans of beans and peas, they could have a meal. To start with it was just for the men: you could have been starving at home.

We didn't push our way into the kitchen. Now I work in school meals, I'm a good cook, we're all good cooks, and this cook was not a very good cook but the men never tried to get rid of him. We should have had a rota, and let him cook one week in four or something.

Suzanne: We ran a play scheme that summer. At the start we had been promised that if it was raining we could have the hall for organised games for the kids. But it just so happened that it was a great summer and we didn't need it. Until one day it rained. We asked if we could tidy up after the meal, and put the tables back. 'Tables back? What for?' 'For the hall, for the kids.' 'Oh, nobody asked us for the hall.' We just went home.

In Fife we got passes to take the children to the facilities:

swimming and things. We wanted to take the children out, but we would need the minibus. We could pay for the petrol, because when we made some money we kept some to take the kids out; all the rest went to the men.

Margo: They wouldn't let us use the minibus, it was always going somewhere. We had a big argument about that. It was the strike committee, they didn't want us there at all. The chairman of the strike committee said that women were only good for one thing, lying on their backs, I remember him saying it. I was furious, it was terrible. He was basically a nice guy, too, a super family man, but he was in totally the wrong position, he wasn't suited to it. In the centre, I disliked him a lot. The men at the centre, the majority, were with us, they really were; we were unlucky with this minority on the strike committee.

Suzanne: In fact they kept putting obstacles in our way. It is not as if we even tried to take over or anything like that. We had nothing to do with the men's side of it at all. All our husbands backed us, but there were only a couple on the committee that backed us. We'd ask to have a meeting with the men, and they would sit through and say, 'Oh, yes, we will try that then.' And things would be a wee bit better, but the next thing we would be back where we started.

Margo: You have no idea of the trouble we had. They really took the piss out of us as if we were incapable of doing anything. We proved them wrong and they didn't like it. They just wanted us to serve their meals and that was that.

We managed to get through the summer holidays without a lot of arguments, but the minute the children went back to school there was a big hullabaloo, we were banned. We'd all been coming to the Dysart centre anyway for some time, so we just shifted to here. We were very angry.

Suzanne: We had a girl, she was really very good, she'd four kids, and her man was picketing. She was very active and a grand speaker. But she had the heart knocked out of her.

Margo: She had been to many places, speaking, in Dundee and everywhere. She took it all personally. She just dropped out.

But after it was all banned, I don't know how many men

have said to my husband, and not just mine, 'Is Margo still involved at Dysart?' They even talked of putting up a vote of no confidence in the committee.

Suzanne: Even after the meetings when there would be a big row, you would come out and some men would say, 'You are doing a good job,' but they wouldn't stand up in front of the other men and say it. It was our men who stood up.

Margo: It was pointless in a way for them to stick up for us, because if we had a grievance it was taken to the committee and the committee would just throw it out.

Suzanne: A lot of the meetings were committee meetings, and the ordinary men didn't have a say. They didn't even get in to the meetings.

Cath: In Cowdenbeath, right from the very beginning, a couple of us thought we were going to have a big hassle. We realised what some of the men in the mining communities are like. So we made sure at the very beginning that we got our women's committee set up. We had a hell of a week, shouting and swearing at each other, men and women. But we *had* to get ourselves established, we had to make the men see.

Some of us had been involved in other areas where we had seen the men put a damper on things. We insisted, but it still wasn't perfect. Sometimes the men would come to us and say, 'Right, you women, you have overstepped the mark, you should have come and asked us first.'

The men in the mining communities don't work with women, they've never worked with women. Even some of the leading activists who have been 100 per cent in support of the women's groups have said they wouldn't actually like to work beside a woman, because they have never done it and it would be a bit of a strain.

Margo: You say you were expecting this hassle. I'll be quite honest, I always feel that, as a woman, I can handle men. I was not expecting the hassle we got. I've said it for months: we were too soft in the centre.

Every centre had some problems with the men. The women at Bow Hill had exactly the same problems with the men as we did. But those women are harder women. They told them

where to get off, and they were in that centre right to the end.
We were too nice. We didn't go in and say 'Now then,' but we
should have. We let them off lightly. Next time, we'd be in
there first, soup kitchens, the lot!

Margo: I detest the police. I work beside two policemen's wives,
and what I went through! I came home from my work at night
to get drunk. I used to bring wine in with me, and my mother
always came with the whisky on Friday night.

Cath: A lot of people hit the bottle a bit during the strike. You
sat and said, 'Well, how could they go out and buy a bottle of
whisky and then sit there, when the bairns are doing without?'
But the pressures that people were under! You didn't think
about tomorrow, you could only think about today. You've
got bills piling up at the door and there's no way you're going
to be able to pay them.

There was a tremendous burden on the woman in the house,
because she handled the finances. In a mining community the
women handle the money: he brings his pay home, that's his
responsibility finished. If money isn't being managed properly,
well, it's the woman's fault. So that was a pressure on the
woman.

Margo: I used to say that at the end of the strike, the women
should get a medal, because I felt I was the morale booster in
my house. I was the accountant, I did everything, I was the one
that had to try to get him up: he had a lot of down days. I
always felt I was the one who kept our house together. When
you wakened every morning that was what came right to my
mind. It was depressing, but you couldn't show it.

Cath: Because of the strain a lot of women must have said to
their men, 'Away back to your effing work.' Just to inflict pain
on them. And because the men equate their masculinity with
having a job, a lot of women went through big problems
during the strike, even sexual problems or whatever, because
the men were feeling down. My husband would get depressed
at times. I'd say, 'What is it?' 'Nothing, I'm alright, there is
nothing wrong with me.' But it was getting him down. I was at
work and he was watching the baby. I'm glad in a way, because
he had a relationship with the bairn, which he wouldn't have
had before; he is close to him. He can tell me *now* what he went

through, but that didn't help me at the time. I was working, I was coming home to make up to the bairn what I hadn't been able to give him during the day: I felt guilty being back at my work and should have been at home with the baby. Then I was trying to cheer *him* up as well. I was coming to Dysart, I was attending meetings; I felt as if I was bionic. A lot of women were like that during the strike.

Margo: We couldn't have done as much if our husbands hadn't been on strike, because they *had* to help out in the house.

Suzanne: Our men were totally committed as well: they were hardly ever at home anyway. We had to have the bairns down to the meetings, some Tuesday nights.

Cath: Mining women in particular have a protective attitude to their husbands; when you get married or go to stay with someone you take on the role of mother. I remember feeling outraged when my husband came back from Orgreave. I had seen how much he had developed during the strike: he was able to address meetings, a couple of hundred people and I thought he put the case across as well as anybody could have. I felt, how *dare* they treat him with such contempt, when he is struggling for all the principles we hold dear. Sometimes you so desperately needed somebody to be on your side. At work they used to say, 'You'll be glad when it's all over,' and I would feel like saying, 'No I bloody well won't.' They seemed to be writing you off before it was finished.

Suzanne: Last June my husband was arrested at Lochgelly, the same place as Cath was knocked to the ground.

Cath: There were about 170 arrests over two days, and there was absolutely no trouble. The most trouble they had was people running on the road; there was no violence.

Suzanne: My husband was taken to Cowdenbeath, and later to Dunfermline cells. He was charged with obstruction and breach of the peace. He was let out on bail, with conditions. There was a young boy of about sixteen arrested too; he was crying. He was on a YTS job at the council workshops and he was going for his wages, and just happened to be there at the time. He hadn't done anything, but they wouldn't listen.

Then in October, at the Francis pit in Dysart, he was

watching the pickets. The pickets had to stay on the main road, and he was on the grass verge, and he was arrested. It was just coming up to Christmas time, and there were a lot up in court at that time. If they had broken their bail conditions, they were getting sent away for six weeks, so rather than plead innocent, he said he was guilty. And that's when he was sacked.

It was all in the papers when he was arrested: they were full of it. Some of my neighbours cut themselves off totally from us. When they went back to work a lot of them thought he was on constant night shift because they saw him in the garden during the day. A lot of people were saying, 'I bet you're glad they're back at work, I bet you're glad its over.' That was terrible: it's not over.

Cath: We can sympathise, but we feel alienated from how they are actually living. This man has been sacked and there is no guarantee that he'll ever get another job again in his life, because he has been sacked for gross industrial misconduct. How's that going to affect a family? We're at a stage when all the support we were getting during the strike is not coming in any more on the scale it was. People are saying, 'You've not done badly, all your men are back, there's only a few who've been sacked. You should thank your lucky stars.' A lot of women have lost heart. The majority of women who come to the Tuesday night meeting now are either sacked miners' relations, wives, or daughters or friends, or the women who were involved on the central committee. It isn't really an attractive prospect, coming and sitting talking, because the men are back at work.

There are a lot of women whose husbands have gone back to work and the first thing they have done is to put in their notice for redundancy. I was listening to the breakfast television and this man was saying, 'I'm a scab, I was a scab during the strike. But I went back to work because I was trying to save my pit. I believed if I went back to work I was going to save my job. Some of those boys that call me a scab have put in for redundancy and sold their jobs.' That hurt me when I heard it, because it is true.

Margo: But there are also the scabs who went back to work saying they went back to save their pit, but they didn't, they only went back to get their redundancy. They nearly all did.

Cath: Intentions were very good at the beginning of the strike, there was this solidarity and the feeling that we were going to be there to the bitter end. I remember writing this thing, I had have never written anything in my life in the form of poetry, but when Gordon was eight weeks old I wrote this thing for him, to be put away, telling him how his father was on the picket line, fighting for his job, and we were going to keep fighting because it was for his future.

I look back and I could break my heart with what has happened since. The thing I wrote wasn't exactly optimistic, it was more defiance. The rallies and the meetings were there to lift you up. But you really knew the situation was different, you didn't want to think about it or discuss it with other people. You wanted to keep up the morale as long as possible.

Margo: Spirits were high and we were really optimistic to start with. But once the winter set in ... They started dribbling back after Christmas when the propaganda started on the television. About losing the Francis and the Seafield: they were frightened for their redundancy. They made out that they went back to save the pits; did they hell.

It was men you could never imagine would scab, men from the strike centres, men we knew. I have spoken to some women who were not involved, and they felt the way I did: we could have stayed out another year.

Suzanne: The whole of the strike we had been saying, after the strike we will have a great big party, and the kids were looking for a big party. They could not understand why we weren't feeling like a party.

Cath: Everything isn't rosy in the women's groups now. In the strike we were all saying how the women's group are going to go on and on for ever, we were never going to stop. It isn't like that. The women are tired, a lot of them are shattered, and they couldn't wait to get back to what they were.

Suzanne: They had a lot of conflict with their men. And now they have got peace. They don't want to start it up again.

Margo: I miss that involvement. I'm sure I am not alone in that, there must be women who feel like me. I joined the Labour Party in the strike, I go to their meetings, but that's not what I am looking for really. This is the first time I have been motivated to do something, and I really enjoyed it. But nobody's leading on from the strike. Maybe, once the sacked miners' situation is cleared up, one way or another we can start doing something.

Suzanne: All through the strike we kept promising one another that after the strike we'd do something. But we haven't. I think it is because it is not over, we are still fighting, we can't possibly think about anything else; we got a phone call from Sheffield: good news! [The Scottish Coal Board had agreed to a review for each sacked miner during that week.]

A couple of weeks ago we were at Lauden Tech on a women's day: women's rights, women and health. It was really good, I really enjoyed it. It was something I had never had the chance to do before.

Margo: I feel I would like to get educated a wee bit more politically, and about the trade unions. I didn't know one union from another before the strike. I do now, but there are so many of them, I don't know a fraction of them. Even to learn that, where do we go from here?

Cath: In Dysart we are going in for a big meeting to try to get men and women to come and talk about women's issues, because women's issues are for the men as well. There is no point educating just half of the population.

The strike committee is no longer there, because the men are back at work (well, the majority of them), and now it is the new sacked miners' committee that's there. We've got to try and establish a relationship between the women's committee and the men's committee all over again. It is quite hard. But this big meeting is one of our first aims.

During the strike, you felt to a certain extent that the men appreciated what you were doing, but not totally. What demonstrated to me how the men felt was the night that the Seafield miners went back to work. They didn't walk in through the gate, it's buses that actually go right into the pit. So on the Tuesday night we took a decision that we would go down and hold a banner up and cheer the men back to work, to keep their spirits high, because obviously the men were so down.

Margo: We were all feeling down, I shed buckets that night and for days, weeks after it.

Cath: All the men, their eyes were dripping going into their work, and they were banging on the windows to us and waving to us. There were only a few of us, but it demonstrated to us that we had had an impact on them.

It is a highly emotional thing that all the women have gone through, we have not just been politicised, but were actually emotionally involved, because it was for us and our community. It was a bread and butter issue, yet we were fighting for all the things you believed were right: for the community and for the future of your children. That's why when the strike was over a lot of women were relieved, but at the same time so desperately disappointed that it hadn't been an outright victory.

July 1985
(*Written in collaboration with Vicky Seddon*)

Women Against Pit Closures:

Kath Mackey

From Local Groups to National Organisation

Kath Mackey has been working with
unemployed people for six years, in community
centres in Sheffield. She is now employed by the
Employment Department of Sheffield City
Council. She was one of the founder members
of the Sheffield Women Against Pit Closures
group, and chaired it throughout the dispute.
Her husband is a steel-worker and trade union
activist, and Kath has lived in an atmosphere of
trade union and political activism for some
years. This is her account of how Sheffield's
group started and developed, and how the
national Women Against Pit Closures
movement came into being.

Women Against Pit Closures – what a mouthful! Little did we
know what that name was going to signify in the history of
women's development and struggle!

The strike was about two weeks old and nothing much was
happening in Sheffield in terms of organised support. It was
fresh in my mind about my husband Paul, a convenor and one
of the leaders of the occupation at Firth Derihon steel works. I
had experienced first-hand how the state treats workers on
strike. Their particular dispute had been about enforced
redundancies: over the previous eighteen months the
work-force had been cut in half by voluntary redundancies
with enhanced payments but the shop stewards had refused to
discuss the sale of jobs through big hand-outs.

The form of industrial action taken was to occupy the
factory, which was done successfully, and after ten weeks the
workers won. Of course, not only this single action brought
success, but by winning the political argument with workers in
factories who handled their work in other parts of the country.
During this time I had felt very strongly about involving the
womenfolk of the workers. The People's March for Jobs (1983)
was coming into Sheffield and we were expecting Margaret
Thatcher at a Chamber of Commerce reception: it was an
opportunity to link the issues together. Paul communicated my

50

views to the shop stewards' committee, but they voted against the proposal. For a number of reasons, NUM branches along with many other trade unionists had provided financial support, and the feeling of solidarity had been tremendous and obviously crucial to the outcome.

Having lived all my life in Sheffield's industrial area (I was brought up amongst the steelworks), it was horrendous to see what was happening to our steel industry and our economy. Unemployment was rife and very few prospects lay ahead for our children. It was with all these experiences combined with my own political commitment that I recognised what the NUM was embarking upon in taking on Thatcher in the fight for jobs and communities, and against unemployment.

Pat Berry and myself had been talking to Jean Miller who had explained that in Barnsley some women had set up a group to support the miners. The next morning Pat was on the phone: 'Why don't we collect food for the miners like we've done for the Greenham women?' Within an hour we'd got a plan of action – she was to contact local pits (Treeton and Brookhouse) and we would meet in the afternoon with another woman to draw up a leaflet. We decided that if we were going to collect food, we had to have dropping off points, so we spent that day and the next getting a list of about twelve dropping off points agreed, places like advice, community and unemployed centres.

We needed a leaflet, appealing for practical support: a friend did this for us. He drew images of a family, the woman looking something like a Cindy doll! We eventually changed the image of the woman, to be more lifelike. He disagreed and argued that miners' wives wore mascara and looked glamorous. We explained that it was the stereotyping of women we didn't like. It took us around two hours to think of a name. Barnsley had initially called their group Women Oppose Pit Closures, so we thought it best to work along the same lines.

We were anxious to produce the leaflet to present to the Sheffield Trades Council delegates meeting where Jean had been invited to speak, so it was an opportunity for us to explain what we were doing locally. The Trades Council initiated a broad support committee and we were eventually invited to attend meetings. This we did throughout the whole of the dispute, working within the labour and trade union movement within the city.

Only a few women were involved at this time so we agreed to
have a public meeting to encourage other women. I had had a
week's holiday and we had worked solid for six days without a
minute to spare. Everywhere we had gone Pat's three-year-old
son accompanied us, and by the end of the week he kept
saying, 'I want to see a miner.' He thought every male we came
into contact with was a miner, and would loudly ask the person
in question.

We had another leaflet and some posters produced at a
community workshop, and then we went all over Sheffield
delivering to libraries, drop-in centres, trade unions,
community centres and similar places. Things started to get
going, and we started to collect a bit of food. Of course,
because we had dropping off points, we had to organise to pick
up the food. The new leaflet which we distributed on the
special train going down to Democracy Day advertised our
public meeting in the local centre against unemployment
(Democracy Day on 6 March 1984 was a day of action in
support of local democracy, a very successful protest in
London with a march, rally, lobbying of MPs and a festival).
We did a lot of publicity for it, including the mining areas and
their strike committees; about forty women came. Mostly, they
were women interested in supporting the strike, not
predominantly women from the mining communities.
However, a few women did come from the local pits: Treeton,
Brookhouse, Dinnington. At that stage we weren't aware of the
NUM structure in relation to the area panels. We invited a
miner from Maltby to speak and inform us of the NUM's
position and the background to the strike. I was pushed into
chairing the meeting. From then on, the women met weekly.
With me back at work, Pat did a tremendous job contacting the
areas daily, and I worked evenings and weekends. More
women attended our next meeting: the response was fantastic.
Although Sheffield had historically had a few pits within its
boundary (we now have two), we are surrounded by mining
communities. The background of the women who attended
our meetings was diverse to say the least: local authority
workers, unemployed, nurses, engineers, housewives, pensioners, students, bus drivers, and also the mining women
from the villages. The atmosphere was electric. Pat contacted
the area strike committees and requested the names of women

who were beginning to be active. Not many area groups existed at this time, it was more individuals. We invited them all to our meetings and we started to make the links. Our group was still not organised in committee terms, our meetings were open to anyone. It was a tremendous job organising the picking up of food and delivering it to the areas, and eventually supporters gave money which we in turn turned into food, buying in bulk at warehouses. One of the women was requested to open a bank account to record all our finances and I continued to chair meetings, so we had a chair and a treasurer. Other women took on the jobs of picking up food, distributing leaflets, writing letters and so on.

By this time we had become aware of the NUM structure and agreed to work with the fifteen pits and two workshops within the South Yorkshire area on a rota basis. We were about five weeks into the dispute and there was a big lobby of miners at the National Executive Committee, in Sheffield at St James House, headquarters of the NUM. We heard that there would be a demonstration by some of the striking miners to lobby the NEC in support of the strike, and Pat said, 'Let's put on a few flasks of soup and a box of sandwiches for them, like we did for the steelworkers.' Then we heard that 500 miners were coming! The meeting that week decided to cater for all of them, so we did a big ring round of trade union branches, asking for money, and we spent £400 that day. Trade unionists came in all that morning, bringing money from the different factories and we spent it as it came in. We were based in the Centre Against Unemployment. A week later we heard that there was going to be a delegate meeting in the City Hall with a mass rally of miners in support of the strike, and we again said that we would put on the food. I think we must have catered for thousands of people that day. Many of the men from the local strike committees came in and helped, along with Sheffield women plus the mining lasses. It was a tremendous feeling of solidarity, meeting the miners from Scotland and Wales.

Our group continued to grow. We were working at a terrific pace in terms of organising and delivering food to communities, attending rallies and demonstrations. Various women took minutes of each meeting, and we had a packed agenda every week. The treasurer gave financial reports weekly and as the strike progressed, supporters gave money instead of food. We took a decision to distribute money in allocations of £100 on a rota basis. We always worked through the women's organisations in the areas. Our meetings were open to anyone who wished to show solidarity with the mineworkers and their families. Women from many political organisations attended. We worked on the principle that the group as a whole took decisions – and decisions were made after open discussions with the mining women. It was the mining women who were at the sharp end. It was the NUM's dispute so it was vital we worked on those guidelines. Wherever possible it was always a miner's wife and non-mining women who would speak when invites came to attend trade union and Labour Party branches, and when we eventually started to go picketing sometime in May, it was always on the basis that the majority were mining women. Although this could mean in practice organising picking up points around South Yorkshire, sometimes very early in the morning, we achieved this. For weekly meetings, a minibus would go out to the areas picking the women up. Many of the drivers were volunteers – not particularly involved in our group – but who saw this as one of their contributions to this new women's movement and to the NUM dispute. The village groups developed quickly as the women began to realise it wasn't a dispute about wages and conditions, but about jobs, the communities they lived in, and their children's future.

Groups became really organised around food, and the whole process of the fund-raising and food distribution became a full-time occupation, a way of life to some extent. Many needed help in relation to welfare benefits so advice sessions were set up in areas to help cope with the financial demands being made by gas and electricity boards. Advice centres from Sheffield organised many of these sessions. The state benefits were minimal, which is how workers are treated when in dispute. What the women did with the support was to set up an alternative welfare system. For many it had been their first contact with the 'Social', it opened their eyes, particularly with reference to unemployed people living on the dole and supplementary benefit. It was a taste of what could be the norm if the NCB were successful in their closure plan.

Rallies and demonstrations were happening each week. Because of the need to organise for any emergency or event, the group had a telephone tree; within hours we could contact groups and mobilise quickly.

One of the first rallies we attended was in Chesterfield. A community minibus was hired and we dressed it up in suffragette colours, purple and green, and put posters and stickers all over. There were balloons and ribbons, it looked fantastic. We were all very proud of how it looked. Other women from the villages were attending, but on this particular day it was the Brookhouse women in the minibus. The women wanted to travel together, so their husbands came behind in cars!

When we arrived in Chesterfield, after having parked the minibus, the women decided we should do a tour. Having taken great pains in decorating the minibus, they wanted to display it. We were greeted with cheers and waves from the miners, and eventually we walked to the assembly point carrying a quickly made-up banner (probably a bed-sheet!) that was also purple and green. Rallies became a contact point for women's groups from other areas, and the links began to take place.

A few weeks later it was the women's rally in Barnsley, a truly exhilarating and electric experience. Full credit must go to the Barnsley women who organised this in less than a fortnight. For this we organised a bus, through the TGWU with a woman driver who was also a member of our group. 10,000 women attended what was a truly moving occasion: the women's determination flowed. And all we received from the media were shots of women kissing Arthur: they didn't show the hall packed solid with women singing and chanting, women in action. It was too threatening, working class women getting organised, when we are brought up to be passive and think we have one role in life.

It was around this time when heavy picketing was taking place in Nottinghamshire. The men were being turned back at the borders, and the mass arrests had started to take place. Our weekly meeting discussed picketing. Some women were afraid and didn't want to be involved initially, however, other women did and so the meeting agreed to go picketing once a week. All the money we received went to what it was given for, practical support. To enable us to afford to go picketing we had a weekly raffle to which women donated the prizes in turn. Also, women who were working would donate to the petrol costs.

Women picketing at Thurcroft Colliery, Sheffield

Yorkshire was solid. We had already made links with the Nottinghamshire women who were a minority and they asked us for support. They were a bit more organised than we were in picketing, because their pits weren't all out, and so they had to picket their pits, whereas we didn't have to picket ours. We agreed to meet in a car park in Mansfield at four o'clock in the morning. We all set off in different cars and minibuses, with a map and a torch. We were a bit scared but quite excited. The police were stopping people from moving around and especially going into Nottinghamshire, so we were scared at every corner that we would be stopped and turned back. We were stopped by the police three times and asked where we were going. We said we were going to a conference in Brighton – there was a woman with us from London and her accent was just about right. They must have thought we were crackers, but they didn't stop us. We were to meet up in the Fine Fare car park, but when we eventually found it, there were two police cars waiting. We couldn't see any of the other women, so we set off to find the pit.

I knew the name of the colliery where we were going – Bentinck, one of the biggest pits in Nottinghamshire, where most of the men were working. We had taken posters, leaflets, NUM literature, and our intention was to speak to the miners as they went in to work. We took a decision that we didn't want to get arrested, but we wanted to speak to the miners. When we got there, we found another of our minibuses had arrived. At first, the police were alright with us, though it was an odd situation. One side of the road was Derbyshire and the other side was Nottinghamshire. The Nottingham police were really hard, but the Derbyshire police were not as bad. The official picket of six was down the pit lane, but they let six women go down too. All the other women had to stay at the top of the lane. There were about twenty of us, and some more police vans arrived. Unbeknown to us, all the women had got split up, so instead of doing a mass picket, we must have covered about twelve pits. The police must have been running around all over the place!

We managed to speak to the miners who were going in, and gave them our leaflets. Lots of them said they didn't really want to go in to work, but they had been moved from one pit to another as that pit had closed down, and they did not see it as a threat to them, as they did not think they would be next on the list. Many of them just held their heads in shame, and didn't look at us at all. Then the police inspector started to be funny with us, and he made us stand on the other side of the road. When all the working miners had gone in and the police moved on, the striking miners came up to us and said we would be more valuable if we went and picketed the big transport depot of the NCB, South Normanton Transport Depot. We set off in the car, and they showed us where it was: quite a big depot just off the motorway. We parked up the road and crossed the dual carriageway carrying our posters and things, and by this time everyone was getting into the picketing. 'What about solidarity?' we were shouting, 'What about the union?' We could see the brazier burning, and we thought it must be the pickets. But when we got there, there were twenty police minibuses, and they were just setting off to go. The superintendent came up and said, 'What the so and so are you doing here? We have been here all night and we are just off.' You could see they were all seething. Anyway, the NCB vehicles started to leave, and he made us stand on the grass and said he would arrest us if we stood on the roadway. That was very heavy policing for that early stage in the dispute. Of course we had been followed from Bentinck by police cars all the way, and as we stood outside the depot, we kept seeing cars with pickets in them driving up and down the dual carriageway, each and every one 'supervised' by a police car. They were running the police round and round. The police could see we were not going to lie down on the road with the lorries coming so fast, but they had to stop at the road junction, so we could at least try to shout and stop them. When all the lorries were out, the police began to leave. They were London police and as they went by they started to shout at us and call us prostitutes, bastards, whores, effing so and sos, and spitting at us. We swore back, which was quite naïve of us, because we could easily have been arrested.

In actual fact, this was really a key place to have picketed, but we didn't even know what we were doing, or the implication of it. Anyway, when we got back to our own transport, we found that I had a puncture, due to a six inch nail driven right into the tyre, and the minibus had something wrong with the gears. The stick had 'somehow' come out of its socket, so we were stuck for transport. We managed to change my tyre, and the other driver could move the gears up to second, so we had to try to get home in that state. The police followed us so far, until we got onto the motorway: the motorway junctions were just covered with police, and at Woodall service station we phoned the AA for the minibus and went home – and back to work. From then on, we knew we needed to know our rights on picketing.

We listened to Greenham women talk of their experiences, women solicitors were contacted to give advice, and guidelines were drawn up for the women to study in relation to their rights. It became the norm for our group to go picketing and more women eventually became involved; links with Nottinghamshire women were very strong. To picket successfully, we had to organise properly. We felt it was not safe to use telephone contact when referring to pits we were planning to picket, so we devised a contact list. Nottinghamshire women would write to a couple of us, inviting us to 'a party', and we would not divulge the name of the pit until we all met up to actually set off. This procedure was adopted for a long time, until we started to picket locally. It was very important, the women's picket. The atmosphere was very different. When on a mixed picket, the men seemed to want to defend us and some at first didn't like us being there. We would sing songs. Initially the police didn't know how to handle us, but of course it changed quickly and we were treated like the men. Eventually when we went on mixed pickets, the men would welcome our support and accepted us totally.

As we became more organised locally, we recognised the need to develop regionally and even nationally. Women in other areas were thinking likewise. A Nottinghamshire/ Derbyshire/Yorkshire co-ordinating meeting was arranged and we would attend fortnightly meetings in Chesterfield. Sometimes, women would travel to Mansfield and other areas to attend group meetings, making links, helping one another with problems, and gaining increasing confidence in their own abilities. Eventually, informal structures grew within the women's movements and regional co-ordinating groups emerged, which supported and organised on an area basis. At this regional group meeting ideas and initiatives were put forward. A national demonstration was mooted. There was a tremendous push to show nationally the women's strength and determination: the media had ignored to a large degree the growth and development of the women's groups and the crucial role they were playing in the strike, and also the number of miners on strike. One would have thought the striking miners were in a minority, not the majority!

Betty Heathfield, along with other women, initiated the first national conference at Northern College. A steering committee was elected on a temporary basis and it was agreed in principle that we should work towards a national women's organisation. A demonstration had been planned for August and it would be the work of the steering committee, in conjunction with South East Regional TUC (SERTUC), to carry out those plans. Although this meeting can't truly be said to have been totally representative, it was the first meeting in which women from different parts of the country took part: it was a beginning. At steering committee meetings the demonstration was planned to be different from the usual trade union and labour movement demos. We were aiming for a carnival atmosphere. The speakers who were to be invited should march with the women's delegation in their area. The running order for the women's contingents was actually drawn out of a hat! SERTUC took on a major role in organising the London end. An office had been allocated to the women within the NUM headquarters in Sheffield and this provided the central contact for groups. Articles went into the *Miner* requesting women's groups to register in order to collate a national list. There were problems about the office being accessible. Strict security prevailed in the headquarters and quite understandably not just anyone could walk in.

The August demonstration was magnificent, a tremendous boost to everyone. In the park where the rally was held the continual contact and dialogue with other groups was evident and the solidarity and sisterly feelings were beyond description.

The work of the steering committee then was to plan a further National Conference to elect delegates on an area basis. More women's groups had been contacted and a structure was agreed which was very similar to how the NUM works with respect to its delegates. This has continued, though some anomalies appeared. For instance, in Yorkshire, each panel (district organisation between branch and Area level) would have one delegate but this proved to be really difficult, given that one area went from Barnburgh, near Doncaster, to Manton, which is near Worksop – twenty miles, as the crow flies. It is virtually impossible for one person to work between seventeen pits and workshops on a reasonable basis in terms of meetings. Kent would have one delegate covering three pits, so it would be far easier to make contact.

Now that the strike is over and other demands are made on the women, an efficient communication system is vital. It is proposed within the draft proposals for the national women's organisation to have area committees. Although we have worked in a fairly *ad hoc* structure throughout the dispute, some form of guidelines are necessary to work to. The coming conference in August to be held in Sheffield will discuss the draft proposals and aims and objectives. The composition has always been 75 per cent mining women and 25 per cent non-mining women, and this will continue. Groups have been discussing what they want a national organisation to do: educational links with other women's struggles; the coal and community campaign; support for the victimised miners. We have talked at great lengths about the need to have a democratically elected committee. Other contentious points have been the relationship with the NUM. How much of an autonomous movement do we want? What would associate membership of the NUM mean in terms of the women's development? Of course the primary role would be for the women to continue to fight for mining communities and the environment they live in. But other aspects, like education, are also important: how we begin to understand the politics of our society and translate that understanding into practical initiatives.

Throughout the dispute, working class women have made many gains. The experience of organising, being able to put over the politics of the dispute, and gaining confidence by speaking at meetings all over Britain and abroad, taking an active role such as on the lobby of the TUC at Brighton, attending women's conferences: all this in addition to coping with family demands and personal relationships which have real implications when roles begin to change. The women now have experience of group activities and of collectively making decisions. They are also learning lessons.

Problems have been enormous and it hasn't been easy, but many aren't problems in the usual sense. They are struggles about how we work collectively on common issues in order to challenge the system we live in, and how we make changes; about how we continue to develop and address ourselves to other issues, and to challenge the role women traditionally play.

Thousands of women from mining communities are still active on issues ranging from the sacked miners to fighting for community centres. Many have become involved in local politics, though of course some women have accepted their traditional roles back, but even so they cannot have lived through the last year without learning something; and perhaps later on they will take up some activity again. Coping with huge debts and surviving financially through each week takes up most of the time.

Women Against Pit Closures will indeed go down in history. The labour movement and trade unions need to learn lessons from this initiative in the politics of Britain today, as to how we mobilise and build a broad movement against Thatcherism.

July 1985

Holding it Together:　　*Janet Hudson*
Strategies for Broad Based Work

Janet Hudson is a miner's daughter and a
member of the Communist Party. She works in
an old people's home, is a member of NUPE
and has been active in many campaigns in the
labour and progressive movements. Recently
this has included the campaign in Sheffield for a
mobile well-woman clinic to offer cervical
smear testing. As a Communist, Janet considers
that to make a decisive change in the balance of
power in this country, action on many fronts is
necessary to draw into activity the broadest
sections of people. She believes that only by
seeing the links between different kinds of
struggle, and developments in solidarity, with
wide-scale participation by very large numbers
of people can the government of Margaret
Thatcher, and the powerful interests she
represents, be checked and turned back.

When the dispute started some of us (women in the
Communist Party), started to think about what *we* could do to
support the miners, because the media has always tried to use
women to act against strikers. In the steel dispute, for instance,
we had taken soup and copies of the *Morning Star* onto the
picket lines, and there had been a good response. So we
wanted to do something similar for *this* dispute. The first idea
that was suggested was that we use the Communist Party's
women's group as a women's support group, but I
immediately said "No", that it needed to be broader; I saw the
need to work in a broad way around the dispute. The
group was actually set up under the auspices of the Trades
Council after a very good response to a report from Barnsley
on what they were doing there. I got up and congratulated the
lasses, and got very good support because I spoke from the
heart: I think the dispute affected me not only because I am a
Communist, but particularly because I am a miner's daughter.
The leaflets printed for the first meeting invited any woman
who was interested in supporting the dispute to come along.
About 50 turned up, including several miners' wives from

· Brookhouse pit, after we had made contact with the NUM
secretary there. At the next meeting there were a hundred
women. Of course Sheffield isn't a pit village, but there are 17
pits in South Yorkshire. The women who came were from very
different backgrounds, and that was what was very
encouraging about it. There were feminist women, mostly
those who were active around the Women's Employment
Forum, there were women from the Labour Party, there were
some politically unaligned women, as well as women from the
peace movement, Greenham supporters. There was a group of
Communist women, mostly with traditional life-styles, and
some other women with traditional family lives. Of the women
who were neither from mining communities nor from the
peace movement, most had connections, one way or another,
with the trade unions. We hold our meetings at SCAU
(Sheffield Centre Against Unemployment), and some unemployed women got involved. It was when the new centre was
first opened in its new premises, and it came alive and bubbled
because of the involvement with the dispute.

Throughout the dispute, there were new people joining the
group. But there has been a solid core, about half mining
women and half non-mining women, of about thirty in all.
The group immediately involved itself in collecting food, and
in the first few hectic weeks, contacted libraries and community
centres, to arrange collecting places for tins of food. But there
were the rallies too, and with the NUM headquarters being in
Sheffield you saw fantastic rallies with miners coming from all
over the country, and we arranged to use SCAU to provide
sandwiches and hot drinks. And those were tremendously
hectic days. It wasn't just providing the food that was
important, it was the contact with the miners, being able to say
to the lads, 'We support you, we are women and we support
you.' We had done a lot of hard work and we were pleased with
the outcome. The women who turned up to help were really
enthralled with all the excitement and the contact with the
miners. We gave interviews to the *Guardian*, and even at that
time it was recognised that this wasn't just a tea-and-biscuit
exercise, but something important that women were doing
that had never happened before. There was a lot of good
political discussion, especially with the older miners. Really it
was a very exciting and inspiring time for us all.

Looking back, there were three things that we tried to stick to in working in the group: firstly, that the mining women, and their understanding and wishes must take precedence; that we should work through the official trade union movement; and that we should do our utmost to keep the group together, achieving agreement about how to work.

The mining women's background and understanding was very different from that of many of the other women in the group. And we had to recognise that. We had to demystify what we were saying. 'We don't know what the hell you are talking about,' the mining women would say when we talked about the 'T&G', 'G&M' and so on. Those of us who were more experienced in the labour movement had to learn to speak in ways that they understood. Most of the women who came from the villages had no experience of political activity, and were suspicious of it. Their attitude was, 'We are not coming here to have anything to do with politics. We have just come to raise the issues about the dispute, and to raise money for food, and the kids. We don't want to know about the politics; we are raising money and supporting our men.' So that was our starting point. The mining women weren't used to the orderliness of labour movement meetings and would start talking among themselves. The meeting would break up into conversations for a while, and the business would be side-tracked, but there was nothing that could be done about it, though some of the women squirmed at not being able to process business. For it was most essential that the mining women should not be alienated from the group, and you couldn't just tell them to shut up, so we had to go along with it.

The dispute was, of course, an official NUM dispute, and supported by the trade union movement, though not always in the direction you could have wished. The mining women were very much tied up with the NUM. They looked on the NUM as leading the strike, and though you might have criticisms of what the leadership was doing, again it was important to take their views on board. The group, being officially set up by the Trades Council, had to be aware of the reaction of the trade union movement to what we were doing. And that meant looking very hard at anything which was proposed which could be labelled controversial, or critical of the NUM. In any case, the mining women wouldn't have stood for it. Working through the official trade union movement meant, in Sheffield, working through the shop stewards and their committees. That wasn't always easy either; there was a push to move away from that. Some women wanted the group to be completely autonomous – of the Trades Council, of the national Women Against Pit Closures movement, of the NUM. I was always opposed to that.

Adopting a position of always working according to the wishes and development of the mining women has meant making compromises, sometimes working in ways that I would consider reformist, particularly in opposing the different ways different women and different groupings have wanted to push the group. You tried to hold it together, without having a go at any of these groupings (mainly far-left groups), accommodating where it was possible, and welcoming good ideas. But also, where good ideas did come up, to ensure that it wasn't just the women at the centre of the group who took these on board: it was suggested that the women who had raised them should work on them. In this way the 'leadership' in the group could not be berated for failing to put that idea into practice; it became the responsibility of others in the group. Holding it together wasn't always easy; I sometimes felt we were near to losing it, to going overboard by doing things which we would have had our knuckles rapped for, and which might even have led to the disintegration of the group. Because, at the end of the day, to stay together and to grow was very important.

The miners' wives didn't go out to work, or worked part-time, and were in no shape or form trade unionists, which is very, very typical of women in mining communities. And none of them were used to meetings. So that women's group had a style all of its own. It was hard going, but we did get to know one another. On several occasions, we would celebrate someone's birthday with a cake and a bottle of wine. We've had cups of tea half-way through a meeting, and someone would make a cake: they liked baking, the mining women, and it was important that they could bring something, contribute something to the group. There was always a lot of chatting, but we always had our meeting. Eventually, as there were new people coming all the time, we decided that everyone who was new should say why she had come, and whether she was a miner's wife or daughter. And that helped people to get to know each other.

Kath emerged right from the beginning as a person with a particular role. In fact, she chaired the meetings from the word go. And being a working-class lass with an easy manner, it was quite relaxing for a lot of the women for her to be the focus. She, like me, was anxious to put the mining women's wishes first, and to make sure they had a proper say.

Of course, there were times when meetings couldn't be all hunky-dory, with an agreed consensus. When people didn't agree with something that was important the group could be uncomfortable, and sharp words were sometimes said.

In thinking about how to involve the mining women, I thought back to how we had organised in the tenants' movement. We had to be careful not to assume that the standard way of organising was appropriate, with a formal chair and minutes and so on – that could have been so off-putting. We had to ensure that the meetings were convivial for them and adopt a form that was appropriate.

The question of whether we ought to have a committee or not arose. Some of us thought that having a committee would exclude the mining women, because it was difficult for them to get into Sheffield twice a week, particularly because at that time they were busy setting up groups in the villages, as well as coming to the main Sheffield group every week. If they weren't on the committee, or there were only one or two, then the frictions which were there in the group, political differences, for example, would have been sharper on the committee and we didn't particularly want to get into that. So we were against it.

Whenever there was an invitation to speak at a meeting we always insisted that a woman from the mining communities went. It was hard for them to speak to meetings, especially large meetings, even our own meetings. Someone always went with them, but they always did the speaking. We used to say: 'It's your dispute, you can talk about it best because you are there when it is happening, with the police; it is *your* husbands and sons who are involved, not ours. We cannot talk about it in the same way as you can.' And it was fantastic to see how those women developed, how they learned to speak to audiences. So when an invitation came it was an unwritten rule that one of the mining women would go. But then there was the question of choosing a non-mining woman. Lots of the politically active

women would have liked to go. But some of them, especially
the far-left women, would have used the opportunity to put
over their own political views instead of the views of the group,
so we had to be careful who we proposed.

Sometimes, for one reason or another, there would not be
very many mining women at a particular meeting. If something
important came up then to make sure that the mining women
were happy about it we would defer the decision. Again, we
stressed that it was *their* dispute and that they must be fully
involved in the major decisions, even if it meant waiting a week
for an answer.

At various times there were attempts to hive off some of the
work of the group into separate groups, or to get the group to
take on issues which were beyond its scope. Keeping the right
balance between overall control by the group and encouraging
new initiatives was not always easy. First there was the question
of whether or not we were to have a committee. Then there was
the question of picketing.

The picketing was very important for the development of the
group, and for the mining lasses, some of whom wouldn't go
in the beginning. Gradually, they built up the confidence to
go. Some of the unemployed women who had joined the
group had more time than some of us to go picketing and they
loved it. Initially there were a couple of meetings, special
meetings, called to arrange picketing. They came back to the
group and said, 'We are going to do this and that and the
other.' They wanted to start a separate group, just to organise
the picketing, but under the name of the group. I thought it
was important to ensure that nothing was done in the name of
the group that it hadn't agreed to. So we said, 'No, the main
group makes all the decisions, whether it is about tee-shirts,
food, money or picketing.' The mining women agreed with
that, so the principle was established that on all issues the main
Wednesday group would take the decisions.

Then there was the issue of the Defence Campaign. Two
young women were brought to the group one night. They had
been coming away from a picket and started shouting at the
police, who had had them in. Now they had fines to pay and no
money to pay them with. Who was going to pay? So this was
when the idea of a Defence Campaign came up. There was
certainly a need to do some work around the trials and the

outcomes of them. Some of the women wanted a Defence Campaign under the auspices of the women's group; in fact, that we should split in two, and half work on the Defence Campaign and half continue to work on the things we were already doing. I didn't think that it was a very good idea to have a split group, and I proposed that since we already had too much to do without taking on a new responsibility, there was a need for a quite separate organisation. This should be properly set up so that it could be properly represented with lawyers and other interested people, to get it organised through the Trades Council. That would mean someone from their trade union branch sending a resolution to Trades Council, to be discussed there. They asked me if I would do that, but as it was not my idea, and in any case I wasn't sure about it, I said it was up to the people who proposed it to do that. There were several black women involved in the discussion at that time who had not previously been to the group, and the similarities between the problems of the miners and of black people with the police were raised. In the end the Defence Campaign was set up separately, and is working around the miners, particularly the victimised miners, and making the links between the harassment of black people by the state and the harassment of striking workers by the state.

Our connection with the trade union movement has been a permanent and important part of our operation. Because we were set up by the Trades Council we started off with good publicity and good contacts with the trade union movement. In those first exciting days it was to our own personal contacts in the factories and shop stewards' organisations that we turned, to raise money for the refreshments for the miners' rallies. At those rallies we made contacts with many NUM branches and branch officers, and because we were there, visible, when it was all happening, that put Women Against Pit Closures on the map as far as the mining communities were concerned. In those first days we received many donations, but one which particularly touched us was £100 from the Socialist Medical Association in Sheffield, and that made us proud that we were doing something that the labour movement in Sheffield respected.

When the Defence Campaign was discussed it was natural to suggest it should be floated through the local organisation of the trade unions, the Trades Council. And we have had tremendous support from some of the local union branches, NALGO in particular.

But that contact with the trade unions has also given us something to think about, and something to be answerable to. Some of the activities that have been suggested in the group, or the way of going about them, would have been very controversial indeed to the trade union movement. And that would have meant trouble with the Trades Council. So those links have acted as a kind of brake on some of the proposals, of keeping our work acceptable to the labour movement. We have had to be aware of that, those of us who have considered the links with the trade union movement to be of fundamental importance, in thinking about tactics.

Divisive issues have arisen, and they have had to be dealt with. Our practice of asking new people why they had wanted to come, and who they represented (if anyone), has been useful, because people have usually announced which political party or grouping they belonged to, if they belonged to any at all, so we could see who they were, and then *we* knew where *we* were. At one stage some women started to bring all their newspapers to sell at the meetings. The miners' wives had had them shoved at them at all the rallies, and got a bit fed up with it so they didn't want them in the meetings. So fairly early on was agreed that we should have nobody selling political papers, and that anyone who wanted to announce anything which was not specifically about the dispute and our work could put it on the table; there was to be no getting up to announce it. Anyone who wanted to look could do so if they wanted to. So instead of falling out about those things, we came to some kind of compromise, some way of accommodating everyone, without anyone being forced to listen to anything they didn't want to.

There were lots of occasions where we had to think on our feet about potentially divisive issues like that. Sometimes it fell to me to say things in point-blank terms, which hasn't always been easy, and makes you a bit unpopular. I know I have upset people at times. But I am quite shrewd at seeing the tactics behind what people are saying and doing. I see the tactics because I am used to working with them. And that has helped us avoid some trouble.

The decision not to sell papers included the *Morning Star*, of course. But we were at an advantage in introducing it to the mining women because there was always a lot of coverage of the dispute, and specifically about Yorkshire. Martin Jenkinson, who takes photographs for the *Morning Star*, went to Brookhouse, one of the local pits, and photographed the women's group. When they printed it in the *Morning Star*, we took the cutting to show the women, and also the coverage of the various rallies they went to. They met some of the reporters, too. Most of the women in the group knew that I, and some of the other women, were Communists; we had made it clear from the very beginning. In the main, they didn't approve of our politics, but they got to know us and I hope they learned a bit more about our views. Certainly, if there hadn't been Communist women there in the group some of the mining lasses would have been led up the garden path and into all kinds of adventurist politics. The party women didn't meet separately, which meant we weren't always pulling together. But it was very positive to adopt that way of working, of not 'fixing' things but dealing with things as they arose. Our tactics were informed by our politics, rather than our politics dictating which tactics to pursue. I think that is the correct way to work in that kind of group.

When it came to tactics the mining women wavered all the time. They still do. They were not used to assessing different suggestions of ways to do things, so found it difficult to judge if there were disagreements on the sensible thing to do. Because Kath and I had a kind of guiding role in the group we found it difficult even to miss one meeting. So much was going off all the time, and there were so many decisions to make, and ideas, such spontaneity, and on the spur of the moment you had to pull something from deep inside you as to how and why we should do it this way and not that and hope you were making the right decision. Although the responsibility for the group lay with the group itself, we felt that responsibility lie on us quite keenly, for keeping it together and seeing it progress.

One result of that is how I have been seen by the group. I know that some people have seen me as Kath's body-guard, as the person who puts the hard things in. That has been hard to take. There has been a great temptation, because you yourself knew which way the group ought to go, and because you had been given some responsibility by the group, like co-ordination or looking after the money, to keep many things in your own hands. That way you knew that they would be done properly. But of course people would then think you had too much control, that too much of it was in one woman's hands. So in the long term that was no answer: it had to be shared responsibility with people answerable to the group.

Working with miners wasn't without its problems. When we made sandwiches for the miners who attended the rallies there were some problems. They were given money for subsistence and went out and had a drink. When they came into SCAU they were beginning to be quite sexist in their remarks, which didn't surprise me because I know miners. But I didn't like it. The Scottish and Welsh lads were wonderful; with the lads where the unions were better organised it was a better atmosphere. But some of the younger lads were quite worrying.

The older men who had been active in the trade union movement for a long time respected what we were doing, and we had a lot of very good discussions. One of the great things about the dispute was the way the young lads got involved. But some problems arose over their attitudes to women, especially after they had been drinking. There was some touching and things. Some of the women, especially those with traditional life-styles, enjoyed it and didn't see anything wrong with it. They thought they could get themselves a bloke, and of course you cannot stop that kind of attraction to one another. So because of that, and because there was some rowdyism and the police were being heavy, we decided to shut up shop. Some of us were quite upset that it had to come to that, but there was nothing else to be done.

Ireland and the Troops Out Rally was another issue that was very divisive, and over which the group could well have broken up. We heard that Troops Out were organising people to attend a rally in Belfast at which Martin Galvin, the American Noraid leader banned from Northern Ireland, was due to speak. Some of the women in the group had spoken about the links between the position in Northern Ireland and the miners' strike, with the use by the state in both cases of oppressive policing and detention methods. Those links were important of course, and having made those links the question arose of the Troops Out rally, and whether someone from the group should attend in solidarity and to raise some money. The problem for me was, should we have a discussion in the group about Troops Out? How do we persuade people that although Troops Out is a separate organisation from the IRA, that the connections are there and that the Troops Out Movement effectively supports the IRA? Again we were faced with the difficulties of discussing it with women who had no idea about how front organisations work, nor of the implications of withdrawal policies for Northern Ireland, nor any inkling of the mastery of political manipulation that the IRA and Sinn Fein possess. Talking about it over their heads wasn't on either. So we had to do our best in the circumstances.

Ireland interests me and I have read quite a lot about the subject. It is a very difficult and complex situation. Many of the people on the left who sound off about it just don't appreciate the complexities. So when the question of the Troops Out demonstration in Ireland was raised I made it clear that whilst I supported the Catholic minority in its confrontation with the state and the tragedy of Bloody Sunday, I would not support the IRA, or IRA tactics, which included the Troops Out Movement. There was horror on certain people's faces, from people who saw Troops Out as some kind of organisation for progressive change in Northern Ireland. I asked who was organising the demonstration, and said that if we were to go to Northern Ireland we ought to do it through the trade union movement there. We were working for the NUM and it was to the unions we were looking for support. I said that I was very suspicious of going to and speaking at rallies for Troops Out, but I lost the argument on that one. The ideological links between state power there and here were clear; some of the mining women had never been out of Yorkshire, and a trip to Northern Ireland to speak at a rally and to raise money for the dispute was very attractive. In the end one of the women, a miner's wife from Thurcroft, said she would go with the woman who had raised it. But in the end it turned out that the woman who had arranged it all couldn't go because of the national women's rally, so this woman from Thurcroft ended up going in a car with three men she didn't know. When she came back she came up to me before the meeting started, put her arms round me and said, 'You were right, Janet. My husband's gone crackers. It was the IRA I went and supported, and I nearly got myself killed.' She had been there at the rally when the police stormed the crowd to try to arrest Martin Galvin, and they had fired rubber bullets. She had to lie on the floor with the man she had gone with on top to protect her. It frightened the life out of them both. She had been to a meeting organised by Troops Out the night before, and there had been people there from the IRA. They had made a collection and said they were going to divide it up between Troops Out and us, and would send on our part. She was there for two or three days, and when other organisations ask us to send a speaker we go to try to raise money, not just to speak. The Sheffield group never saw a penny from her trip to Northern Ireland. As I was the treasurer I kept asking the woman who supported Troops Out if the money had come, and she was always going to get on to it, but it never arrived. Of course it exposed the women who had been pressing for someone to go, and I think it was around then that some of the mining women began to realise that not everyone in the group could be trusted politically.

The woman who had been to Northern Ireland reported back to the group how frightened she had been, but although she talked to me about how wrong it was to have gone, she didn't know how to raise those criticisms in the group: it was very hard for her to do that.

It was one of the non-mining women, Caroline, who brought the idea of picketing to the group, and she did a wonderful job around it. But the way she and other women in the far-left circle in the group handled some of the arguments for picketing demonstrated the far-left's tactics. They couldn't win the support of the group as a whole as it existed, so they wanted to split it to form a new section where they thought they *could* win. They tried that with the picketing and with the Defence Campaign.

I have used the terms 'Communist' and 'far-left' to label certain women. The differences in the group certainly showed as some women opposed to other women. But the differences were actually about strategy, about the right way to proceed with that kind of group. All of us wanted to support the dispute, but we had different ideas about how best to do so. The tactics of the far-left were to use every opportunity to push the group as far as it could be pushed into supporting other

anti-state movements, to engage in the most 'revolutionary'
activity possible, even if that meant the division of the group
on political lines. Communist tactics were to support the
mining women in their development and their own struggle
around the strike, and to work at the level of their
understanding and political consciousness, trusting that that
would develop as they were engaged in activity. Our position,
trying to hold the group together and moving unitedly didn't
fit in with how the far-left women wanted to work, so it was
inevitable that there would be conflicts.

The mining women were the key to how it would be
resolved, of course. Some of them immediately rallied to the
anti-Communist position, which wasn't surprising given the
widespread ideas about reds under the beds. But we worked
with them and talked to them in a way they understood, and
every time there was a demonstration, or any help needed,
there was always Kath or Pat there to help, or me and Sheila.
We never ever asked them to associate themselves with the
Communist Party or to speak to Communist Party meetings:
we were determined not to use them. We were only going to
ask them to speak at proper trade union meetings where they
would get a lot of support. So the mining women were hearing
one thing and yet the reality was different. The whole thing
came to a head whilst Kath was in Germany.

At that time there was a sharp division within the
non-mining women into the two tendencies described above.
Whenever there was a need for someone to be chosen to
represent the group the far-left grouping would never propose
Kath but always suggest someone from their grouping. It
became as polarised as that. So I would nominate Kath,
especially when it was for something like who was to go across
to Chesterfield to co-ordinate with Betty Heathfield. I would
say, 'Well, I think Kath should go, because Kath is the central
contact person, everyone phones Kath.' And the mining
women would say, 'Yes, Kath can go, she does all the work.'
But they didn't at that time really see what was happening, so
they wouldn't have thought of nominating her themselves.
Then we would suggest one of the mining women should go as
well, to get the balance between mining and non-mining
women. I had to do it that way as Kath couldn't nominate
herself, but you felt deeply hurt that the mining women were

not standing up for her, after all the work she had done for the group, until they were encouraged to do so.

The NUM contacted Kath, saying they wanted a couple of women to go to Germany to speak to meetings and so on. They wanted Kath and a mining woman to go. So Kath rang round the groups, saying that the NUM had asked her, and that we needed the name of a mining woman, asking them to bring names to the next meeting so that we could choose. And that is what we did. But there were a lot of undercurrents at that meeting and a lot of talk later about why it was that Kath was going, with people asking what right she had to go. I was away myself around that time, on a trip to Belgium arranged by the Communist Party, so I missed at least one very stormy meeting. When I came back I was asked to chair a meeting, not a WAPC meeting, but a special meeting about starting a Defence Campaign. There was a difficult atmosphere anyway, but I must have been a bit sharp and tactless about asking the two young women about where else they had been to ask for help with raising money for their fines. I was attacked for being unsisterly, and we had a great big row then. So it was all boiling up.

At the next WAPC meeting, with Kath still away, the whole thing about who chaired that meeting and how it was handled was raised and criticised, and I was accused of having set it up, through the Communist Party. It was alleged that the party had worked out beforehand what to do about the Defence Campaign. I was very angry and let rip. I said that I thought I was being challenged because I was a Communist, and I asked a pointed question, about whenever I had used the group to push the party, 'because everyone of *you* [looking in the direction of the accusers] has pushed your politics here.' I cried and other women cried, and everyone was very upset. Then it was suggested that when Kath came back we should have a discussion about whether we ought to have a rotating chair. The mining women said they didn't want that, *they* didn't want to chair meetings. But I said we ought to put it on the agenda and discuss it. There were several other points that were agreed for the next agenda. It was a very emotional meeting, but good for the mining women to see that some of us were not the hard, manipulative characters we had been made out to be, but human beings like the rest.

When Kath came back she raised the point about chairing, saying that she was upset that it had been raised whilst she was away, and that if people hadn't wanted her to chair meetings, why hadn't they said so? There was a discussion about it, and by the time the mining women had said that *they* didn't want to take a turn at chairing and that *they* were perfectly happy to see Kath in the chair, the whole thing became a dead issue. Although it had, on the surface, been an issue about a woman in a particular role, it was also a symbol of the tensions between the opposing tactics in the group, with specific relevance because Kath, as effective co-ordinator, had had a lot of the threads of the group in her hands. It was a classic anti-leadership manoeuvre.

I think the lesson we should have learnt from that is that we should share out the work more, not have so much concentrated in one person's hands. We could have headed that confrontation off if we had been a bit sharper on our feet.

The mining women were very, very confused about it all. As I have mentioned before, they had precious little political experience between them when they first came into the group (they have a lot more now, of course!), certainly not of work in that kind of broad group. From the beginning they had made it clear that they didn't want to have anything to do with anything 'political', they were very suspicious of that and all political activists. All the time, even now when different suggestions are put forward as to how to do the same thing, they listen to what the different groupings are saying, unsure which is best. They probably all started off with the usual ideas about Communists, and wanted to steer clear when it was put to them (by people who had their own political axes to grind) that we wanted to use them. But all the time it was us, and women with ideas like ours, who insisted on the mining women being involved at every point, on *their* wishes being given precedence, on *their* speaking at meetings, on working in ways that *they* felt comfortable with. They didn't like women like Kath, who had worked so hard for the group, being attacked: they trusted and respected her, and because they didn't understand, at least initially, what was going on, reacted according to who they trusted.

I also think their husbands had something to say too. Many of their husbands were branch secretaries, or branch officers of one kind or another, who had encouraged the women to be involved. I remember, in the very beginning, the women had said things like, 'I hope you aren't using us, our husbands say you haven't got to use us.' Those lads would be well aware of what far-left tactics were, and I guess that when the divisions in the group became very sharp, they would have advised the women to stay clear, to stick to the Communist Party lasses. So gradually we have found that many of the mining women have sided with us in terms of the tactics. Also, some of the non-mining women who were unaligned, and who have swung one way and then another, have come to see very clearly why we have done certain things and that it has been our tactics that have kept the group together. That is very gratifying.

There has been a tremendous amount of warmth in the group, and there have been exciting times, exhilarating times, as well as painful occasions. It has been hard graft some of the time, but with a lot of joy too. Seeing the mining women coming on has been fantastic, and looking back, we have achieved tremendous things. First, there has been the money raised (over £75,000), and the practical things which we have done which have been important in materially sustaining the strike. We have kept the group working together, despite the difficulties. We have been influential in setting up a national network and organisation of women's groups in mining communities. We have maintained our contacts and credibility with the trade union movement without excluding any women. And, perhaps most importantly, we have demonstrated that it is possible for women to organise themselves around what could have been a very male dispute, to play a vital role in sustaining industrial action and to have a voice in matters that affect their communities.

(*Written in collaboration with Vicky Seddon*)

Grub Up for the Miners! *Sandra Taylor*
Women's Contradictory Role in the 1984-85 Miners' Strike

Sandra was born into a mining family, with both grandfathers, her father and her brothers working in the pits. She was brought up in mining villages in the Midlands and Lancashire, but broke away from tradition by going to college. She is now a community worker in North Nottinghamshire and treasurer of her local trades council. Living in Nottinghamshire during the strike was very painful as she watched the NUM torn apart. She writes about the contradictions for women, having seen both the sharp politicisation of the striking miners and the women who supported them, isolated as they were in their communities, and the desire, following the strike, to resurrect traditional personal relations.

Within a few days of the strike starting, women had undertaken a leading role in supporting and encouraging their husbands in industrial action. Their watchword was 'our husbands shall not be starved back to work'. Very quickly women who had previously had little experience of collective action and organisation had banded together in support groups, running kitchens and arranging the distribution of food parcels. This was more than mere self-preservation, for miners' wives were quick to identify with the principles behind the strike, especially the right to work and retain communities. They joined picket lines and experienced for themselves the degree of police brutality used in opposition to the right to strike, and many toured the country speaking publicly of their determination and commitment. Many will admit that the experiences of 1984-85 have revolutionised their life-style and the way they now view society. From being 'traditional' housewives, many feel that they have expanded outwards, learning and developing from their daily experience of the strike.

The most frequent phrase you will hear when talking to

miners' wives is 'I would just never have believed it' – a sentiment which sums up the full extent of the educational process which has been taking place. Many may well have started the strike thinking that the struggle was that of a fight for their husbands' jobs, but the majority now see the wider context and issues involved. Their view of the police, for example, has altered radically and they now perceive the extent to which the police are used for political ends. Their recognition of the vital role they themselves have played in the solidarity of the NUM has led many for the first time to have a positive evaluation of themselves and their potential.

By November 1984 the organisation of women throughout the coalfields was such that it warranted the establishment of the National Women's Organisation, a body committed to the fight of the NUM, but also to the strengthening and continued retention of those women's groups which had sprung up throughout the country. This body sees its role as campaigning on issues of jobs, peace, health and education, and also for the specific promotion of education for working class women.

The clarity of vision and articulation shown is a reflection of the months of learning that the strike offered. Significantly, this body, whilst totally supporting the NUM, has recognised the value in organising separately and consciously as women. In breaking away from the idea of merely servicing those 'actively' involved, not just serving tea for pickets but experiencing picket line duty, the women's support groups have developed a political style whereby active involvement and positive education go hand-in-hand to develop and support each other. This very process has led to a positive evaluation by miners' wives of their value as women.

The miners' strike was not about wages or productivity bonuses. It was not related to bargaining over the labour process within the pits. On the contrary, the strike was motivated by a strong commitment to those basic human rights to which all socialists aspire; the right to work; the right to live in a community of one's choice; the right to raise one's children with the expectation of a decent future; the right to take industrial action in defence of one's beliefs; the right to be more than a commodity to be bought or discarded at whim; the right to demand an energy policy which does not confront the world with the possibilities of nuclear holocaust, and which is based on need rather than profit. These issues are not 'owned' merely by miners, they effect us all, and women in mining communities were quick to identify with them.

Ten years ago, or even five, it would have been difficult to imagine that a body of workers would choose to take industrial action on such issues. Yet 1984-85 saw miners and their wives undertake and withstand the longest and most bitterly contested strike this century. Never has a *wages* strike elicited such commitment and determination and never has a *wages* strike won the enduring support of women in such a way as the 1984-85 strike. This is no coincidence, for those human rights on which the strike was based have as much, if not more, significance for women as they do for the miners themselves. It would be unrealistic not to expect deep contradictions within such a strike, for at its very core it challenged the ideological hegemony on which capitalist society is based, and that is why the government used every available tactic to defeat it. The contradictions are many: issues of democracy, attitudes to violence, relations between the organised and unorganised labour movement, etc. Within the NUM there has been evidence, both amongst officials and the rank and file, of different levels of awareness of how pertinent the strike is. Some miners saw the strike as based narrowly on the issue of pit closures, whilst others acknowledge its wider aspects. It is within these divergent views of the strike and wider social issues that some of the contradictions that face miners' wives can be found.

The formation of the National Women's Organisation and the recognition of the value of women organising separately from men accepts implicitly that women can and do have a specific role to play in the political arena. Whilst engaged in a campaign of support for the miners' fight for jobs, miners' wives began to identify the extent to which they, as women, are oppressed and exploited. A frequent comment of women activists during the strike was 'I can never go back to what I was. You know ... behind the kitchen sink.' Many wives are now stunned by what they call the profound boredom of their lives before the strike. Their commitment to the strike forced them to undertake duties which previously they would never have dreamt of attempting. The miners' wives I know were terrified about addressing trade unionists many miles from their homes, but having forced themselves to do it they enjoyed the experience and found rewards in the admiration and respect which they won. Their confidence strengthened and blossomed on the basis of such experiences, and they have been encouraged to express themselves in a wide range of ways. They have written poetry which has been published nationally. They have visited the Greenham women and recognised the common bond of sisterhood in struggle. They have made new and valued friends amongst women in the wider labour and feminist movements. These and other experiences have opened up hitherto unimagined horizons.

Towards the end of the strike some of those women who had been most actively involved talked openly of their fears about the difficulties to be faced on the return to 'normality'. Some felt that life could never be the same and that whatever happened to the pits their own lives, as women, would have to be different. This strength is both an asset and a challenge to mining communities. It is an asset that women, many of whom were previously passive and only involved in living in the private sphere of home life, have become organised and are striving for a political forum in which they can have a voice. It is a challenge in as much as the mining industry is almost exclusively male and contains large sections who have failed to see the wider issues contained in the strike. These sections have had a tendency to view debates on the role of women in the labour movement as esoteric and diversionary. Before the strike there had been examples of an antagonism between some sections of the NUM and the women's movement, most notably over the 'pin-ups' in a NUM Area paper, the *Yorkshire Miner*. At times it has appeared that women have no right to express an opinion contrary to that of male trade unionists. These same men have rather pursued the image of women as wives and home-makers, creatures who should keep clear of the harsh world of politics and work. Some women who have played an active role in the miners' strike may no longer be prepared to accept this role, and only time will tell whether or not this leads to changes in the attitudes of miners as a whole, or whether it leads to tension and antagonisms between men and women in mining communities.

The role of miners' wives in the 1984-85 strike was at one and the same time new and not new. It was *not new* to see working class women organising in support of the interests of their menfolk and their communities. In all the major strikes in the mining industry this century miners' wives have shown solidarity and support. But the 1984-85 strike saw women take a *new* role in that they consciously organised as women. There is a recognition, by both the women themselves and in part by the NUM, that women have something specific and vital to say and need a forum to express themselves. The strike provided this for miners' wives. Possibly for the first time, miners' union leaders recognised the crucial importance of women to their own solidarity. The strike also saw many national and local NUM leaders consciously link the strike to the rights of women in our society in a way that would have been unimaginable prior to the strike.

How far these changes in attitude will persist after the strike is a significant question, and one which will only be answered by the extent to which the NUM changes in the post-strike period. It was not encouraging to see the 1985 national delegate conference of the NUM reject a proposal for affiliation by women's organisations, although support for the Chesterfield women's action group's petition, 'The People's Petition', has been positive. It is legitimate to ask whether the new horizons opened to women by the strike will be extended further and whether they will continue to have a forum for the expression of their views, or whether the return to work will bring a 'return to the kitchen sink' for miners' wives. Some women who have gained enormously in confidence and strength may well resist this and demand a new direction for their lives, even if this involves a re-evaluation of their relationship with their husbands. It would be a tragedy if such women were forced to seek fulfillment outside the communities that they have been committed to, but unless their communities change, some may do so. If women have to resort to such change, that would in itself be a defeat for the collective strength which the women have developed over the previous year. Will the NUM recognise the potential and value of women and support their development, or, with the end of the strike, will the 'man's world' image of the mining communities and industry once more prevail?

In the early months of the strike I asked a friend who had played an active role in supporting her husband on strike and in running a local support group what motivated her determination to see the miners win. She told me that her main concern was to see that there would be jobs in the future for her husband and her sons. 'What about a job for your daughter?' I asked sheepishly, and she replied with some confusion as to what I meant, ' ... well she'll have a husband and so if you like I'm fighting for his job. The main thing is to ensure that the men have jobs. Without that we're all sunk.' The traditional attitude to women's role revealed by this comment is strong within mining communities. By and large there is little attention given to daughters' future careers and the usual expectation is that they will 'get married'. Indeed it is hoped that they will not have to work. I know this from first-hand experience, for I was born and brought up in a mining family. Whilst the world of work was made very real for my brothers it was something that was never really discussed with me. The long-term consequence was that I had no plans for my own future, I merely expected that in due course I would get married and that that would be that.

The 1984-85 strike opened new possibilities for all women in mining communities; it provided a vision of a different role, one which would be more fulfilling and which would arm women with confidence in finding an identity of their own. As the strike entered its eighth month I asked my friend whether she had had any further thoughts about her daughter's future. All confusion was now gone and she smiled in understanding of what I was asking. She simply said, 'She is going to have one.' How far this is typical I cannot say, nor can I possibly say how far the NUM will support a constructive future for women in mining communities. It is possible, however, to identify some of the structural aspects of those communities which may well provide barriers to women's development.

Mining communities have a very male character. The social and cultural life is geared largely to those who toil beneath the soil. Between shifts many communities appear like ghost towns, the men at work, the women at home. There are few places where women can meet and so their social life revolves around the kitchen which often becomes the place for all kinds of discussion. In the traditional mining village few women work, partly because there are usually few employment opportunities, but also because many husbands oppose their working and see it as a challenge to their ability as men to provide the family income. As part of the division of labour accepted to recompense men for the hard graft of face-work, most miners' wives undertake all the housework and child-rearing. Precisely because mining communities are close and supportive, several generations of families live in close proximity and the traditions of family life are observed and repeated. Because one's father did little around the house one does not expect one's own husband to do much. Indeed the older generation of women can be dismissive of younger women if any attempt is made to organise home life differently. My own grandmother suspects that I am a failure as a wife because I expect my husband to share in the household tasks. Because he does the hoovering, my brothers claim he is either 'hen-pecked' or not quite 'a man'.

In mining communities women rarely have an identity that can be called their own, they are either miners' wives or miners' daughters. You are always introduced to new people by reference to that relationship and always have to live with the fact that it is assumed that your opinions are identical to those of your menfolk. In my experience this definition of women by your relationship to men undermines your self-confidence and sense of identity.

Always to define yourself as relating to an industry which offers no role for women, or recognition of your value outside of the home, means that it is difficult to have an image of yourself or your future, except through a man. At one level it means that you always view yourself as of secondary importance. My own family has been in mining for at least five generations, and I have known three generations of the women. All have been strong women with great human potential. None has realised that potential and all have thought that this was inevitable given the importance of ensuring a secure home for their men. All of them have deferred to the choices made by their men in decisions about their lives and all have a very low concept of their own importance.

There is a major contradiction here, for there is legitimacy to be gained, both within the community and the wider labour movement, by being able to identify oneself as a miner's wife or daughter, as if somehow this relationship gave women some credentials, some respect for knowing the harshness of existence in mining communities, but also working class solidarity. Indeed, this seems to have been the case throughout the strike period. There is, from either perspective, inequality for women as women, either as not important or as important only in their relationship to men.

The NUM, the miners on strike and miners' wives in women's support groups have all committed themselves to the fight to retain their communities, and the labour movement has rallied behind this call. But let us look unsentimentally at those communities. They are hardly designed to expand human potential; they have poor services, poor communications, and more often than not, poor housing. On a whole range of community issues, mining areas fall behind the advances which have been made in other urban areas. My retired grandparents, now in their seventies, still rent an NCB house which suffers from severe subsidence, has no bathroom and only an outside toilet. Such conditions would not be tolerated in the public housing sector, and yet in mining communities, where too often community issues have taken second place to the interests of men as expressed through the NUM, such conditions still exist. Legislation which gives consultative rights to council house tenants over a wide range of housing issues does not give any rights to NCB tenants, and thus the community once more has to rely on NUM officials rather than encouraging greater involvement of all people living in the community. Campaigns which have been important elsewhere, such as opposition to the 'right to buy' council houses, have been entirely absent in mining communities, despite the massive sell-off of NCB houses to miners.

Whilst there are undoubted strengths to the traditional mining village, there are also the weaknesses of traditional family life, a family life all too often built not on an overt exploitation of women but on a subtle tradition which does not allow for women's personal development. Those women know only too well the limitations of their communities. They live in the houses, they have difficulty in getting buses to the nearest big shopping centre, they know the services which are lacking, they experience the boredom of being stuck at home with little to do. If mining communities are to be worth saving, they have to be more than a geographical place where a pit can be found. The NUM could pledge itself to support campaigns which will make them worthy of the people who live in them. Increased centralisation has meant that even *basic* welfare and cultural services, like libraries, doctors and clinics, are sited a long way from the villages. Access to them will be even more difficult when the Transport Bill is passed, for it is expected to bring a deterioration to already inadequate bus services. But the villages do not only need *basic* provision close at hand (though that would make a considerable difference). Arguments for *additional* services should be raised: for pre-school child care, for adult education, for welfare rights advice, for plays and exhibitions. If it is sincere in its fight to save mining communities, the NUM should recognise the importance of fighting for those services. Such issues should be given priority, and not designated as secondary to those which revolve around work underground.

But that cannot happen unless there is a wider involvement of different sections of those communities. Women have known these things for generations, but their voice has hitherto carried little weight. The respect that they have won during the course of the strike and their ability to organise themselves could provide a recognisable base so that they could be encouraged to play a vital role in those community struggles.

These prescriptions sound easy and glib, and many miners and NUM officials would say that of course they have supported and will continue to support such moves. However, there is much more at stake than appears at first sight. I am arguing for a recognition of alternative, although complementary, community organisations to those run by the NUM – the Welfare, the Labour Party and, of course, the NUM itself. The NUM is rightly concerned predominantly with issues around the work-place. It does not and cannot represent the interests of women in mining communities, and often does not concern itself with wider community issues. The NUM has often closely guarded its right to represent these communities and has jealously guarded against the establishment of alternative community organisations. It has looked suspiciously on what are often termed 'outside influences'. Local Labour Party branches are swamped with NUM delegates on any occasion when decisions seen as contrary to the interests of the NUM are to be discussed. More often than not elected Labour Party representatives are careful to ensure that their activities meet with the approval of the NUM whilst showing very little concern for other sections of the community, and for women in particular. This domination of the local political arena by the NUM and its interests has often prevented the development of other channels for political struggle and change. The National Women's Organisation may be seen as a threat to the NUM's authority, or more likely that it will be seen as of secondary importance. Both possibilities should be resisted. If they are to make any advances, women in mining communities need to take on an identity which does not define them in relation to men, either as wives or daughters of miners, and they should be encouraged to seek a forum in which their own ideas can be expressed.

The 1984 May Day miners' rally in Mansfield was for me a most depressing day. A day set aside to celebrate the solidarity, strength and determination of the miners saw chauvinism and sexism abound. Placard after placard floated down the street showing cartoon caricatures of Nottinghamshire miners' wives wielding rolling pins and glowering over their small hen-pecked husbands. Those carrying the placards confirmed this derisive image – Nottinghamshire miners were not on strike because their wives would not let them strike. In other words, Nottinghamshire miners were not 'real men'. In this view the only reason a miner fails to respond to a strike call is because he cannot assert his dominance over the wishes of his wife. Assured in this interpretation, Yorkshire miners shouted abuse at Nottinghamshire women standing at kerbsides, even though many were there to show their solidarity with the miners. The role of men and women presented by this caricature does not bode well for the future of women in mining communities now that the strike is over, especially with their being allowed and encouraged to seek an independent identity. Indeed many of the marchers made it clear that if their wives did not agree with them and their decisions they had plenty of ideas as to what should be done with them.

Implicit in this was an attitude of tolerating some autonomy for women as long as they express views in agreement with their menfolk. This is a long way from recognising the fundamental need for that autonomy as a lever for social and political change, let alone as an essential part of that change itself. This incident, although extreme, is symbolic of a certain attitude to women and expectation of their role that is common amongst miners. Too often women are seen as servicers and the appendage of men rather than autonomous and valuable human beings. Their political awareness is frequently seen as irrelevant, and there is certainly no recognition of any need for specific political education for women, which is surprising given the importance political education has for men within the mining industry. The expectation is that women do not need to think politically, as their husbands will instruct them on such matters. Indeed there are those who find it unthinkable for women to have views different from those of their husbands.

Let us take the position of working miners and working miners' wives. I do know of examples of working miners' wives who had great sympathy with the strike, but who did not challenge their husband's decision to work. These women are vilified and abused in their communities, as it is automatically assumed that they are opposed to the strike ... After all, their husbands are at work, aren't they? These women are disenfranchised because they are married to a man who has taken a given course of action.

Such women may be rare, although this is merely an assumption, as to my knowledge no one has considered the possibility that mining wives may differ from their husbands in their political outlook. We do, of course, hear a reasonable amount about those wives opposed to the strike who 'force' their husbands back to work, but this is a convenient excuse of using women as the stooge, the political scapegoat, to explain why men are not conforming to the NUM's view. This inability to allow the expression of women's political views independently of their husbands is not merely a question of male suppression. Women themselves seem to find difficulty in asserting their own identity and opinions. Loyalty to husband and family is seen as of paramount importance and to propagate different opinions would be seen as an affront to that loyalty. Traditionally, women in mining communities have subordinated their own opinions in order to stay loyal to their husbands, and if they disagree, they keep it to themselves.

So, the norm has been that the woman will back the stance to the strike taken by the husband. Much of the strength of mining communities is built on that loyalty, but a loyalty built on subordination and repression is not a strength but a weakness. Women creating their own forum in which their ideas can be expressed independently of men, and then implemented within the policies and strategies which are made for mining communities, directly challenges this weakness.

The issue of democracy was given a central role in the miners' strike, and was used by those opposed to the strike as a weapon to attack the union. Much of this debate was hypocritical and opportunist; suffice it to say that if the union *can* be seen as undemocratic, then it is in relation to women in mining communities. Women, who have shown throughout the strike how integral they are to the NUM, have no platform within the NUM to engage in discussions determining policies. They have no vote except through their husbands. They have no control over the major issues affecting their lives except through their relationship with men, more often than not, their husbands. It may be argued that women can join the Labour Party and thus have a voice. This side-steps the key issue that miners' wives have demonstrated by their actions throughout the strike – the need for *their collective* input within the community – not as expressed at one stage removed through an external national organisation.

The position of women in mining communities is one riddled with fundamental contradictions. On the one hand they are admired and respected for the solidarity that they have shown throughout the strike, on the other hand they are, in practice, dismissed from having any significant role in decision making. Standing outside the local Miners' Welfare waiting for a union meeting to finish in order to find out what the next steps would be, one was only too aware of how excluded women are. As the ranks of miners descended from the hall the absence of any female face reaffirmed the subsidiary role women played.

Night after night the male image of the dispute was confirmed. The television screen was filled by besuited men discussing the future of the industry and thousands of lives, and women were rarely seen, let alone heard. For those whose only contact with the strike was by watching television, there would be no idea of the dramatic role played by women. The exception, of course, was the role taken by women in providing soup kitchens or organising Christmas toys, significantly 'traditional' women's roles. When was a woman asked her political views on the strike? Except Ann Scargill, who was almost certainly only asked because of her legal relationship to a particular man, I have yet to see any programme which focuses on women's *political* perspectives of the strike. That is, looking beyond their support or non-support, to their political attitudes to energy policy, unemployment, community affairs and the future of our society. Those miners' wives who fought so hard to sustain the strike have not done so merely out of loyalty, but because they have strongly and deeply held opinions on all of these subjects, and yet rarely have they been allowed a voice.

Throughout the strike the labour movement tended to depict the miners' wives and children as passive victims of a vicious government. This was especially so in the weeks before Christmas, and there was certainly political mileage to be gained from this portrayal, but it denied the strength and vitality of women in the mining communities. More seriously, it revealed the lack of recognition of the changing role of women, and the need of the labour movement to respond to those changes.

Take the poster published by the Joint Chapels Liaison Committee in support of the Mineworkers Hardship Fund in December 1984 reproduced on p.92. The poster confronts us with major contradictions. While there is a recognition that the organisation of communal kitchens thwarted the government's hope of undermining the strike by disallowing miners' entitlement to DHSS benefits, it also shows a gross and exploitative portrayal of women's role. We see the passive and ever-willing miner's wife serving up food for the waiting miner and children sitting at a table clutching their knives and forks. It should also be noted that there is not even a place set for the wife. This image of women's role indicates how far the labour movement has to go in changing its thinking.

Further contradictions can be found in women's attitudes to work, and the attitude of the labour movement to women's right to work. Some miners' wives sought temporary employment during the strike. The reason they did so was the

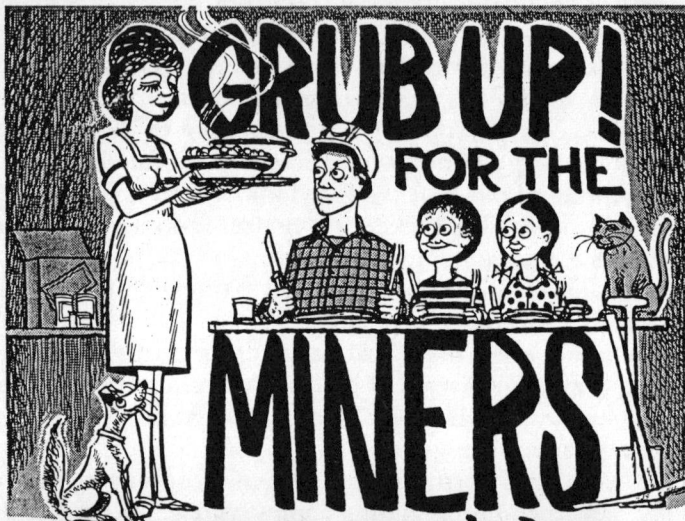

Poster produced by Joint Chapels Liaison Committee

need for money, not a desire for fulfilling experiences outside the home. For many miners' wives, the lack of employment experience and formal educational qualifications, means that the available jobs are often soul-destroying and, more often than not, a negative experience. To them, the idea that a job could be fulfilling, or at least satisfying, would seem absurd. Indeed, many women get married as a positive attempt to escape from such employment. In such circumstances women expect, and are expected, to find fulfilment in their homes and marriages, and many of course do. For those women in mining communities who were actively involved in the strike, there is now a desire for other things in their lives. Many will want to remain involved in community activities and issues, others may seek some form of further education, whilst still others may now wish to seek meaningful employment outside of the home. What employment opportunities will there be for such women? Saving women's jobs and ensuring training and employment opportunities for them has not been a priority for the labour movement. I have seen how, in mining communities, manufacturing industry has consciously exploited the ready availability of women workers in mining areas over many generations. Precisely because of the geographical isolation and poor public transport provision in mining communities, it has often proved impossible for miners' wives to get employment. 'Kind' and 'generous' employers have arrived and been only too pleased to provide employment in the home: assembling Christmas crackers, sticking faces on action dolls, over-locking chain-store jumpers. Look at the piece-work rates for this type of employment and the face pales at the gross exploitation. Hosiery employers also have a 'marvellous' scheme for over sixties: the wages are so low that they make no difference to your pension! This is appalling, but the conditions of home-workers are not unknown to the labour movement. Why has there never been an attempt by the NUM to unionise these women? Why has the NUM never addressed such gross exploitation? Why has the NUM never fought for adequate employment opportunities for women within their communities? One could go on and on, but the point is made. During the course of the miners' strike women have shown solidarity with the NUM. We have to hope that the NUM has learnt valuable lessons about the role and potential of women, and that they will offer reciprocal solidarity to enable women to achieve their emergent hopes and aspirations.

The importance of women's involvement in the miners strike is not only of relevance in its relation to the labour movement. The miners' wives' achievements provide important lessons for the wider women's movement, and add considerably to its history and culture. Over the last ten years the feminist movement has had to face the fact that it has been unable to attract and to be nurtured by working class women. Efforts have been made to attract working class women into the movement but they have largely proved unsuccessful. But now, working class women have suddenly been organising themselves in a vibrant and powerful manner, and finding great strength in themselves and one another. During the course of the strike, strong and sisterly links were woven between many miners' wives and women in the labour and feminist movements. These links were mutually enriching, but mining women still do not easily identify with many of the wider issues raised by the women's movement.

This has proved a disappointment to a small section of the women's movement which has been impatient to 'open the eyes' of the mining women to feminism. Instead of celebrating the mining women's achievements, they have alienated them by insisting that their movement is not a feminist movement, and could only have value if certain prescribed formulae were adopted. For these 'purist feminists', there appears to be a 'true and 'false' feminist consciousness that is very reminiscent of the Leninist idea of 'true and false class consciousness'. They have presented themselves to miners' support groups almost as a vanguard who could demonstrate the correct path forward. This stance was quite rightly resented by miners' wives and seen as élitist and dogmatic. The condescending attitudes of this small section of the women's movement (which should not be confused with the women's movement as a whole), to what they term the 'limited consciousness' of miners' wives, is in certain respects similar to those patronising attitudes shown by some NUM members, and perhaps explains some of the reluctance of mining women to identify with the wider issues of feminism.

There were other groups of women who sought no involvement whatsoever with the support groups, as they saw no common identity of interest. This was sad, for women in general have a great deal to learn from the experiences of miners' wives who brought a specifically woman's perception to the miners' strike. In making their case, they have touched the hearts and minds of the labour movement in a way that no sociological or theoretical analysis could ever have done. They have brought human emotions into the arena of 'respectable' politics, and in doing so have done in practice what the women's movement has for so long argued from a theoretical standpoint. A feminist assessment of the achievements of the mining women must take as its starting point the position of women in the mining communities: the role defined for them by men, the ambiguity with which they are at one and the same time valued and subservient and the impact of their experiences during the strike on these dynamics. Only by comprehending those mining communities and women's position in them, and by understanding, accepting and supporting the struggles those women took on can feminists develop constructive and enriching relationships with the women in those areas.

At the moment the vast majority of mining women would dissociate themselves from the Women's Liberation Movement, though they have been happy to engage in women-only organising, and in developing their own styles of organisation. The way a negative image of feminism has been projected, the way men have interpreted it, the way in which the media manipulates our image in order to fragment the interests of the working class and women: all these filtering devices need looking at and challenging and overcoming, if the links between women inside and outside of the mining communities are to be strengthened.

Miners' wives have shown a potential that must be built upon, by feminists as much as by the labour movement. Working class women have too often been alienated from the women's movement precisely because some parts of that movement have taken a rigorously critical attitude to the traditional labour and trade union movement; too often the 'enemy' has been portrayed as being men as individuals, rather than a society in which men have been allowed advantages denied to women. In devising its strategy, the women's movement has too often attacked men and not often enough the political and economic system which feeds off the division between women and men. Feminists have taken this stance for understandable reasons. Too often excluded and patronised within both trade unions and political parties, women have seen the issues they consider important being relegated to second place. Women have thrown up their hands in desperation and committed themselves to independent action as women. There is one flaw in this – that women do not necessarily have a common identity of interest merely by virtue of being women. What miners' wives have shown is that certain sections of women can have a common identity not merely by virtue of their sex, but also because of their class and their community. As they have shown in practice, they have a million things more in common with Arthur Scargill (a man) than with Margaret Thatcher (a woman).

Whether miners' wives have perceived the extent to which they are discriminated against by being women is open to question. It is clear that they have understood and responded to a perception of class issues, but how far have they developed an understanding of sex divisions? I believe that they have moved a long way in this direction, and that is precisely why they have recognised the value of organising separately from the NUM. This may differ from a purist's view of the correct way to organise, but purism and practical politics have little in common. My concern is that whilst feminists worry about whether we can see 'real' feminism emerging, whilst the NUM concerns itself with the miners' lot, and the labour movement considers the wider effects of the strike, no one will reflect on the real value of the lessons taught by the miners' wives. The strongest lesson has been that of solidarity and support, a practical recognition that patriarchy and class are intricately linked and a living example of how the 'personal' may be brought into the political. It has been a fine lesson in what women can bring to an industrial and economic struggle.

Not All the Strikers Were Men

Liz Marshall, Barbara Drabble

Although women cannot work underground in Britain, by law, the NCB does employ women: as clerical workers, as canteen workers, as cleaners in Coal Board premises. Some of these women are organised by COSA, the Colliery Officials and Staffs Association, which is part of the NUM. COSA asked its members to come out in support of the NUM strike call, and Liz and Barbara did. They were both very committed to the aims of the dispute, they both stayed out to the bitter end, unlike many of their colleagues. Neither of them works for the NCB now. They met whilst on a solidarity visit to Northern Ireland. These are their accounts of their year on strike.

A Canteen Worker On Strike

Liz Marshall

I come from a valley in Lanarkshire, about thirty miles from where I now live in Netherthird, Cumnock, which is in Ayrshire. We had to move when the pit there closed, and my father came to the Killoch Colliery to work. My mining ancestry can be traced back to 1805. There are two pits here, Barony and Killoch. Barony is quite old. Killoch is supposed to be the big pit, open since the mid-1950s whilst the others were being run down, but it has never made a profit because they have never put money into it. It is very difficult geologically, but they knew that when they sank the pit.

I went to work in the canteen at Killoch four years ago, as a part-time worker: 27 hours a week. I have always argued that it is not really part-time, and that I am entitled to the rights of a full-time worker. All the canteen workers are COSA members; some of the office workers are in APEX, but we were all COSA members. We were called out on strike in support of the miners. It was a very difficult and confused situation over the nature of the call. For the first week and a half we went to work, and I felt really bad. As a single parent I need my job, but even so I didn't like it. Between the other women, three out of ten (including myself) supported the strike. One of them had brothers-in-law out on strike and there would have been family hassles if she had wanted to go in. The other was as strong and committed as I was, though she did not maintain that.

For me, crossing a picket line is going against something that you have always been brought up to believe in. The men were out and I felt we should be out with them. There is a COSA branch at the pit but the men do not keep us informed about where the branch meetings are held and when. I have had this argument about not being informed of branch meetings many times. Then they would tell us, and they would have it maybe on a Sunday afternoon when you were either cooking the dinner or you have the kids to watch. I have had many an argument about it, but when you are a minority you don't win.

We in the canteen had our own wee meeting to decide, and the vote went that we were not going on strike. I came home on the Friday night and spoke with my dad.

'Dad, we're not going on strike.'

'Well, what are you doing?' he asked.

'I don't know,' I replied.

I thought about it all weekend. I really didn't know what to do. I got up Monday morning and phoned my manageress and told her that I was going on strike with the men, and she said, 'That's alright because we have all been picketed out.'

It was just the canteen workers who came out, the office staff and the cleaners didn't come out. They worked in the offices right through the strike. And the cleaners who are NUM members refused point-blank to come out. In the canteen you are in constant contact with the men, you know them, you are friendly with them. On the picket line you can see them and think, 'Och, I ken that man,' you are meeting them every day. The office staff didn't have that daily contact, but still I could never understand why they didn't come out. There would have been nothing for the canteen staff to do, only the office workers to cook for, but you would have been a number for the Coal Board propaganda, a statistic.

I was very pleased that day, I went to one of the fellas who lives down the road, a miner, and said, 'The Killoch women are on strike!' and they were pleased because they knew how I felt about it. I just couldn't go in, I felt it wasn't right. I could see what they were fighting for, I had had to move away before. People in this wee village, Netherthird, are all incomers, they have all had to move before. They were not born and bred here and it has made this place special, the last to have scabs. We have all lost jobs and had to move before to come to Killoch or Barony, and we don't want to keep on moving. We know there are no jobs down in England for us, because for the past two or three years there has been no transfer south. There are tremendous coalfields around here, but they want to open-cast it, not deep-mine it. So there is nowhere to go and people know that, especially in this village.

The ten of us in the canteen were mostly local, not incomers. But they all had fathers, sons, friends in the mine: they realised the importance of shutting the pit. But the office workers also lived in Ayr and round about …

The Women Get Organised

I went up to the local strike centre, the local community centre: Strathclyde Region allowed us the use of the hall and the cooking facilities free. It served miners from both the pits in this area, this village. There were 24 strike centres in Ayrshire. When we got up there the men had got themselves quite well organised and said, 'We're managing fine …' Yet they had potatoes in the soup this big! Dinner was for any striking miner or if his family was in need. Whoever needed feeding would get fed, while we had things to make. So the men did the cooking themselves until they had the mass demonstration at Hunterston and all the men from this area went. It was about five or six weeks into the strike and they went to try to close the oil terminal at Hunterston. Therefore they had nobody left to make the dinner. I was up at the strike centre one day and they were talking about going. Ellen and Isabel were there, and we just said, 'Well, we'll make the dinner that day.'

We had a great relationship with the men at the community centre – we were together, it was not them and us. We had a banner made at Glasgow University which was for both of us, men and women. We have our own wee banner but that is a bit battle-scarred. It was too much for the men, organising the food when they were going out picketing, hours a day sometimes. And then other women, when they knew there were wives, women already there, going about the strike centre, they started to come up and the ball started rolling. Before we knew it there were about thirty women all wanting to help, so we organised a rota for kitchen duties and going speaking. There were only two or three of us that would actually go and speak. I had never spoken anywhere in my life, but I did it to get money, clothes, anything. You just had to take the bull by the horns.

The first time was completely out of the blue and spontaneous. I am a member of the local Co-op Women's Guild, and I went to the Congress in Kirkcaldy as our delegate: it was the middle of May. They had brought in an emergency motion on the miners' strike and a woman whose son was a policeman had been up talking about the police (this was just after Hunterston). There was an old, old woman who I remember very vividly, she must have been nearer eighty than seventy, and she got up and started belling off in full support of the miners, and I thought, 'Just look at that!' Before I knew it I was at the rostrum, I just went up there and it was tremendous, there were people standing, clapping and I wasn't at all nervous, not until I came down. They even had a whip round, but I was mad because the money went to the delegates from Francis colliery up in Fife, where the Congress was held, and I wanted it to go to Hillside Crescent (NUM Scottish Headquarters) where it would be shared out equally.

The women's group got organised in May when things were beginning to get together. It was called 'WASH', Netherthird 'WASH': Women's Action and Self-Help Group we called it. We took advice and went under 'WASH' so that we got grants from the local district council; otherwise we wouldn't have had access to such funds. We could give the kids a holiday, and it seemed quite appropriate for a group of women!

Then they asked us from Miller Road, which is the Area NUM headquarters in Ayr, if we would set up an Ayrshire Women's Committee, if such a thing could be set up. I think I am not being big-headed when I say that the Netherthird women's group was the best organised group of them all. We got our act together quicker than some of the other places which seemed to have some animosity running through them.

We were just all united in a common cause, but don't get me wrong, we didn't all love one another! But it was great if you needed somewhere to go, there was always somebody at the strike centre, and if you wanted to have a blare it was okay because they all had the same problems as you.

The women were together, strikers and wives, and that was it. I always felt I had the best of both worlds because I was in with the men *and* the women, and I never lacked any information on the strike. Not through my union delegate: I'm not very enamoured with my delegate, I didn't see him at all.

After the day when the women were picketed out they stayed out until about New Year: there was myself and a woman from Auchinleck who were convinced that the strike was right and got involved, doing what we could in the strike centres. The other women didn't seem to get involved, I don't know why. Perhaps in other areas the men weren't as willing to let the women in to help. It was 'You're doing the dinners and that's it, you're not getting involved.' Whereas we were on the picket lines, going speaking and so on.

The first picket line I went on was at Killoch Colliery where the NACODS men were going in. (NACODS is the organisation of pit deputies and foremen; it is not part of the NUM.) I don't know what happened in England, but in Scotland they were told that if they did not go into work they would not get their holiday pay. I have friends who are NACODS men: the management was hassling them and the union was not being supportive, so they didn't have much choice. They were supposed to go and get their holiday pay and the women picketed the Killoch pit, and not one of the NACODS men would go through the women's picket. It was about July, the women's group just got itself together and said, 'We'll go and picket.' It was the first time and I was ecstatic. That was Friday and we were back out only two or three times, though we weren't there constantly, having families and the men going out. But most of the mass pickets had women there.

At first the men discouraged the women from picketing. I was not there at Hunterston, the men were not letting us go. But the men had tried to get the NACODS men out and they had got nowhere. If the men couldn't get the NACODS men out, it was time for us to try. We said, 'We're going' and that was it. Really, the men were pleased. Make no doubt about it, that first picket was the most successful even though the police were there. The police didn't know what to do, they didn't know where to touch you because if they grabbed you in the wrong place you could have them for indecent assault. You could be cheeky with them and they would just laugh it off, and we shouted at the men. Later on it was not like that, you weren't even allowed to shout 'scab'. Then, we were treated the same as anybody else; they were horrible, nasty.

We were going on demos, marches, to London to demonstrate. Every thing that happened was completely new: I don't think my life has ever been as exciting before. But I don't think I could go through that year again because during that time we had nothing. I was living on my child benefit; my rent was being paid but apart from that I had £17.95 to keep the three of us, myself and my two children, for a week. If I never see another peas and chips, fried egg or sausage again it won't worry me: I put on two stones in weight because of the food and the fact I wasn't working. We got food parcels which helped, we even got food from Russia. A huge consignment came in, it was held up at Hull and they wouldn't let any of the meat in.

I was doing kitchen duty that day, being used to dealing with large numbers from working in the canteen: it is a lot different from just cooking for two or three. I was also in charge of buying very large amounts of food, and I was there that day when the stuff came in. We were sorting it out, you know, 'This will be good for feeding large amounts of people, these cans we can divide up individually amongst people.' And then we opened this sack, it was full of corn, grain! They must think we still actually grind the corn! But we were grateful for whatever we got. SOGAT sent down food supplies regularly, mainly tinned food from London, and also from local areas. The people of Glasgow were wonderful, they supported the strike and we were up there every Friday doing collections. There were collections at Paisley and other places which were really good. Different coalfields had different areas for support and Glasgow was our big city. It was tremendous.

We also got great support from members of Militant, they were very good here, and I would say more supportive than the local Labour Party of which I am a member. They were more dedicated.

Even the children got involved, they helped us in the kitchens or if there were any toddlers to be looked after, the likes of lasses Andrea's age (my daughter, aged thirteen) were able to help out. Both Andrea and Tommy went on holiday to Ireland where the Irish people were really good, and it was both sides of the community. They came over and took the kids back with them to stay. Andrea stayed with a Protestant family, Tommy with a Catholic family. It was the biggest surprise of my life when I went to Belfast, it was lovely and the people were so nice. (Andrea: 'The second time I went, I stayed with a Catholic man and a Protestant lady.')

There was a small token picket there at the pit all the way through. None of the canteen women worked until January. At the beginning of January I got a phone call to say that the opinion of the rest of the women was that we should return to work. I said, 'I'm not going back. As long as the men are out, I'm out.' That was quite acceptable to them, that was my course, and there was no hassle. I asked, 'Are you all going to go back?' and I was told that the woman who had been so involved with me was going back to work as well. I phoned her and she said she wasn't going back, but then she did, so did the other woman who voted to strike. I didn't usually bother going to the men's meetings because I would get all the information through the women's group: if there was anything new about benefits the men would keep me informed. But this night I went up and told them what had happened. They said, 'What are you going to do?' I said, 'I'm not going back to my work,' so they decided to phone round all the strike centres and set up a mass picket. So the picket was set up, but it did no good. I was there on the picket line and I thought all of them went in but me and this woman, I kept looking for her on the picket line but she wasn't there. I felt more about that than about any of the others, because she had been so solid and active. She had been on holiday in Ireland and she had a fantastic time. To me, she has abused all that hospitality, she has simply thrown in with whatever side was winning.

I can get on with all the other women because I could see they were never committed from the start. And many of them were never given a chance to get involved. The COSA branch didn't involve them and the men in the different areas just didn't treat them right, they didn't give them the chance to join in. Whereas I was welcomed with open arms because I had come out on strike, that didn't seem to be happening everywhere, and it should have been. The women should have been counted as striking miners, but they weren't. I was, though. Now that it is after the strike, and we are talking about it I can accept why the other women went back. I think they have a higher respect and regard for me for sticking by my principles. I can get on fine with them, though I still think they let the union down, but they have to live with their consciences. They were all better off than I was because they all had husbands working, so they weren't so financially badly off as I was. For me it was desperate. My mum and dad are pensioners and it was they who fed me and my kids every weekend. My sister paid for the television rental every month, and my other two sisters came down every week and they always brought something, especially if the kids needed a jacket or a new pair of shoes. They made sure that the children didn't do without.

So I was much worse off financially than the other women, but to me it didn't boil down to finances. I look at it this way: my son is nearly fifteen and he wants to join the merchant navy, but there is now virtually no merchant navy because this government has done away with it. They have done away with such a lot. I don't honestly think that even mining families want to see their sons going down the pit, they don't want to see them live in hell. But they would rather they did that than nothing. And they are not going to replace the pits with anything else in this area: there is little hope for youngsters here. The only other work is at the Bata shoe factory which is where I am now.

Back to Work After the Strike

When I went back there were new rules and regulations. The part-time women had to start at 4.00 a.m. every morning. The manageress knew that that was virtually impossible for me because it meant my mum watching the children all the time. Before the strike I did back-shift, night-shift, day-shift alternately, and every third week my children would go and stay with my mother. I relied on her to watch them, but I didn't want her to watch them all the time – she's getting on, she's 72. Four o'clock until eleven every morning: impossible. So they said if I couldn't do that they would transfer me to the Barony. It was in the area, I would be doing days and afternoons, I would still have my job, so I said, 'Okay'. Then they weren't going to let me do 27 hours.

I wouldn't say positively that this was deliberately designed to get me out, but I think it was a hopeful exercise! They were trying to ease me out because they didn't want to make me redundant: they would have had to give me redundancy money, and they knew there would have been trouble from the men because I know a lot of the men from the 24 strike centres. I cannot give my manageress all the blame, because it goes further up than that, to Green Park, Edinburgh (Headquarters of the Scottish Coal Board). So I went to the Barony and it was terrible. They had been working for weeks and weeks and weeks there whilst the men were out. They came out after the Killoch women and went back before, so there was a lot of animosity there and I felt it towards me. Also, there was the attitude, 'If the Barony shuts, you were the last here, you are the first to go.' I am not the sort of person to sit and take it, and I just decided it wasn't worth it. I left in May.

I am working at Bata now. I am a member of NUFLAT, the National Union of Footwear, Leather and Allied Trades. The large majority of workers are women. It is semi-skilled, even the kids could do it after six weeks.

I would rather be at Killoch. If I could have been left working there I would have, because I enjoyed working at the pit. There was nothing skilled about the work there either, but before the strike it was a nice friendly place: management and mineworkers. Now it's horrible, horrible. I think a lot of the men would be glad if it shut down tomorrow. The atmosphere is so bad because the men who stuck out the strike were in the minority. The majority had gone back before the strike had ended. The men are having a rough time, especially the union men, the activists. They are having to watch every step they take. They cannot put one action or word out of place otherwise they are up the pit.

Looking Back

I don't think the union let the men down, I think the men let the union down. They just deserted the union: I cannot see it any other way. The union was saying and doing the same thing all through the strike, that never altered, so the men must have changed their minds. They were out a long time, but if they had just had the sense to stick together the Coal Board just couldn't have hung on. It goes back to the old motto Unity Is Strength.

I think the union, COSA, should have given the women more recognition. We got more from the ordinary men than the union. The delegate didn't come down at all, there was no attempt at communication whatsoever. I still think that if there had been more communication the women wouldn't have gone back to work. I wouldn't have survived the strike without my local strike centre and the women and the men that were there. A single parent is in a funny position anyway, socially unacceptable because you don't have the compulsory man at your side. But it has made such a difference to my life. Take our working men's club. A year ago I would not have walked into the club alone and expected to sit in company. Now I could say, 'Oh, it's Saturday night, I think I will go out to the club and have a drink.' And there would be loads of people I could sit with and not feel in the least embarrassed. I could say, 'I decided to come out for a drink tonight,' and nobody would think it the least bit funny. It has opened up a whole new world for me. Educationally, it has told me I am not as stupid as I thought I was. Not having had an education I always thought was a drawback, because I have two sisters who have university degrees. I always felt slightly less able to put myself forward. Now I feel I can make a valid point, and I've talked to people and not made a fool of myself.

Things have changed for women, in this village things have changed a lot. Before I would have said that miners in particular are chauvinistic, they like to keep the women in their place. But the men have seen that the women are not just here to make the dinner. The strike centre wouldn't have been as well run if the women hadn't been there, because we dealt with the money, the food and looked after the children. They realise now after seeing for a year just how organised their wives have got their lives. And they know they are not going to be shut up in the kitchen again. You notice more sharing, more couples going down the street for the messages [shopping] together. And families going out together. I don't think the men ever realised just how much organisation the women put into their lives, they are not brought up to see it.

I found out about a week past about the decision of the NUM not to offer affiliate status to the women, and I wasn't happy about it. I feel they have gone back on what they said. They never promised it to us, but they took all the help we gave them and they praised us up no end. It is as if they are saying, 'We've used you for as much as you are worth, now back you go, we don't really need you now.' I don't think it was a nice decision at all, I don't think it was the right decision. There will be an awful lot of disappointment, including on the Scottish Women's Committee. I was one of the delegates from Ayrshire, and I used to like going up to the meeting in Edinburgh. When I left the pit, I had to give it up. There are still decisions to be taken about membership. There is talk about widening it. But there is no way we could accept the wives of miners who scabbed.

We now have a campaign for the sacked miners. There is hope for them, because not one of these boys is charged with anything serious. For me, there is no way that a wife who could countenance her man going scabbing can go and sit in a meeting where we are discussing what the procedure is going to be for helping a sacked miner: whether you are going to pay x amount of his electricity bill or whatever. I don't think I would like to be in the position of a scab's wife: I would have left him. We didn't lose any women from our support group through scabbing, but then again we only lost about four men from the strike centre that way. Netherthird had the name of being the most solid and active in this area. It had to be here, because we have all moved before. The village where I come from was only a wee village, but it was a thriving community; when they closed the pit it just died. The coalfield there is really massive, they are doing borings for an open-cast pit in that village. They don't need a lot of men for open-cast, because the men work twelve-hour shifts. They have to, to make a living. They are paid less than underground workers.

I can still go and talk to the women at Killoch, and they will tell you the strike was right even though they voted not to come out. The whole idea of women going on strike had such a lot to do with it. I think there was some influence from their husbands, though no one would come out and say it. They said, 'What would I do in the house all day? I would get on our Bill's nerves,' those kinds of comments. It is the men that go on strike, women don't do that, it's not like a woman. Our jobs are not important enough to merit a strike. I think that maybe if women did, society would treat them a lot better.

I didn't feel like that, and I still don't. I gained a lot personally; I have more friends in this area now than I have ever had. What I got from the men, I gave back in return. I gave value; I did what I could.

July 1985
(*Written in collaboration with Vicky Seddon*)

Office Workers Take Action   *Barbara Drabble*

I can trace my involvement in the miners' strike back to 1980 when I joined the Labour Party. I joined as a reaction to Margaret Thatcher's government and what they were starting to implement. I began reading left-wing newspapers, and one of the themes running through these newspapers was the importance of being active in the trade union movement.

I started work for the NCB in March 1981 at their Pensions and Insurance (P&I) office in Sheffield, on a two-year contract. Now, looking back, there seems to be an inevitability about my involvement and commitment to subsequent events.

The NCB operates a closed shop and there was a choice of two unions to join: APEX or NUM/COSA (the Colliery Officers and Staffs Association organises white-collar workers in the industry and holds the status of an Area within the NUM). I quickly decided that NUM/COSA was the union I wished to belong to. I got involved with the union committee and after I felt I had done my committee work well enough I allowed myself to be nominated as branch president. The start of my presidency coincided with the start of the overtime ban, November 1983.

90 per cent of the union work at our branch had been done by a marvellous woman called Audrey Godfrey. She had been nominated (unopposed) as secretary year after year, and most people had the attitude 'Leave it to Audrey'. She had started to suffer with her health and had, over a period of time, sought to involve other people in the union at branch level. She had quite a degree of success in this, but she was still seen as the mainstay of the branch. She retired quite suddenly because of ill health and we, the committee, were left to feel our way.

We held branch elections and I got the position as president, Adrian was chair, Marion secretary and Sue Treasurer, and we had about six more people as committee members.

At this time the approximate number working at P&I was 570 COSA members, 340 APEX, 170 BACM (British Association of Colliery Management). At least half the clerical staff were employed on a fixed-term contract basis, especially to work on the Iron and Steel Employees Readaptation Benefits Scheme and the British Shipbuilders Benefits Scheme.

These were two contracts that the NCB operated on behalf of the other nationalised industries but the staff were NCB employees, with exactly the same terms and conditions as staff working directly on NCB work. The P&I office was the only NCB work-place or unit which employed staff on fixed-term contracts. Here was a work-force divided between permanent and contract, clerical or management, different grades of clerks and three unions. At least three-quarters of the staff were women, and they were concentrated in the clerical grades and lower management grades.

Contracts were constantly being renewed, but only for one year at a time, and in March 1984, when the strike started, I had just signed another contract: my fourth year at the NCB. As a union branch we had started to put pressure on the NCB to make existing contract staff permanent and not to take on any more people on a fixed-term basis. We had already held preliminary discussions with the Staff Department at Doncaster, and a petition signed by the majority of staff at P&I had been presented to one of the staff managers. So here we were, a new batch of union branch officials with a reasonable amount of goodwill towards us from the members ('let them have a go') and we were going for a fairly high profile in terms of our branch.

When the instruction was issued by the NUM to ban overtime we, as a union committee, decided it must be implemented at our office as a sign of our credibility and solidarity.

Some weeks before we had invited Arthur Scargill to address our branch meeting and the date was fixed for the end of October. Management were really worried about this and thought the timing was to coincide with the overtime ban, but we had just been lucky with the date. Arthur was really impressive at the meeting and swayed a lot of people who were wavering. Our high profile was paying off and some of us were really enjoying ourselves. The only job satisfaction we were getting came from our union duties and putting a brake on management!

A further branch meeting was held to explain the situation and our regional committee member, John, spoke and was well received. Branch officials were called into meetings with management who tried to persuade us to ignore the instruction. We decided to counteract this by printing and issuing our own leaflet. This caused quite a stir on the morning when committee members stood outside our office leafleting staff going in. It was absolutely unheard of in our office, but nevertheless several leaflets were displayed on desks and pieces of office equipment by sympathetic staff. We had also started obtaining regular copies of the *Miner* for internal distribution round our office, and *Unity*, the Doncaster COSA panel's own magazine.

The first Saturday morning of the overtime ban arrived and all the union committee and branch officials arrived at 7.30 a.m. for our first picket duty. We were frightened and unsure of ourselves, and did not know what to expect in terms of staff turning up for overtime. Rumours had been flying about all week about people who were going to work regardless. About ten more pickets arrived from the Doncaster COSA panel, so we felt much more confident, as they had experience of industrial action and none of us had. Lunch-time arrived and we could hardly believe our luck: no one from our union had turned up for work! A handful of APEX and BACM members had gone through our picket line with the excuse that their unions were not involved. We were aware that this could be a danger to us, as COSA members would soon feel why should they observe the ban when members of other unions did not.

We had talked and argued our case to these people crossing the picket, but had been unsuccessful in turning them back. In the afternoon we broke the picketing into shifts and we all reassembled at 4.00 p.m. to observe the last staff to leave the office. We were elated with our success and decided to display on the union notice boards in the office a notice which informed staff that no one from COSA had worked that Saturday, and the number of other union members who had.

This pattern continued more or less until Christmas. The office was even opened the Saturday before Christmas, but by then the numbers working were down to two or three. We had scored an immense propaganda victory with the notice displayed every week, as no one in COSA wanted to be the first to spoil the record, and we had threatened to name people who did.

Early in the new year Arthur Scargill heard about our picket line and promised to come one Saturday to stand with us and help to get us some national publicity. We really appreciated him finding time to stand with us and it boosted our confidence. Reporters and photographers arrived from the *Sunday Mirror, Times, Observer* and from the local papers. The people that we worked with were impressed with the publicity and also with the fact that Arthur was interested and cared about what we were trying to achieve.

The following Saturday, some of the staff from NUM head office joined us on the picket line and agreed to organise a mass picket for the following Saturday, which would involve miners. We felt this was important, as we wanted to maintain the pressure and the initiative.

The mass picket took place and about twenty miners from High Moor pit stood with us. They were successful in turning staff back because they refused to give way verbally or physically as we had done when people insisted on going through the picket line. A couple of incidents took place which illustrated the gap between our solidarity and thinking, and some people who wanted overtime at all costs, who could not, or would not acknowledge any connection between clerks and miners in an organised front. One lad's parents had brought him into work from Barnsley and they insisted that he went through the picket line. He kept walking over to their car and telling them he could not get through and they shouted at him to keep trying. His mother was the worst and gave the pickets some verbal vitriolic. One of the retired miners tried to talk to her and came back saying, 'She was a real hard-liner, a *Sun* reader.' The lad eventually gave up and went away but not without threatening to be back next week.

Next, a woman was dropped off at the picket line by a man in a car and she panicked and tried to push her way through. The miners did not touch her but stood firm; the man got out of the car, walked over, rammed her through the pickets and then walked back to the car. Someone threw a stone at the car and there were a few seconds when the incident could have escalated. We held our breath; we were speechless that someone could want three or four hours overtime so desperately that she would allow herself to be manhandled in that manner. The moment passed and our tempers held.

The following Monday at work rumours abounded: rocks and bricks had been thrown; the woman had been hurt and ended up in tears; staves had been driven into the ground. This aspect of the industrial action I found really difficult to handle – working normally with people during the week and taking action as an active minority at the weekend. I found it hard to accept that people would believe the rumours, and be so quick to jump to conclusions. Aided and abetted by the media, pickets were easy game for hostility, and we were portrayed as people who would throw away our usual behaviour and morals to be 'thugs', and 'hooligans', 'the rabble' or 'mob'. Management called two of the branch officials to a meeting and told us how shocked they were that staff could arrange such an event, and how damaging it was to our image as a city centre office, that we were quite beyond the pale. It was the usual management propaganda of 'let's be reasonable, our aims are the same, common-sense,' and all that moral blackmail. I think it struck a chord with the branch secretary, Marion, as later events were to prove. The main outcome of the picketing was that overtime was not worked again, a management decision, until the dispute was settled.

I have dealt at length with the preceding events as an indication of what united union action and hard work could achieve. I also think it is important to remember our successes in light of what was to come.

When we heard about the Yorkshire Area strike being made official we were convinced we would not be involved without a ballot. We spent a lot of time reassuring COSA members about this and later in the dispute the lack of a ballot hung round our necks like a millstone, and proved a useful weapon for strike-breakers to beat us with. At a COSA Yorkshire delegates meeting on Saturday 3 March Trevor Bell instructed us to come out on strike with the Yorkshire Area on Monday 5 March. We were told to meet our members coming into work Monday morning and inform them we were on strike. Looking back on it now, that seems totally ridiculous and there are strong feelings that COSA activists were set up by Trevor Bell and the COSA General Council who wanted to ride two horses.

They knew the activists would try and implement the instruction and that the membership would react against it. Trevor Bell could therefore go back to National Executive of the NUM and say, 'My members have been instructed to support the Yorkshire Area strike.' But at the same time there was such uproar and bad feeling about pit closures that anything seemed possible. I can't begin to describe my feelings over that weekend, waiting for Monday morning to arrive. I knew the strike was right and the lack of a ballot did not bother me, the feeling was there that unofficial action and rebellion against the Tories and the NCB was unstoppable and could not be contained by any demands to wait and see, compromise, or time taken to do things by the rule book. The Tories had issued the challenge with the Cortonwood closure and we were going to answer it with strike action. But I knew most of the people in our office would not see it in this light and that I would be playing a leading part on Monday morning with my head well and truly above the parapet, a very unpopular person. We couldn't get any help on the picket line for that Monday morning as all the other activists were too busy at their own office, pit or workshop, in exactly the same predicament as we were. And so we were on our own.

So on the Monday morning we talked to our members as they came into work, and it was utter chaos. Some didn't believe us and thought we had set it up as militant individuals; others, confused, milled about outside, wanting to support us and the miners but uncertain about the way we were doing it. Some hung about until 9.55 a.m. (end of flexitime) and then made a mad dash into the office. We made an especial appeal to our members in the typing pool, as we had recently won a flexitime dispute they had with management, but they didn't want to know. I drew the connection between their united and militant stand which had been successful, and what we were now embarking on for a far greater prize. I can remember standing on top of the office steps and really laying it on the line to the people milling about outside. There was a deadly silence and a small clutch of managers was across the road listening. I told them we had aranged a branch meeting at 4.00 p.m. and that our regional full-time official would be taking the meeting and explaining the situation. I appealed to them not to go into work, to come to the meeting and to support the strike. It was the first time I had spoken in public like this. I just felt impelled to do it. I could see around me various branch officials and committee members who were wavering and thinking they had taken on more than they could handle. I felt very alone, as only two or three others had put their backs into it like I had. About 140 people did not go into work, and towards mid-morning managers mingled with the people outside, telling them that the staff at Coal House, Doncaster, had held their meeting and voted to work.

At the mass meeting our regional officer interpreted the union position as a request not an instruction and allowed the members to vote whether to work or not. The membership, seeing the chink in the armour, flooded through it and voted to work. It was a very hostile meeting, like a modern gladiatorial ring where the activists were thrown to the membership. About forty people voted not to work and a few of us activists stayed out on our own for a couple of days whilst seeking clarification from Trevor Bell. He backtracked so we all returned to work, but we arranged a branch meeting for him to speak about two weeks later. During this period he was under pressure from the Yorkshire COSA Regional Committee, and from the activists, to support the stance he had taken at the 3 March meeting. He addressed the meeting and urged full support for the NUM position although not instructing members to strike. Some of us felt this position was sufficiently strong for us to come out on strike again, as we were finding it more and more difficult, morally, to carry on working. Our office had not been picketed by other NUM members so we knew we would have to put ourselves on the line again. Forty of us got it together and took strike action again.

Up to this point all the branch officials and committee members had been united, but the second strike action split us down the middle and some of them crossed our picket line and worked throughout the strike. It was really hard to picket again; not hard to take strike action, but hard to try and further that action and influence other people to support us. We were asking people to take a principled trade union stand, and we were just laughed at by most of the membership. The mystique of the picket line had been broken and people realised they could do what they wanted as even the activists were not sticking together. Within the first week all but nine of the forty had drifted back to work. It was heart-breaking to see people break away and return to work. This affected me very much as I had put in so much effort. I shed a few tears on the picket line and at home; I felt let down. But I wasn't supposed to have feelings: I was a hard-line picket, I ate babies for breakfast according to the media!

It was a very small group that stayed solid: there was Adrian, the branch chair, who was only 21. He lived with his parents. Tricia was 26 and lived in her own house in Maltby; John lived with his parents in Chesterfield; Julie was from Ebbw Vale and married to a redundant steel worker. Peter and Richard were both single; Roger was engaged and had just bought a house. Then there was me, married and in my late thirties. So we were a mixed group of people. Some of us were involved in politics. The others believed in the strike and would not cross a picket line on any account.

So a pattern emerged; we would picket our office from 7.30 to 10 every morning, Monday to Friday, standing there with our placards, shouting 'scab' and 'support your union'. There was no turning back now and we would not talk to the people going into work about anything except the strike and why they should support it. Lots of them tried to say 'Good morning' and actually wanted to talk about other things, to pretend we could all still be friends. One man on the picket line had to contend with his girl-friend crossing it nearly every day! We used to have odd days when some people would not cross and would stand with us, especially in the early days when there was still talk of ballots and mass lobbying of the NEC meetings. A COSA member from Hatfield pit and one from Hickleton came to picket with us every day, initially at the request of the Doncaster COSA panel and then because we all got on well together and were committed. It was difficult getting the wider labour and trade union movement in Sheffield to take an interest in our picket as most of them were involved picketing at the pits and raising money for the miners. We were seen as a bunch of clerks, quite insignificant in the broader spectrum of things. I was a delegate to Sheffield Trades Council and used regularly to harangue delegates about their lack of interest in us. I say 'harangue' because I got very cross about our isolation when we thought what we were doing was worthwhile. We could have worked, there was nothing to prevent us as we were the only pickets. But we stayed out for the sake of the highest principles of trade unionism: solidarity and loyalty. We were committed trade unionists who had taken branch and committee positions and who could not turn our backs on this responsibility because the going was getting tough.

I would like to acknowledge the help that Sheffield City Council gave the miners in the form of food vouchers and the Christmas hamper. We used to receive food vouchers from the Doncaster COSA caravan collection and from the regional hardship fund. We had a couple of large donations from Sheffield NALGO and some members of NALGO used to stand with us regularly on the picket line and bring toast and flasks of soup and tea. It was important that other people joined us as it boosted our morale and we didn't feel quite so alone. After a couple of months we had stopped attempting to talk to staff going into work as it had proved so fruitless, and the confrontations so wearing and provoking. Once again we, as pickets, were an easy target for people to abuse, not only for people going into work but also for complete strangers passing the picket line. We cut ourselves off as a form of survival and made a special point of laughing and joking and talking to regular passers by who were sympathetic. Word came to us many times from people inside our office that we were enjoying ourselves: we were too cheerful and well dressed to be suffering unduly from the strike. According to these people, we should have been in the gutter and dressed in rags, a cup of cold water in one hand and a piece of dry bread in the other. But survive we were determined to do, and also to carry on the picketing which had now become a presence or a vigil. It would have been the easiest thing in the world to stay at home for the rest of the strike. Many times I could hardly face dragging myself to the picket line; I wanted to pull the blankets over my head and sleep until the strike was over. But as long as we were turning up on the picket line it was a reminder to the people going into work about what they should be doing and we were certainly not going to let them off the hook. It was also a good way of the pickets keeping in touch, and nearly every day there was some new national or area development to discuss and analyse. We didn't feel disenfranchised or powerless; we were part of a national strike and as a whole we felt strong and confident we would win.

Around June 1984 I started going to Sheffield Women Against Pit Closures (SWAPC) meetings. It was just what I

needed. Our picketing had settled into a routine but I needed
to be involved in the wider support. The Sheffield women were
doing so much that my head was spinning with dates, times
and suggestions at the end of the first meeting. They were so
supportive of one another, and when we moved into action as
a group there was such a feeling of solidarity that we could
achieve anything that I was lifted. I started speaking at
meetings as a representative of SWAPC all over: Sheffield,
Manchester and Ripon. Just before Christmas I went with two
other women to Belfast to do meetings that coincided with
women's week in Northern Ireland. We were each put up in
individual houses and treated as one of the family. On our first
night there we held an impromptu meeting in an amazing bar
called Kellys in the Short Strand. We asked permission from
the landlord to speak, leaflet and take a collection. He said we
could do what we liked, so we did. Afterwards various people
came and spoke to us individually about the strike and their
troubles in Northern Ireland, all the time drawing parallels
between the policing methods. This understanding continued
throughout our eight-day visit, and we hardly met anyone who
did not support the strike.

The next high spot on the picket line was Christmas. We
decided to hold a Christmas party in the street on the picket
line. We had a Christmas tree, paper hats, a trestle table laden
with food and drink. Our friends from other unions who stood
with us regularly supplied most of the food and drink and we
all entered fully into the spirit of the 'pavement party'. The
local press heard about it and a reporter and photographer
hotfooted down to the picket line to do a story on the
'forgotten pickets' enjoying themselves. Once again word
reached us from inside our office that our party seemed better
than the one they were allowed to hold. There was one main
reason why our party was better than theirs – that we all got on
together well and we were bound together in a common cause.
This was apparent to anyone who spent any time with us.

Unfortunately after Christmas the strike appeared to be
crumbling a little at the edges. The media played on this and
the numbers game started for real. The strikers had gone to
great lengths to have as good a Christmas as possible, and so
had their supporters, but no one seemed to have looked
beyond Christmas. There were no new strategies and it was

hard to raise money on a great scale after the emotional appeal of Christmas was over. Various groups tried their best with the Derbyshire women's 'Strike Alive 85' week-long event, and the Hatfield Women's March. Things settled down again into a pattern of just carrying on, raising money in SWAPC, selling calendars, a jumble sale, street collections. The February Day of Action resulted in me addressing a meeting at Doncaster from the top of a lorry. It was a bitterly cold day and we had marched around Scawthorpe, Doncaster, for a couple of hours. When we reached the field where we were to gather for the speeches I thought most people would drift away because it was so cold. When my turn to speak arrived I was amazed to see the number of people who had waited. Before I could start to speak after my introduction some wit shouted, 'Get them out at P&I!' and I responded, 'I wish you could. I have been trying to get them out since March last year.' There was a lot of sympathetic laughter and I was away. I very rarely prepared anything for these speeches. I just had it all in my head and it usually just flowed out of me.

The reason why there was sympathetic laughter was because we were now all in the same position. In conversation with miners from various pits early on in the strike, they used to vie with one another as to who had the most militant pit and could not understand why our members were not solid. On the whole they were contemptuous of our part in the strike. Now Yorkshire pits were experiencing, to different degrees, scabbing and fragmenting of solidarity, and they started to respect us for staying the course and for picketing in such soul-destroying circumstances.

Just before the strike finished I started to feel the NCB's heavy hand. During the time I had been on strike, all contract staff graded CO3 who had worked throughout the strike had been offered permanent employment by the Board. Naturally Adrian and I expected this to include us, as we had always intended to return to work when the strike was over. I did not want to as I had found the work and the atmosphere soul-destroying prior to the strike, and it would be even worse afterwards, but I intended to return and rub their noses in it and then get out as soon as possible. The NCB would not clarify our employment position until the strike was over and it began to look as if we were going to be victimised.

I lobbied the delegates at the COSA Yorkshire delegates meeting and got their support. We also spoke to staff who had been made permanent as they went into work, and told them that we were being victimised for our part in the dispute. We asked them what they were going to do about it. This was very difficult for us as we had not spoken to these people for nearly a year, but we realised that we had to try and gain some response from the people working in our office or management would ease us out if the anger was only on the picket line. The response we had was good, considering the yawning gap between us. Most people said it was unfair, and whilst they had not been prepared to strike they did not see why we should be penalised for doing so. We also spoke to the branch treasurer and she was very concerned and said she would do what she could. We printed our own leaflet and gave it to all working members of staff in our office, which meant that everyone was put in the picture. I think management were surprised that we still had the initiative and guts to do this, but it activated the pickets again. Apparently it caused uproar in the office, and we were told the place was absolutely buzzing with it. It was hard to maintain the level of concern and interest now shown by our strike-breaking colleagues as the real leaders and activists who would have tried to do something about it were out on the picket line. We had been prodded into activity again but could not raise any positive response inside, so the issue died in respect of rank-and-file activity. We decided to pursue it at a legal level and let the bureaucracy of our union take its full course.

On Sunday night when the announcement was made by the NUM that we were to return to work on Tuesday I just couldn't believe it. It *couldn't* be over; we *hadn't* won, we *couldn't* give up. For my part, I could have stayed out for as long as it took to win, and so could all the activists I spoke to. We were stunned. For a year now we had built another way of life which was, by turn, hard, depressing, exciting, exhilarating, new. We never knew what each day would bring: a phone call in the evening could send us anywhere the next day. As far as the establishment was concerned, we were free, unaccountable to a large degree. Even our families and friends found our movements unpredictable: we could no longer be tied down.

Working had got to be boring after this eventful year! That Sunday night I wept and wept and despaired: where was the rabbit in the hat that the NUM had managed to pull out from time to time? We *couldn't* have come to the end of the road.

On Monday morning we gathered on our picket line for one last defiant gesture. I was pleased to learn later that this was happening all over the coalfields. All our regular pickets turned up and there was no question of whether we should or shouldn't picket; we were in tune. Different people who had picketed with us from time to time came and stood with us. A way of life was coming to an end. We all swapped names, addresses and phone numbers and said we would have regular reunions, and at the time of writing we have had four or five. It felt good to be among such friends at a time like this. However we were really worried about the return to work next day. Not for us a return behind banners and a band alongside the hundreds, but a handful of stubborn people who would have to try to integrate themselves back into work. We decided to meet at 8.30 a.m. outside the office and all walk in together.

Tuesday 5 March. I got out my regular office clothes which I had not worn for a year, and prepared to put on my Coal Board skin. No sooner had we stepped inside the foyer than we were separated and whisked off to different parts of the office. Adrian and I were escorted to a manager's office to be interviewed about our employability. As I suspected, the NCB went for the middle option so as to appear reasonable. The three choices were: sack us; offer us a one year contract; offer us permanent jobs like the other staff. We had already decided that if we were offered a year's contract we would turn it down. That is what they offered, and we were outraged by their manner. We were given 24 hours to think over the offer of a year's contract. We were asked to return the next day and the offer would then be made in writing. The year's contract was a bitter pill to swallow. For Adrian and I this would be our fifth year on contract if we accepted it. We were aware that we would be monitored all year and there was a strong possibility that after a year we would be given the push. They wouldn't be able to fault us on our work as we were both efficient, or we would not have been promoted to CO3, but they would get us on our attitude. We weren't broken and I personally had felt more confident, assertive and strong about the strike as time had gone on. We also felt we were being asked to accept less than we had been able to achieve for the other contract staff who had been made permanent. Most activists and people in COSA urged us to be 'sensible', to accept the offer and fight from within. We just couldn't do that, and insisted we take our case to a solicitor with a view to taking the NCB to an industrial tribunal. The solicitor sought barrister's advice and he was very sympathetic to our claim for moral and natural justice, but there was no legal case for the NCB to answer. So, end of the road. In the aftermath of the strike the NCB has taken every opportunity to dictate to its staff, and even two striking clerks could not escape the NCB's heavy hand. It seems they have learnt nothing about industrial relations, nor does it appear that they want to.

I have been lucky since the strike finished. I have managed to find another job and I have been accepted as a student at Sheffield Polytechnic on a full-time, three year course for Applied Social Studies. I have been chosen to be part of a group of women and children who will have a month's holiday in the Soviet Union, paid for by the Soviet miners. I have had choices, unlike lots of people involved in the strike who now feel trapped in jobs they hate. A year is a long time to be off work in circumstances I have described. It breaks the hold that paid employment has; it breaks the fear of industrial action; if the opportunities and the personalities are right it can be heady and liberating.

I have been lucky, as things have generally worked to my advantage despite unfavourable circumstances. I have never seen myself as a leader, but when opportunities have occurred and I have been pushed to the fore I need little persuading to act. I continually said on the picket line, 'I don't want to be the leader, we are all in this together. Any one of us should be able to take initiatives.' I could feel myself developing and responding, and I very much wanted other strikers to recognise and respond to developments too, as a confidence builder. I felt it would be healthy for the labour and trade union movement if there was more stimulus from below. We do not have to wait for leaders to tell us what to do, most of the time we know what needs to be done and we should take the initiatives. For too long working class people have allowed the establishment of the ruling class and of the labour movement to set the parameters for action and debate and we have lacked both the education and the confidence to set our own. During the miners' strike there were many examples of strikers, women and support groups setting the pace when so-called leaders had turned their backs.

I am bitterly disappointed by the lack of support from the Parliamentary Labour Party and the TUC. As in 1926 and 1945, we trembled on the brink of moving ideas and expectations but most of our leaders who had access to the media and other influential institutions lacked the vision and courage to seize the opportunity to argue socialist ideas. This was seized on by some of the British public as a let-off and the Parliamentary Labour Party and the TUC were exposed once again.

The way forward for the NUM now seems unclear. I believe the only way to fight the NCB and the Tory government proposals is through further strike action, carrying many sections of the public with us. But surely the union cannot afford to dissipate its resources trying to convince people who are not our natural allies. We must recognise that some groups will never be convinced that it is right for a fight for jobs and communities to be undertaken in the only manner this government found frightening. The union needs to be united and the whole membership convinced of all-out strike action with appeals to the trade union movement to join us.

30 June 1985

Spirits High and Stomachs Filled:
Women and Solidarity Work

Caroline Coles;
Sally Davison;
Polly Vittorini,
Nicola Field
and Caron Methol

A Miner in The House

Caroline Coles

Caroline Coles is 'doing the knowledge' –
learning to be a London taxi-driver.

At the beginning of April 1984 my partner Jim and I moved out of a tiny flat into a spacious house we had decided to buy together. I was very excited by this prospect, especially as it coincided with a change for me in terms of work. I was to stay in my job at Hackney Community Action (HCA), but part-time. I needed a break from the sort of pressures it involved: campaigning, going to untold numbers of meetings and, though by far the most enjoyable part of the job, the constant need to be helpful and receptive to people.

These two changes meant I felt I had a lot more space both physically and mentally. This coincided roughly with the start of the miners' strike. Six weeks after the start of the strike Jim and I were asked if we could put a miner up for a couple of weeks. 'No problem,' we said. Glen Turner from South Wales stayed with us for over ten months: ten months I won't ever forget. Now it's hard to remember life before the strike.

A local Communist Party branch, Stoke Newington, had a member who had connections with someone from South Wales and the branch agreed early on in the dispute to adopt a pit from that area and make contact with the people there. Oakdale was chosen and when contact had been established the miners from Oakdale decided they should send four men up to London to see what could be done. They were not simply representing their own pit, but were working on behalf of a larger area for the Gwent Food Fund.

The meeting in a local pub was the first between miners and hosts. I must admit to feeling a combination of excitement and anxiety at the prospect of meeting miners, and I realised that I had a romantic impression of miners. I had recently finished reading *Wigan Pier Revisited* by Bea Campbell and remembered being particularly struck by the chapter on attitudes to miners.

When it came to the crunch, however, it hadn't changed the way I felt. I saw these men as working class heroes who could do no wrong, and who had the strength to deal the Tories a severe blow. It seemed they only had to sit there in the pub to inspire us all to great effort and commitment. This was a view I later had to grapple with, because I wanted the strength of support for the miners that seemed so easily inspired, to be transferred to everything I cared about. I didn't realise then that the reason they were here in London was because they knew they were going to need all the help they could get.

That first evening was a torment to me! I had expected to meet huge great men: I didn't know it is an advantage to be small if you work down a pit; I had never thought about it. I didn't have a clue what to say, I was in such awe. Also, I could hardly understand a word they said because of their strong Welsh accents. Humour, however, won out at the end of the day. The Welsh men soon picked up on our fascination, particularly among the women, with the fate of the pit canary. What happens to the bird? Where does it live? They teased us unmercifully and found our curiosity very amusing. Canaries, it seems, have a better life than miners! The laughter put us at our ease; the longer, more serious discussions and debates came later.

Because Glen Turner came to live in our house it transformed my involvement in the strike virtually overnight. I began to learn about miners and mining by asking basic questions about what they did. My romanticism was soon replaced by an enormous amount of respect and admiration. I felt myself to be in a privileged position, being able to learn so much so quickly, and being able to see the miners as human beings as well as heroes gave me a greater sense of solidarity.

I finally plucked up courage to ask the miners how much money they earned. I shall never forget how appalled I was at their low wages, particularly because of what I had learnt about the reality of working down a pit. And all they were asking for was a future for their communities.

In the first couple of weeks the four men, Colin, Glen, Fred and another Colin, were introduced to as many potentially sympathetic local groups, individuals and local trade unionists as possible. The local Trade Union Support Unit specifically allocated the time of one of their workers to help set up a support committee, food and money collections and so on. Soon after they arrived a Hackney Miners Support Committee was established.

Another early event was the introduction of the miners to the leadership of Labour-controlled Hackney Council. The miners were looking for office space of their own to deal with the enormous amount of support that was being expressed. All the legal aspects of this had to be checked out first: a sad, almost commonplace practice for left-wing councils under attack from central government and threatened with surcharge over many issues. But it seemed that all was okay. They moved into the office of the council rate-capping campaign at the Town Hall.

Collections, meetings and benefits were happening all over the borough. A number of local groups offered their premises as food collection points. I even remember competition amongst different groups about collecting outside certain supermarkets on the same evening. Our house often seemed dangerously loaded with the money that poured in from collections. We hid it away as best we could, and even resorted to storing some of it in the fridge. That was in the early days. It began to seem that almost everyone in Hackney supported the miners.

But there were problems as well. In the first couple of months there was a spontaneous eruption of support. But this was followed by confusion and disagreements about organisational matters. Confusion, for instance, about where to send the money collected. The men from South Wales were not the first miners to stay in Hackney, but they were the first to establish an office and were very involved in setting up the Hackney Miners Support Committee and, most importantly, in making a large number of contacts in a very short space of time. This meant people knew them, and knew that money given was going to the Gwent Food Fund. Some on the support committee thought the money should go to a central pool; the miners argued they had permission from the NUM to collect in specific areas for Gwent and South Wales, and one of those areas was Hackney.

I had some sympathy myself with the idea of a central fund because the NUM itself did not seem clear about the allocation of areas, and I felt there might be a danger of one area not getting much support. However, I agreed with the majority on the support committee that the problem could only be solved by the NUM itself. The issue became confused and local political in-fighting surfaced, with attempts to control and dominate the group by people who seemed to have the view that, because of their experience, they knew best what to do in any situation. Of course it was the miners who felt the brunt of the discomfort in the committee, and they felt it was their responsibility to sort it out. Many people did not want to become embroiled in squabbling, but were not prepared to see the group pushed around. It was dealt with, but unfortunately some people withdrew from the committee altogether as a result. The miners then took over the chairing of the meetings. Another group of miners from Nottinghamshire had in the meantime also arrived in Hackney and were working quite happily with the men from South Wales. So work continued, support grew rapidly and the amounts of money and food collected rose each week.

The miners from South Wales seemed to have a unique approach to their work, perhaps because they didn't have what I would call the 'London left' approach. They had few preconceived notions of how things 'ought' to be done, and were prepared to listen and learn as they went on. At the same time they were teaching us about the politics of the NUM and mining communities.

They were prepared to speak to anyone who wanted to hear their case, no matter how small the meeting or benefit. This attitude gained them a tremendous amount of respect. Glen worked flat out in the office, discovering a natural flair for administration and organisation, while the others raced around meeting people and making new contacts, attending meetings and collecting food from all over. But no matter how busy they were, they always had time for individuals who would pop into the office. Glen, obviously moved, would often tell me about some of their supporters and their particular circumstances. For instance an elderly lady came in once a week to give fifty pence. One week she didn't come, but the following week arrived with a pound note to make up. She told

Glen she was sorry about missing a week, but she had had to go to her sister's funeral. Accounts of that sort of commitment were frequent, but their impact on the miners never diminished.

This openness of approach exposed the miners to a certain amount of attempted manipulation by various political groups. Some people tried to involve the miners in their own disputes and though they might see the justice of their position, the miners would not allow themselves to be drawn into taking sides in a local dispute, and always took advice about such problems from the head office of the NUM. They must have felt under pressure in those situations, but nevertheless showed great integrity.

For my part I was collecting twice a week with my own CP branch and helping to organise a benefit for the miners set up by Hackney Community Action. The benefit was a huge success, raising its target of £1,000 and showing off the vast array of talent in a multi-cultural borough like Hackney. Though demented with worry about the benefit and the organisational details, I was extremely proud of the communities that took part in making the evening such a success. It wasn't just the presentation of a miner's lamp to the people of Hackney, or the Afro-Caribbean and Asian food, or the Irish dancers or any of the other groups and individuals who participated that made it so good. It was the coming together of all those people to support the miners that made it so fantastic. The people that came up from South Wales for that evening were impressed by what they saw, and quite rightly. It was an integrated and communal effort to be proud of. I myself was a nervous wreck at the end of the evening. I hadn't realised the extent of the emotional commitment I felt towards the dispute, made more acute by my contact with yet more people from mining communities in South Wales. This all happened quite early on in the dispute, and gradually I had got to know a few women from Oakdale. A number came up to Hackney on quite a few occasions to speak and to raise money, and it was always a joyous greeting. I remember times when 14 miners were sitting in my front room, but the first time a woman came to the house she followed me downstairs to the kitchen to help make the tea. We *both* felt more at ease in the kitchen doing something useful, but I also felt that we could

Women from North Derbyshire planting a commemorative tree at an East London school

talk in a different way away from the men. Their hearts and souls seemed to be in the dispute, and I had great admiration for these women who coped with families, ran their homes, were a pillar of strength and wit *and* managed to become effective political activists. And, of course, they were not intimidated by romantic notions of miners. They were their backbone, and held their own with the men very well. Of course, they carry the same oppression as all women, but their approach and attitude to life I felt to be more stoical than my own. I loved to see them, but unfortunately this happened only rarely and I had far more contact with the men in the dispute than with the women.

Initially I went out collecting twice a week with my party branch: once a week knocking on doors, and once on the street. At first I felt nervous about collecting, but after a couple of weeks I started to look forward to it. It gave me an opportunity to be involved in the sort of political work I feel most effective in, practical activities.

I shall never forget the response of the people of Hackney; it left a deep impression on me. Despite media hype and general feelings of despair about the state of Britain, I have always remained an optimist at heart. But the effect of collecting for the miners for the first time made me feel proud of people in this country. It wasn't just the extent of the support, it was also the way people identified with the miners' struggle and how much they wanted to make a positive contribution. In particular, the support in the ethnic and black communities was tremendous. For many of us it came as something of a surprise to see the extent of the concern in those communities for the miners' struggle. Not surprise that black people supported the miners, but that the support seemed unanimous. For the miners it was a real eye-opener. One day Glen was in the HCA office collecting contacts. One organisation we suggested would give a lot of support was an African organisation based in Hackney. Glen told me he had never spoken to a black person before. During the first few months when the miners themselves came out on collections with us (before they were booked solid morning to night), their amazement at the response of black people was very noticeable. It was talked about endlessly, they marvelled at it. So did I.

Glen told me one night how humbled he had felt by the collections themselves. It was the amount of poverty that got to him. He said he had knocked at one door of a very run-down house and was greeted by a man who, when asked if he would like to contribute, went and asked his family if they had anything to spare. They came back with a can of corned beef they said they had been saving but had decided the miners and their families needed it more than they did. That one instant moved Glen enormously. But many others like it started to change his thinking, not only about black people but, I suppose, about politics in general. And what was interesting to me about the miners' reactions was the effect this in turn had on many of us in London. We, too, were forced to reflect on our relationship to black and ethnic people and their politics.

The collections made a tremendous impact on us. At the time I wanted everyone to go out collecting to see for themselves the level of commitment from people, and I wanted everyone to be as convinced as I was that there was real hope for a united and socialist Britain. The collections and the contact with the public kept me going throughout the dispute and made me believe that there was no way the miners could be defeated.

Another important aspect of the collections was the contact I had with the people I collected with. I was greatly encouraged by others in the group with more political experience than myself. Many members of our branch came collecting but there was a core of people who would turn up whatever the weather, even if they were ill or had horrendous hangovers! I came to feel a strong loyalty to the group; we were proud of our work and, despite some political differences, the collections acted as a great equaliser and gave us respect for each other. The only other area of political activity that gave me such a sense of purpose was activity at Greenham Common. The similarities were a shared experience, a united collective action and a lack of battling for power within the group.

Like many others I knew, the strike became the main priority in my life. Though I was getting on with other things, it was always in my conversations and thoughts. I suppose it was inevitable as I was involved through my work, my politics and because of the presence of a miner at home: it was a personal as well as political involvement. This meant there were benefits and drawbacks, but the drawbacks were heavily outweighed by the positive experiences I gained through Glen's presence, and by the laughs we had. Nevertheless there were times when I thought the strike and all its attendant features would drive me insane. Sometimes Jim and I would escape to the country for a break; there was no such luxury for Glen. He didn't allow himself a break very often. He rarely went home. He even asked us if it would be alright if he went home for Christmas. It became a standing joke between us all that Glen was our 'adopted son', and to be honest sometimes I did feel like a mother. It is hard to describe the relationships that developed between us in the house because it was unique. There were never any ground rules set; all three of us had an involvement in the miners' strike which bonded us. And because the dispute dominated my relationship to Glen, it meant that I was unaware of the extent of the effect on him of being in London: being away from home, being on strike and coming into contact with a whole new array of people and experiences. I don't think it was really until New Year's Eve that I finally realised that our house had become Glen's home.

By that time I think we were all feeling somewhat exhausted. The three of us in the house were getting on with the work around the strike without having much time to deal with personal matters. Glen himself went through an emotional upset which hit him on New Year's Eve. I remember standing in the kitchen with him, trying to alleviate the pain he felt, but feeling useless. I was feeling pretty low myself and tears flowed, followed by one of those rare moments of insight into life. Then we started to laugh: after all, we had made it through 1984!

I often wondered how Glen would cope when the time came to return to work as so much had happened to him, and so many of his ideas and attitudes had shifted. His ideas about women changed. When he first came to stay with us I think I spent the first two weeks arguing with him about whether women were capable of working down pits. He used to infuriate me by saying after hours of argument, 'OK Caroline, you may be right, but it doesn't seem right to me and that's my view!' Gradually, though, he started to discuss women's politics with me. He met many feminists and realised that women in London weren't going to sit back quietly and support the strike without having their say as well. I'm sure many of the women from his own community gave him a good argument, but I think the fact that he heard a lot about women's politics from women outside of his usual sphere of contact who were committed to supporting the miners made him re-assess his views. But in the same way that Glen's reaction to the participation of black people forced a reaction in me, his reaction to women's politics forced me to think more clearly about male attitudes and how to effect positive changes in men's views. Too often I have felt that I have argued with men for my own position and thought I had not made any ground. Seeing Glen's attitude change made me rethink that. Now, I am more hopeful about changing other men's attitudes in that way.

But what of South Wales itself? It was at least six months after the strike began that we finally found time to go. Now it seems incredible to me that I have only been to Oakdale twice in my life. We had history lessons, walks on the mountains, a tour round the pit and visits to pubs and clubs. It was great!

We went down by car and just as we were approaching the village Glen lived in, he said, 'Just about here, below us, is where I would normally be working.' It was several miles to the pit entrance and it left me with an eerie feeling. There we were in the middle of beautiful countryside, and it was below all that that the miners would normally be working. That realisation altered my way of looking at that environment. I was disturbed at the thought of someone close to me working under the ground, and when the miners went back to work that was what I thought of. It gave me a better sense of the relationship of the people to the place they worked in.

We went first to Glen's house where he lived with his gran and two brothers. Glen's gran was a lady to be reckoned with. She is in her eighties, and at that time was still working. I noticed almost immediately her attitude to the 'boys' in the house. She had total control. She had a beautiful sense of humour and when pulling their legs, as she frequently did, she would look straight at me and wink. It felt good! A female conspiracy of secret smiles. The telly was on, Charles (of Diana fame) had gone off and left Di holding the baby. Gran said, 'That's just typical of men,' looking at me with a wink, then at

Glen, 'but you'd be just the same, except you'd be off down the pub to boast!' Then with a twinkle in her eye, 'and I suppose you've brought your washing for me to do.' She loved every minute of it. So did I. The next moment there was a knock at the door and a little boy from next door came in, tearful and soaking wet, locked out of his house. She had him in dry clothes, sat by the fire with a hot drink in his hand in no time at all. She tried to cajole him out of his misery, but he sat there stoically staring at the television, refusing to smile or cry. She looked at me and said, 'Why is it that boys must always try and hide their feelings?' What a good question, I thought. To me she is a live, political woman, rooted in the mining community, much more clear about what she thinks and says than I am. It was great to meet her, especially because of her closeness to Glen.

On Saturday Glen took us on a tour of South Wales. We went miles, met up with people he hadn't seen for a while, went to a food distribution point in Tredegar, went up and down the Rhondda, took a look at the Mardy colliery and visited Aberfan. No one could visit Aberfan without feeling devastated. As I walked round the graveyard I felt like an intruder, and I was shocked by the dates of birth: they would all have been about my age. It struck me as I stood there that the boys would almost certainly have been striking miners and the women would most likely have been out picketing, collecting, organising and supporting the strike. The pit at Aberfan was solidly on strike. None of us in the car said anything for almost an hour.

Later on we went to the most popular spot for a Saturday night, known as 'the bottom club', as opposed to the club at the top of the village. We knew quite a lot of people there, particularly women who'd been up to London. It seemed strange to be introduced to their husbands – it usually happens the other way round! Events in the club took their normal course but to me and Jim it was extraordinary. We played bingo, listened to people singing: everyone took their turn, and what amazing voices they had. Everyone was there to have a good time, and everyone did have a good time. Shirley, who I had met a few times by then, said that it was actually going to the club and being with your friends that was important. The fact that people couldn't afford to have much to drink as a result of the strike didn't matter so much. But Jim and I never had empty glasses.

The second time we went down was after the miners had gone back to work. Lots of people from Hackney and Bristol had been invited to a 'thank you' social. It was a mass get-together, a celebration of the links that had been made and a further strengthening of those links.

Again, everyone had a great time. There were speeches, entertainers, music and dancing, and many, many smiling faces. The entertainment didn't stop at the end of the 'do'. The partying continued in people's homes till very late.

The people I met in Oakdale didn't mind who or what you were: if you had supported the strike you were welcome. I had such a good feeling that weekend that I didn't want to leave. It felt like a goodbye gesture to the days of the dispute, and part of me didn't really want to say that goodbye.

Of the return to work? I call it a defeat in the sense that all of us who contributed, all the miners on strike, all the efforts of the women, have not saved one job. That was a huge disappointment – and didn't the media just love it. They tried to humiliate the striking miners throughout the dispute, and gloated over the return to work in a depressingly assured and familiar style.

Now that it is over, the analysing has started. It is very important for all of us to learn from our experiences of the dispute and what might be done better in any future situation, whoever we may be. But I wish we could do it without mud-slinging and political point-scoring: none of that will save one single miner's job or mining community.

The dispute was not a waste of time, however, and there were many victories. Much solidarity was expressed all over the country: some trade unions and many trade unionists stood firm in their support, and there was a stunning contribution from women. To me the involvement and struggle of women is the most important development: women from mining communities worked hard, won their right to be involved in the dispute in their own ways and taught women like me from London a lesson in solidarity. They gained recognition from many of the men and I dearly hope they will continue to go from strength to stength.

For me, I can take what I learnt from the miners' strike into other areas of struggle that are less publicised and that might seem less heroic: against unemployment, against homelessness, against low pay. Throughout the strike, I saw a fantastic commitment from people in and around Hackney. Despite some attempts to show us all the 'true' way to the revolution, there was a clear sense of purpose and a massive effort to try and achieve a victory for working people.

I am proud to have been part of that effort.

Camping Holidays   *Sally Davison*

Sally Davison is a part-time teacher and is active
in the peace movement.

As the 1984 school holidays were approaching it became
obvious that the strike was going to continue throughout the
summer. Groups of people began to address themselves to the
problem of providing holidays for miners' children. I myself
took part in a four week holiday scheme in Essex in
conjunction with Barnsley Women Against Pit Closures. We
had four groups of children, with accompanying adults, down
to a campsite near Brentwood. One of the weeks was allocated
to children from the Nottingham coalfield because of the
particular hardship there.

Providing a holiday was a way of linking in to the alternative
welfare state set up and staffed by the coalfield women. This
alternative structure included provision for leisure and
enjoyment as well as basic needs: bread, but roses too. The
holidays were a useful service, giving both parents and children
a much needed break, but they also underlined the fact that the
struggle for community survival included the struggle of the
community to organise alternatives in every area of life.

The organisation of holidays was also a way of linking
communities. Those who provided the resources and services
for the holidays were able to support the strike in a new way.
There was a direct human contact between supporters of the
strike and mining families. It helped people from non-mining
areas to understand the community nature of resistance in the
coalfields. And in turn, they were able to show *their* solidarity
as communities.

The international solidarity was tremendous, both in terms
of money sent and holidays provided, but in some ways the
geographical encounters between different parts of the country
were even more illuminating. For example, most of our visitors
had had very little previous contact with black and Asian
people. On visits to London they were amazed at the
cosmopolitan nature of the city; they were also deeply
impressed by the generosity the black community showed
them. In addition, they were agreeably surprised to find that
not all people in the South-East are stand-offish, mean and

unfriendly! And we in the South-East learned a lot about the strong spirit of the mining villages.

The idea and organisation of the camp I was involved in came from the South Essex District of the Communist Party. The campsite we used, Coppice Camp, was left to the Communist Party by a Communist doctor in the 1930s, to be held in trust for the use of young people. In recent years, regrettably, the camp has been under-used. The left seems to have forgotten how to make use of this kind of resource. However the campsite is still in good working order. It has rudimentary 'chalets' with bunk beds, a shower and toilet block that was built by the Young Communist League and a large central hut fitted with kitchen and dining facilities. Progressive Tours, a travel agency with left-wing connections, gave great assistance to the project throughout the summer, providing bicycles, tents, sleeping bags and a minibus. As well as this, there was the experience of previous users of the camp to draw on. It took the stimulus of the miners' strike to bring all these resources together and put them back into the service of the labour movement.

In addition to this pre-existing network of resources, the organisers were able to draw on wide support for the strike within the area. As well as Communist Party branches there were miners' support groups, Labour Party and trade union branches, trades councils and, above all, many, many individuals and families. Pensioners were outstanding in their support, some of them sending in enough money to pay for a child's holiday even though they themselves could not afford to go away. Letters and telephone calls asking for £35 to cover the cost of a holiday for one child for one week brought in a tremendous response. The project revealed all kinds of friendship and work-place links that helped to spread the idea around, bringing in money and many offers of help. Harlow Council provided free use of their recreational facilities, including boating and swimming; a local student union lent a minibus; volunteers came to help in the running of the camp; families invited miners to their homes; a Ford branch of the TGWU contributed a fish and chip supper; a Southend seaside stall-holder provided free ice-creams for all the children every time we visited the beach. The project appealed to people's imagination and was able to draw in new supporters for the strike.

The third vital organising ingredient was the Barnsley Women Against Pit Closures group. They sent nearly a hundred children from all over Yorkshire down to the camp, as well as adults to help with the journey and the running of the camp. They made contact with the Nottinghamshire women so that some of their children could also be given a holiday. In addition to this, the Barnsley group organised a series of week-long trips to the cottage of a CND member in North Yorkshire who had offered help. And they sent children off on trips to Ireland, France and the Soviet Union. All the organisation for these holidays fell on the Barnsley group. They circulated letters to all the women's groups in Yorkshire and to the miners' Panels, and from the replies drew up a list of children wanting holidays. Names were then drawn out of a hat, parents contacted and, eventually, children gathered together at the collecting points. By the end of the strike nearly every child in the area who had asked for a holiday had been away somewhere. The 'travel agency' service was organised at the same time as food kitchens, welfare advice, money collections, picketing, travelling round the country to mobilise support, and organising meetings, rallies and marches.

The holiday scheme at Coppice Camp drew on the skills and resources of hundreds of people. It enabled the organisational ability of the labour movement to be put to a different use. Different groups of people made their own particular contributions. Although the holidays were not the initiative of women acting on their own, the existence of the women's campaigning groups enabled the scheme to take place.

The general pattern of the week at Coppice was that the children and accompanying adults were collected by minibus and brought down to Essex. Activities on the site included sports, bike rides, games, music, painting and cooking. The Nottinghamshire miners built a 'death slide' that was a great attraction. Every week a talent show was organised and there was always a big party on the last night. There were sightseeing trips to London and visits to the seaside, as well as repeated excursions to the swimming baths, which were very popular. The atmosphere was fantastic: the children helped with the chores, sang miners' songs on all the journeys and got on very well together, even though most of them hadn't met before. They were generally an impressive advertisement for their parents. The adult contingent consisted of people from the mining communities who had come down to help, full-time workers at the camp, including an excellent cook, and several full-time volunteers, mainly unemployed people who were able to make the really valuable contribution of time. In addition, there were a couple of local teenagers whose summer holidays were greatly enlivened by the camp. It was a very mixed bunch of people, but, most of the time, everyone got on really well.

Originally the plan had been for a week's holiday, but there was so much support that the scheme stretched to two and then three weeks. Finally we realised that we had enough money for a fourth week. It was decided that this last week should be for women as well as their children. This threw us into a bit of a panic: entertaining adults is much harder than entertaining children. But everyone agreed that it was high time that some of the women who had been slaving away in the soup kitchens should be given a break. In the end twelve women and their families (about twenty children) came down.

Most of the women had never been away before without their husbands. Nor had they previously been on a camping holiday, much less a communal camping holiday, but in spite of this they all contributed to making the week very memorable. The local support groups also rose to the occasion. The highlight of the week was the trip organised by ten London cab drivers who drove out to Brentwood and picked up all the women and children for a round trip to London (20 miles away), together with a sight-seeing tour. Both passengers and drivers were completely knocked out with each other and with the success of the trip. The women were treated like royalty and the cab drivers really enjoyed their personal contribution to the strike. As well as this trip, there were many invitations to people's homes, an all-women party, free tickets to the Albany Theatre in South London, an outing to the Notting Hill Carnival and a quite wild party on the last night. For every one concerned it was a very new experience and it helped to contribute to the feelings of solidarity in the Barnsley Women Against Pit Closures network. I cannot really speak for the mining women, but it was certainly an educational experience for the camp workers!

At Christmas this network was re-activated. Money was raised for £3,000 worth of toys by appealing to the same constituency who had supported the holiday scheme. Because that had been so successful it was easier to collet the money; people felt they had confidence in the organisers, and a personal link with the families who would receive the toys. A group of us went up to Yorkshire with the toys, using the same student union minibus we had used in the summer. The women's group had organised a big children's party and we all distributed the presents. It was quite an emotional occasion and a further strengthening of the links between the two groups.

The strike is now over, but there is still a fight going on against pit closures. The women's groups are still in existence and the support network still functions, though some of the impetus has gone. This was bound to happen given the end of the strike, but it would be a great loss if the network disintegrates, for the alliances that sprang up last year showed the potential organisational capacity of the working class and labour movement when that movement is operating at full strength: that is with the full inclusion of women.

Lesbians Against Pit Closures

Polly Vittorini,
Nicola Field
and Caron Methol

A group of women were invited up to London by the Lesbians and Gays Support the Miners group. The women attended their conference on Saturday where the guest speakers were Sian James (Neath and distict), Kay Sutcliffe (Kent) and Vicky Smailes (Notts). There were various workshops held throughout the day and in the evening a performance of a play called *Shoot*. This play was written by Nigel Young and Stephen Gee. Nigel had been a guest in the Dulais valley on two occasions. On Sunday the women were taken to see an exhibition by Judy Chicago called 'The Dinner Party'. After tea, which was in the Fallen Angel, they attended the Support Group meeting where a further cheque was presented.

We take this opportunity to express our gratitude to this group who are not only generous, but kind and caring and we value their friendship a great deal.

The Valleys' Star, paper of Neath, Dulais and Swansea Valleys Miners' Support Group, April 1985.

Lesbians Against Pit Closures and Women Against Pit Closures and other women's groups have got to keep together and carry on in the future. I hope the links between lesbians and gays and Women Against Pit Closures will be carried on solidly. Lesbian women might need our support in the future, and we're certainly going to need theirs. We'll all be on the Lesbian and Gay Pride march in June.

Vicky Smailes, Rhodesia Women's Action Group, Nottingham-shire, March 1985.

Lesbian women were drawn into support for the strike through Lesbians Against Pit Closures and Lesbians and Gays Support the Miners. All told there were ten of these groups around the country – hardly a mass movement, but certainly a good deal more extensive than anything we had previously experienced or hoped for.

Predictably, the first reaction you got to announcing that you were in Lesbians Against Pit Closures was often prolonged hilarity – on the face of it, who can think of a more unlikely alliance? But of course the strike was about the coal which fuelled the lights we sat under, it was about jobs, not just the miners', it was about a fightback against the government no less – *abstention would have been suicide.*

Organising ourselves *as lesbians* proved vital if we were to involve other lesbians, since, especially in London, the lesbian scene is a thing very separate from other areas of life. One reason for the persistence of the idea that lesbians are outrageous individuals who can be spotted at a distance of six miles or so is that our clubs and meeting places are physically isolated from the rest of the world.

In the event, we made huge inroads into the lesbian and gay movement: a 'Pits and Perverts' miners benefit attracted 1,000 lesbians and gay men, raising £5,000 for the miners; women and men from the mining communities who spoke were given tremendous support from the audience and everyone went away feeling very high. London Lesbians and Gays Support the Miners alone raised £18,000 from lesbians and gay men, and the 1985 Lesbian and Gay Pride march was led by Lesbians and Gays Support the Miners, along with the banner of the South Wales Area NUM and 78 miners and members of Women Against Pit Closures from South Wales. This was the biggest Pride march ever, with up to 16,000 participants, a full third of whom marched in the miners' contingent which stretched from one end of the Haymarket to the other! Sian James, from South Wales Women Against Pit Closures, was given the warmest reception (a standing ovation in fact) of all of the speakers at the march.

We could not have done this had we not organised as lesbians and gays. Nor could we have won the tremendous support for our cause that we did. Up and down the country miners were meeting lesbians and gay men and coming to a real understanding. Our acceptance was so complete that when Lesbians and Gays Support the Miners visited the mining community of the Dulais Valley in South Wales, the two lesbians on the delegation were automatically given a double bed!

In fact that visit was the first of many, all of which are treasured memories, though none are so spectacular as that first one. With the Dulais Valley fighting for us we managed to get our first mass platform, at a thousand-strong miners' rally where we were given a standing ovation. (The television cameras were turned off throughout, of course!)

That night at the Onllwyn miners welfare hall the dance floor was filled with both gay and straight couples, smooching together or barn-dancing. It was one of the most moving experiences of all of our lives.

At the 1984 Labour Party Conference the NUM sent a message of support to the Labour Campaign for Gay Rights (now the Labour Campaign for Lesbian and Gay Rights) fringe meeting, applauding the links that had been made in South Wales, and was one of the few unions to vote in favour of a debate on lesbian and gay rights.

Gone completely were the 'what do you do in bed?' conversations, replaced by a real level of support which was first seen nationally at the Labour Party conference.

Such gains were of course partly made possible by the brilliant example of the NUM leadership and miners in South Wales, who, by accepting support from lesbians and gay men, built for themselves the possibility of massive and previously untapped amounts of support. What a difference from Grunwick where members of the Gay Left Collective were turned away from the picket line by workers who would not link arms with them!

As lesbians and gay men, some of our most immediate and dangerous enemies are the police, who threaten us outside (and inside) our clubs and on the street for the way we dress, even for holding hands together. So lesbians and gays identified readily with the experience of the violence from the police that the miners had to deal with on the picket lines. One of the arguments we never had was over who caused 'picket line violence'. But collecting in lesbian and gay clubs and pubs (in London we managed to cover an average of three every night), a lot of people said, 'what have the miners ever done for us?' and we had to launch into explanations of how a victory for the miners was a victory for the whole working class, and so on. Incidentally, this complaint evaporated as stories of the Lesbians and Gays Support the Miners visit to the Dulais Valley became popular. An especially objection-flattening quote was the promise we were given by the Dulais miners that if we were ever getting trouble from the police, to call them up, and they would 'send up the commandos from South Wales'.

A more frustrating objection we encountered when collecting for the miners was that they were all men, or all macho, and therefore all oppressive to women. Our answer was that our support for such a vital struggle for jobs must not be conditional on every member of the NUM being a model anti-sexist male! It is worthy of more than a little notice that the NUM was the *only* union at 1984 Labour Party conference to vote for women to be able to elect their own representatives onto the Labour Party's National Executive Committee. This is vitally important because in doing so they assert women's right to decide what is best for women – undoubtedly the most feminist thing which any all-male group can do!

Since then media-induced hysteria has escalated the number and seriousness of attacks on lesbians and gay men, despite the fact that lesbians are the least at-risk section of the population from AIDS. The following article appeared in the *Valleys' Star*:

> Christine Crawley, a British Euro-MP, is also likely to question the European parliament on what it is doing on AIDS research and on countering anti-gay reporting in newspapers using AIDS as an excuse. A number of other Euro-MPs are said to be interested. Meanwhile a satirical leaflet circulating among gay organisations has been sent to 'Out in the City'. It reads 'AIDS – Acute Intelligence Decay Syndrome – this killer disease is spreading rapidly among journalists. Most of the victims so far found to be clinically brain dead work for Rupert Murdoch, but other high risk groups include Dr Adrien Rogers, local radio contacts for the BBC and IBA, and all those who take ideas intravenously. The symptoms are moral hysteria, irrational fear of homosexuals and uneven patches of purple prose. Advice includes cutting down on your number of media contacts, avoid social intercourse with middle-aged journalists from Fleet Street and do not carry copies of the *Sun*, *Times* or *News of the World*.
>
> Remember PGQ (Persistent Generalised Queerbashing) is endemic in many countries, Britain is no exception.'

It is rather easy to talk as if the lesbian and gay movement was much of a muchness. Actually this is not true at all, since sexism and the oppression of women divide the lesbian and gay movement in exactly the same way as they divide the rest of the world. There is no automatic basis for an alliance between lesbians and gay men, and in fact it became *necessary* for us as lesbians to work in Lesbians Against Pit Closures as an autonomous grouping, because of the demoralising effect of working as completely outnumbered lesbians in a practically all gay-male group. Of those lesbians in Lesbians and Gays Support the Miners, many dropped out after a short time, while doubtless many women didn't get involved because it was a 'mixed' group. When some of us saw this happening we decided to try an all-women group.

Although there were many lesbians who actively supported the strike through their trade unions, their work-places or through their connections with women's centres which were in contact with women's support groups in the mining communities, there were still many who did not recognise any kind of link between themselves and the striking miners. We felt that it was vital that these women should be drawn into the struggle, and so about ten of us formed Lesbians Against Pit Closures. This group was to be specifically for lesbians who wanted to organise separately from men. A few women believed this move to be divisive, splitting the co-ordinated support that women and men could organise together. Many men in Lesbians and Gays Support the Miners were also opposed to the setting up of our group.

Our response was that if it was going to encourage more lesbians to be involved in supporting the strike, then a separate women's group could only be a positive thing. Many lesbians' unwillingness to be involved with gay men in campaigns and other things is based on the tendency of men to dominate groups, meetings and discussions. This means that not only do women get little opportunity to speak, neither do they have the chance to formulate different and new ways of showing support. Things sweep along on much the same lines as they have done for years, with the same traditions of organisation invented by men and often wholly alien to women. These traditions have structured trade union and political party organisation for years. Coming from non-hierarchical groups in the lesbian movement, this felt strange. It is important to remember that women have been traditionally alienated from trade unions. They are often unemployed, in low paid work where union membership is discouraged if not actually forbidden or, when unionised, they are prevented from being active by the way meetings are time-tabled and run. Child-care facilities have until recently never been a high priority with any trade union. Much of the achievement of trade unions had been undermined and made more fragile by the exclusion of women.

It is hardly surprising then that many lesbians felt that the miners' strike was nothing to do with them. Since it was the initiative of a union whose membership was almost entirely male, they felt that it had no relevance to them. And if supporting the strike meant going to meetings organised on the same principles which had always excluded women, then they weren't prepared to do so. As it was, Lesbians against Pit Closures was a group where lesbians who were in support of the strike's aims could organise outside of the structures from which they felt ostracised. Although the group made a late appearance, in November 1984, it immediately involved three times as many women as had been in Lesbians and Gays Support the Miners. We did organise support jointly with them, as well as establishing stronger links with mining women.

We decided to support Rhodesia Women's Action Group, in Nottinghamshire, after meeting a woman who'd just been in their village and who described how they needed more support. The miners who were still out on strike there were very much in a minority and were quite isolated. So we wrote explaining who we were and offering our financial and political support.

All in all we raised well over £1,000 through collections at women's pubs and clubs, discos and conferences. The largest single sum we raised was at a benefit we organised in early March 1985 to mark the anniversary of the strike, which was also International Women's Day. This was a very successful event as spirits continued to be high even though the strike had just ended. We knew that the fight was by no means over. We also made collections outside supermarkets in Camden and Hackney in London, which ironically were almost better supported after the strike ended.

Our pink banner was seen at many marches, rallies and demonstrations, including Swansea, Chesterfield (what an inspiring day for all the women who turned up!), Neasden power station and also the Lesbian Strength and Gay Pride marches in Central London. Whereas a year before we might have expected at least a mixed or even a hostile reaction to our banner, we were widely applauded and made to feel welcome marching alongside the fighting men and women of the mining communities.

Although people may baulk at the idea of separate lesbian groups in the women's and gay movements (self-organisation within self-organisation, as it were), our experience of them has been totally positive. For lesbians are faced with male sexism in the gay movement, and by heterosexism, or anti-gay feeling, in the women's movement. We found that it was only by recognising these divisions explicitly and organising as lesbians that these issues could be confronted.

We want to pay tribute to Women Against Pit Closures who blazed a trail for us: they were an example and our inspiration. Such solidarity between women, black people, lesbians and gay men, and those of us who are more fortunate to be organised in trade unions, has never before been so strong. It is a new kind of unity. Lesbian women have learnt, through the strike, new ways of fighting our isolation as lesbians, and we thank the mining women who have pledged their support for *our* cause. Tremendous links were forged during the strike, and we must never forget them. They can be the basis for struggles in the future.

Mines Not Missiles: Links with the Peace Women

*Liz Knight et al;
Annie; Judy;
Mary Millington;
Vicky Smailes*

Shared Resistance

Liz Knight et al

Liz Knight is a member of the Enfield Women's
Peace Group and teaches part-time at
Tottenham Technical College where she is an
active member of her union, NATFHE. She has
a nine-year-old daughter.

In March when the strike began the Cruise missile convoy had
just started its exercises outside the base. That night at
Greenham women trying to block the convoy's return had
been hurled against the fence by furious policemen. In the
morning papers we read how hundreds of picketing miners
had used their cars to block the motorways. We were filled with
excitement ... If only somehow all our courage and initiative
could be shared, if all our struggles could be linked in more
than words – how strong we would be, how easily we could
stop either the police or the Cruise convoy from using the
roads!

Of course it's not quite that simple. We are all separated in
so many ways, and no one of us can be everywhere at once.
But, collectively, perhaps we could be everywhere at once.
We'd each be resisting at our particular front line – at the
picket, police station, missile base, or in our own school or
work-place, home or street. But we'd know we weren't alone.
We could help each other out, share experiences, cause
diversions, plan place and time of joint or separate actions.
We'd each be part of the whole resistance.

What resistance?

For most women who identify with the Greenham women's
peace camp, opposing Cruise missiles may be where we start,
but it's certainly not where we end.

We know nuclear weapons are the ultimate threat. But

they're integral to a system based on profits and power, run by an élite of heads of government, big business and the armed forces who are implacably opposed to any challenge they can't control, and who, in order to keep their system going, will inflict any 'necessary' horror on the rest of us: unemployment, poverty, pollution, imprisonment, torture, starvation, and – ultimately and insanely – the threat of nuclear extinction. The real enemy of the system is not the 'Communist bloc' – though promoting external 'enemies' is always useful to our rulers – no, the real enemy is us, the ordinary people of each country, asserting our simple human rights to food, shelter, work, a community, a future for our children. For, increasingly, this grotesquely inadequate economic and political system we live under can't even permit us those basic freedoms. Millions in the world starve. Coal is locked underground. People are locked out of useful work. Nuclear missiles costing billions of pounds are pointing straight at us from inside the wire fence at Greenham Common.

The men – and one or two women! – who run this system use an ideology of male supremacy, the supremacy of muscle, gun and bomb, to legitimise their rule. This ideology works in crude and subtle ways, 'Divide and rule' is central to it, and the first victims are women as a social group ... We are either openly or subtly given to understand that we don't really count: we are just there to oil the wheels and produce the next generation of workers.

Men everywhere have to acknowledge their part in sustaining this ideology which oppresses them too. Every sexist joke unchallenged, every trivialisation of women's life experiences, every set-up which excludes women or puts us firmly on the sidelines – all these are ways by which men, often unknowingly, help prop up the system they may want to end.

Physical violence, or the threat of it, is the system's ultimate sanction against us and all dissidents. Some women feel that answering violence with violence can never be justified, because it again excludes women, perpetuates the ruling ideology and ultimately helps keep the system going in its own vicious circle. Many other Greenham women, while sympathising with this view, think that sometimes the conditions of struggle mean that there is literally no choice, at least in the short term, but to defend ourselves physically, with fists or weapons, against aggression. At Greenham we do have a choice, and we choose non-violence. We resist not with physical force or threats, but with our whole selves: in a sense, with our vulnerability as women and as human beings. Men have to learn to accept their vulnerability too, as women have been forced to do. Out of that self-knowledge, when it is shared, comes strength, not weakness or passivity.

That, for many of us, has been the meaning of Greenham. A shared vulnerability as women in a world that's hostile to women (and to men too in fact). A literal linking of hands with each other, feeling the electric energy of that linking, empowering each of us individually to say 'No'. No to genocide, no to the rape of the world. Yes to life and self-determination. 'Freedom!' was what 30,000 of us shouted when we surrounded the base that day in December 1982 which was for many women when it all took off.

Greenham is about freedom, and continues to be in spite of all the hardships, conflicts, set-backs, hurts and disappointments experienced by women round the camp. It is not about 'an issue', an organisation, leadership or power struggles. What it means personally for each woman who has ever identified with the struggle there, is what it is. Each of us defines it, because each of us *is* it. What we take to Greenham, we find there: sometimes anxiety, loneliness, depression; sometimes a soaring confidence and energy which will see us cutting fences, doing handstands on the runway inside the base. Whatever it is, it's what we bring and find freely as women with other women.

Freedom, non-violent resistance, solidarity. Making connections. Greenham imagery is full of spiders spinning, snakes sliding, dragons whirling – all perpetually in motion, linking tree to tree, earth to sea, sky to fire. 'Only connect' ... and we can undo the rigid, imprisoning divisions imposed on us. This, at least, is how we want it to be – meanwhile we often feel isolated and stuck in our own particular groove.

Building solidarity was – and still is, of course – the key struggle for the NUM and everyone in the mining communities. And we know this is and was an uphill job in the face of the lies of the media, the NCB and the government; the silence of much of the trade union and Labour leadership; and the real fear and feelings of helplessness generated by unemployment.

Divide and rule: one way or another you are told by government and media that if you're not a miner, then it's none of your business. Moreover, 'they' (the miners) are violent, stupid, trying to defend an obsolete industry, living in the past. Similarly, we as Greenham supporters have been portrayed as dirty, ugly, aggressive and crazy – wasting our time on a pointless protest when we should be at home looking after husbands and children.

We know the ways of the media very well: the silencing and the omissions as well as the lies. Women in particular have always been used to being silenced or trivialised. The Greenham protest has been about women refusing to be silenced any more, becoming visible at last, to ourselves as well as to others. The media hardly mentioned the self-organisation of the miners' wives, except towards the end of the strike. It wasn't considered newsworthy … and it might have made women outside the mining areas stop and think. Women on picket lines. Women occupying buildings when they are refused permission to set up communal kitchens. Women organising in every pit village, initiating food and money collections, checking on every striking family's welfare, feeding hundreds daily, sometimes from two gas rings. Women making their own banners, posters and leaflets, marching, speaking at meetings and rallies. Women being roughed up and insulted by the police, being arrested. We knew.

Many women living at the Greenham camp went almost immediately to Wales, Yorkshire, Kent, Nottinghamshire and Staffordshire to give support on picket lines and in the kitchens. Several were arrested at the pickets alongside miners' wives. (One at least was spirited away by the miners' wives before her court appearance!)

Greenham women everywhere, in support groups as well as at the camp, were inspired by the tremendous courage and organisation of women in the mining communities. We understood that the struggle was about the very survival of those communities. And it was about freedom. Who shall decide? Should MacGregor and the government be allowed to destroy whole communities and rob us of our natural energy resources in the name of the god profit? This couldn't be a concern of the pit villages alone. The issues were too great and the consequences of the state winning were too terrible.

The whole question of the expansion of nuclear power and its direct link with the escalation of the nuclear arms race was thrown into focus and made urgent for us by the government's attack on the coal industry. It became dramatically clear that the government wants to close coal mines in order to expand the use of nuclear power. And nuclear power stations not only produce electricity (very expensively) – they also produce plutonium for making nuclear weapons to add to the ever-growing world stock-piles.

You cannot have 'peaceful' nuclear power. Its proposed development as the major energy source in the economy can't now be separated from the whole strategic direction of the ruling class. It's part of the generalised attack we're facing on so many fronts.

Nuclear power implies drastic job losses. It implies an attack on people's way of life and the breaking up of the mining communities. It has already meant the stealing of indigenous people's homelands in Australia, Canada and Namibia, where the uranium which fuels the power stations is mined. It implies a continuous attack on people's health and safety; not only of the people working in the uranium mines and the power stations themselves, but of everyone on the planet. There is still no safe way of producing nuclear power or of disposing of its poisonous waste products. Children are already dying of leukaemia as a direct result of leaks from nuclear power stations in this country. Thousands of unborn children are already sentenced to death or deformity from nuclear radiation, whether from power stations, uranium mines or nuclear bomb testing.

The incorporation of nuclear power into the economy gives the government potentially even more control over our lives. Increasingly, we may see armed police and oppressive laws taking over what democratic rights we have, in the name of 'security' – in reality in the defence of the profits and power of the few huge monopolies and the politicians who serve them. The thousand years' worth of coal still underground may be left to waste. The other natural energy resources – wind, water, sun, earth – whose only disadvantage is that it's hard to make money out of them, may remain undeveloped.

Our planet is being slowly poisoned.

Women as a social group, and of course working class women in particular, are generally excluded more than men (even working class men) from the world of power, money, 'politics' and the kind of alienated thinking which goes with it. Perhaps that's why talk of the 'realities of economics' in the coal industry never confused the miners' wives, just as talk of the 'realities of defence' never confused the Greenham women. For most women the realities of life are not the posturing and the power and the battle of ideas, but the details of daily living which underpin everything else. An industry, an economic system or a defence system which endangers our lives must be a nonsense. No wonderful arguments are going to impress us, because we know.

As Greenham women and as Women Against Pit Closures, we share that understanding and the will to resist.

We have shared experiences: the brutality and lies of the police and the media; the exhilaration of taking action for change with other women; the dogged determination to defend our children and our future, come what may. Also – the incomprehension and sometimes hostility (as well as support) of the men we live and work with, in the face of our new-found independence.

But there are also differences between us.

Greenham started as a movement of mainly middle class women (although it certainly isn't entirely so); whereas the Women Against Pit Closures movement is of course emphatically working class. There are fears and prejudices and real differences on both sides of the class division which perhaps need to be more explicitly acknowledged and discussed so that we can learn more from each other. All of us as women are used to being accommodating and unobtrusive, and to avoiding confrontation. Facing differences, especially among friends, can be very threatening. But while we give in to our lack of confidence, the links between us will not be quite as honest, or therefore as strong, as they could be.

We chose to support the miners' struggle specifically as Greenham women because we understood we had a common cause and we wanted to make that understanding visible. However some of us often felt unable to carry over our experiences and views as Greenham women into our support of the strike. It was not that we wanted to impose 'Greenham politics' on the strike, but we wanted to participate fully as ourselves, with our own particular viewpoint, rather than just as more or less passive supporters.

Having discovered the tremendous power of non-violent resistance at Greenham, we did not really know how or if we could carry that understanding into the new situation of the strike. Having discovered the political power of women acting autonomously, we didn't always support strongly enough the efforts of women in the mining communities to act autonomously in the strike. And having discovered the connectedness of political struggles, we still hadn't the confidence always to challenge sexist behaviour and assumptions, for fear of undermining the struggle against pit closures.

These difficulties, experienced more by some women than others, indicate again how crucially important confidence-building is. Had we been braver, we might actually have given our sisters in the mining communities more valuable support than some of us felt we did, and learnt much more from them too in the open exchange of ideas.

Instead of either bulldozing other women's views aside, or remaining spectators of each other, we need to work more on learning to validate every woman's contribution (without having to agree with her), and on trying to function without a hierarchy, so that every woman can take a full and equal part. It's ideas such as these which help make real solidarity possible, because in their context, differences become just that: differences – they do not have to be threatening. This is not to deny the very real power differences which exist between women of different classes, but we need to find ways to really look at them and understand them, so that they are no longer such great (and often invisible) barriers between us.

Many bridges which will not be destroyed were built in the course of 1984-85.

What links were made?

Many Greenham support groups and individual 'peace women' collected money to send to Women Against Pit Closures, or affiliated to their local miners support groups and joined in street collections. Groups took their peace banners on rallies in mining areas and in London, particularly on the great Women Against Pit Closures rally in August.

Women from the Greenham camp, with women in Leicester and York, helped initiate marches between pits and nuclear power stations. These took place in August in England,

Scotland and Wales, and involved 'peace women' and Women Against Pit Closures in long miles of talking, leafleting, street-theatre and collecting food for miners' families. The slogans were: 'Make the links!', 'Pit closures = job losses + nuclear power + nuclear weapons!', 'Mines not Missiles!'

The Mines not Missiles theme was taken up on thousands of tee-shirts, badges and banners, and in some areas 'Mines not Missiles' groups were formed.

Groups such as these and women's peace groups turned out on picket lines at power stations, particularly on the regionally organised 'days of action'.

Women from both movements invited each other to stay in their homes and speak at each other's meetings. From one such meeting in London women from London Greenham support groups decided to try and make our support for the strike more visible, and, calling ourselves Greenham Women for a Miners' Victory, set about making a banner bearing our message and a red dragon, the Welsh, Greenham, Chinese, ancient life-symbolising dragon all in one. This task we shared with women involved in the occupation of the South London Women's Hospital. The dragon appeared at rallies and picket lines – perhaps most memorably for some of us on a freezing day in February at Neasden power station when dozens of musicians, singers, fire-eaters, jugglers, dancers and comedians, brought together as the 'Pit Dragon', kept the picket line jigging all day.

Friendships were forged and correspondence exchanged between women in both movements. Dozens of women, we know, worked at making links – much of what was done and is still being done is of course unknown by those of us who happen to be writing this. We'd like to take the opportunity here of acknowledging the achievements of all the women involved.

What was generated out of all this feels to us strong enough to survive the difficult times we all, but particularly the women in the mining communities, are now facing. Iris from Yorkshire wrote to us recently:

'Thank you for flying the flag down there; we were afraid you all would desert – what little faith we had! ... Our links are forged with love and sisterhood, and it is wonderful ...'

Jacky from Nottinghamshire wrote:

> 'We are not defeated and it is thanks to you with open eyes that we stayed out for so long. The women's support groups will carry on to fight for our industry and also to return the support and solidarity that you have shown us by assisting you in your struggles ... Yours in unity and solidarity forever ...'

These words make us feel proud to have been able to share, in however small a way, in our sisters' magnificent struggle. In many ways that sharing is only just at the beginning. Already those women's support groups in Nottinghamshire and Yorkshire have worked hard to campaign for the release of Ann Francis, imprisoned for six months for protesting at Greenham. Women from several mining areas have visited Greenham and Molesworth and supported actions there. On our side we need to continue to raise funds and support the campaign for the victimised and imprisoned miners. We need to exchange ideas as well as information, to risk exploring differences as well as the ground we know we share – so that together we can all go forward. The success of both our struggles is in the growth of political awareness and confidence they have generated. We as women have been at the centre of these tremendous changes, and as women we are reaching out to build a larger human solidarity than our divided world has yet known.

July 1985
(*Written by Liz Knight, with much help from Peggy Gosling, Fiona Jamieson, Juliet Nelson, Iris Preston and Jill Robertson.*)

The Women's Picket at Port Talbot

Judy, *Orange Gate, Greenham Common*

I spent some time in South Wales during the summer of the miners' strike.

One of the first things I did was to go to a meeting in Cardiff of women in miners' support groups. There were about a hundred women there, from dozens of different pit villages in the valleys.

The sense of power in the meeting was immense to me. Although there are thousands of women involved in Greenham, working at home in towns or at the camp, there are often quite small numbers of women living at the peace camp at any one time, and calls for a big gathering of women are often communicated by word of mouth and take some time to get through.

Here there were hundreds of women who could hear directly what each other was doing and arrange to meet and get together at very short notice, which made them potentially very strong. There was a sense of urgency; women were making decisions about taking action, stating what they wanted, deciding it was time for them to break the law – taking all these steps very fast. They were being forced into these quick understandings because the state had immediately realised the potential threat of the strike and their growing ability to confront those who expected them to stand and watch while their communities were destroyed. So the media and police were immediately ranged in force against them. In this sense women at the camp have more time to decide when we want to take action, or when to confront the police.

Women who would never otherwise have met and who didn't usually spend much time out of their own village were sharing experiences as they met and talked with other women. This did the same as the camp does for some women who feel isolated where they live, and are only able to visit sometimes – it made a space to see and know the others involved in the same struggle, so that once you've gone back to your usual place you know how strong you are.

Anyway … the idea of a mass women's picket soon came up and took off straight away in a buzz of excitement. Women liked the idea of it being women only; of taking action themselves, not ordered by the NUM. Some women felt that the police would be less violent with women, and that strike breaking drivers would be more likely to be affected by it.

However some women felt dubious about taking action the NUM hadn't ordered; some women didn't know if their lodges or the NUM would agree not to send men to picket that day; some women would have problems getting transport as the lodge at their pit didn't think money should be spent on sending women to pickets.

After some discussion about where the picket should be, it was agreed to ask a miner who had driven one of the groups to the meeting to say which place he thought would be best. 'The Port Talbot steel works,' he immediately replied, and that was agreed without much more ado.

This felt strange to me, largely because of the preconceptions I had brought with me from Greenham. I had naïve assumptions that women working together would magically collect their own power into their own hands and use it without a backward glance. Partly I could think that because living at Greenham in a women-only community, dealing with the problems of working with men politically is something I didn't have to think about – there's obviously no possibility of the women making the sandwiches while the men talk if there are no men around. Although we lead very busy lives at the camp, we usually have the time to give all our attention to something. During the strike the women from support groups were coming home from a picket after being up half the night, making the breakfast and immediately starting some sewing to earn a bit of extra money before they set off for the food kitchens. Women so often have their attention split between the three things they're trying to do at once – that's what needs changing.

It seems that the right decision was made and Port Talbot was a really good place to go to, and it was obviously sensible in that situation to ask a miner because he knew things about the NUM that the women didn't know (like where NUM pickets were likely to be), but the reason he'd been asked seemed partly to get the action recognised by asking a man from the NUM; although women had initiated the action they didn't remain completely in control of it.

meeting of womyn from the south wales coalfield ———
during the miners' strike, July 31 1984

womyn sitting bursting
straining with indignation
each with her own
stories racing round her head

the meeting called to order
trying to sort her

for a moment she listens
and someone says: DHSS

and she nudges your
elbow and out pours the story
of what they said to her son...
the room bubbles with
fifty whispered stories
GROWING LOUDER

the meeting called to order
trying to sort her

for a moment she listens
and someone says: POLICE

and the stories start
smouldering
s c a t t e r i n g
spark off flames of anger ———

me meeting called to order _____

ying to sort her

r a moment she listens
nd someone says:

LAW
COURTS
SEQUESTERING OF FUNDS

and she **ERRUPTS!**

each of her

too full with fear and fury

shouting her story to her sisters

all at once desperate to talk

she is saying:

i am here

this is happening to me

i must do something

i am ready

_____ and you cannot contain her _____ —Annie

So, come the morning of the picket we drove down from the camp very late, had a few hours sleep in Cardiff, and eventually arrived at Port Talbot at about six in the morning and stumbled sleepily out of the van.

The steel works entrance is down a private road, about 200 yards from the exit of the M4. Women were grouped around the top of the road on two triangles of grass on either side, standing with banners or talking in groups, waiting for the first coal lorries to arrive. There were quite a few men around, but many more women. We immediately saw women we knew and ran over to talk to them and found out that a few car loads of women had driven down from the camp that morning. There were also already a fair few police Transit vans scattered about.

About ten minutes before the first of the lorries was due out people started to wander back and forth across the top of the exit road, and a blockade developed when some women sat down in the road and linked arms. As I sat down in the road with some friends I was thinking that this was the first time I'd been in a mixed blockade.

The police used the same old tactics as at the camp – drag us off one by one and then attempt to pen us in at the side of the road by making a wall of navy uniforms. Obviously I'd thought about non-violence as one of the issues that would come up working with people who weren't committed to that as a way of working which is right or effective. It was clear straight away that the situation was different here. How much that was because the police didn't assume we would be non-violent, and how much it was to do with there being men on the action, I don't know, but the police weren't there with the idea of being non-violent and they knew who they were out to get. They went straight for the men on the blockade, made them get up by twisting their arms so that they were forced to move or have them broken, and arrested several of them, although at that stage they were mostly just moving women to the side of the road and didn't arrest any until later.

Then some of the women started off walking down the side of the road towards the M4, spreading out so that the police were no longer able to contain us. As people streamed out down the road, the police had no alternative but to follow. That was when we didn't grab our opportunity – if everyone had walked between the spaced-out police onto the main road they would have had no option but to stop the convoy of lorries while they cleared the road.

If I'd been at the camp I think I'd have been quite sure that every woman who was there would have been determined enough to walk between the police and get onto the road. As it was, not enough people had the faith that we could be effective by direct action and so the police had enough spare men to have three or four watching one person trying to get through them. I wish we had done this again on another day, because I think it's the kind of thing you don't get fooled by twice, but on the other hand several miners told me not to keep walking into the road because they truly thought the lorries would deliberately drive over us. We hadn't quite got to the belief in direct action which makes it work.

As it was I was continually held back to watch the convoys of lorries pass – the drivers high up, staring straight ahead through windscreens covered by grids, their faces often masked by dark glasses and helmets. I got the same kind of feeling as when I've watched the American drivers of Cruise missile launchers go past – they were using the same survival tactic of blinkering themselves from the people shouting to them to stop by becoming as much a part of the machine as possible.

Once all the lorries for the day had gone in we heard we'd held them up for over an hour and a half. It seemed a good beginning.

The other thing I spent time doing in Wales was helping to get together a walk from pit-heads in Welsh mining villages to Hinckley Point nuclear power station, just opposite Barry over the Bristol Channel in Somerset.

The walk was a good chance to meet women from the mining communities and talk with some of them a bit more, and as we wended our way down the valleys to Cardiff we talked with many people about the strike and what we were trying to do at Greenham.

I had some good discussions with people who at first thought it was mad to link the government running down of coal mines with the rising investment in nuclear power and the arms trade but who later began to see the connections. People in Wales obviously understood how centralisation meant loss of autonomy: they have been struggling against domination by the English for centuries. We met with a lot of old people and ex-miners who could remember earlier strikes and saw the same issues coming up again.

The sudden meeting of the two groups – women from the camp and women from the mining communities – at first threw up the differences more than the similarities. Our lives are very different and we looked weird to each other because of silly things like our clothes and hair. Gradually we learnt enough about our differences to begin to see our own prejudices. Both groups had the same kind of wrong ideas about each other, like thinking there were far more politically active people in the other group than there actually were. When women arrived at one pit village the miners had laid on a welcoming meal and were disappointed when only the few women who were doing that bit of the walk came. I was surprised that in some villages where there were thousands of miners on strike there might be less than a hundred women doing the work keeping the food kitchens going.

Some of these women have since visited us and seeing each other in the places we live has made it easier to understand that we are all in different parts of the same struggle and the connections between those parts became much clearer to many people, me included, during the strike.

The Cynon Womyn

Annie, Orange Gate,
Greenham Common

the cynon womyn on the picket line so angry
so determined
not a question now of being behind their men
they are with them
putting themselves on the line
saying: this is our struggle too
we want to keep our pits open to dig useful coal
to keep our town, our village, our people together
not to be closed down, not to be robbed of use
not to be people scattered into thousands of frustrated
fragments …

the cynon womyn know what it's all about:
a government that doesn't want people
to work and produce something useful
or grow strong
a government that wants people weak and
divided
to let it
railroad over them with its nuclear waste trains;
make nuclear electricity make bombs;
pollute the sea the fish the earth the cows
the milk
our children drink leukemia;
make it so when you switch on the radiator
you radiate …

the cynon womyn talking:
nato generals visited the drift mine
what do they want to hide here?
nuclear arms or nuclear waste?
we won't let them hide: let them come out in the open
let's see what they are
the soldiers dressed as police
businessmen dressed as magistrates
multi-national profiteering dressed as social concern …

the cynon womyn know this story:
the welsh tourist board stripping south wales
of its life and liveliness
dressing it up pretty
leisure garden for the english ...

the cynon womyn know your plan:
outwardly the tourist tart
inwardly the nuclear rape
THEY WILL NOT LET YOU DO IT.

The Walk to Hinckley Point

Mary Millington, Orange Gate, Greenham Common

I can't put an exact date to it, but someone at Greenham told me that there were Kent miners' wives at Orange Gate. *They* had come to *us*. *They* saw the connections between us. At first all I could see that we had in common was being women: struggling against the tide of the Tory river, being persecuted for our refusal to follow the precepts of British Conservatism, namely:

1 *Women* are timid, and get patted on the head for their valuable contribution in the background of the Real World, i.e. men's politics. There have been three or four exceptions to this rule, i.e. Boadicea, Elizabeth I and Margaret Thatcher – really *exceptional* women. Ordinary women need not apply for space where the action is, unless to make tea and sandwiches behind the scenes.

2 *Strikes* are just plain naughty, because the good British worker really has nothing to complain about. The state is wiser than she/he is, and any tendency to strike must be the result of lunatic, far-left agitation, master-minded by Moscow (just like the Greenham women).

3 *Violence* is what naughty left-wing agitators do, even when they haven't actually done anything that would normally be defined as violence. What the police do to these agitators is *never* called violence, because they are the police, and *never* go on strike, and are therefore perfect.

Then I heard Annie and Judy were organising a walk from South Wales pits to Hinckley Point nuclear power station in Somerset. I read the leaflet they had produced and realised more connections: Government energy policy → nuclear power → nuclear weapons → poisoned planet → fear of holocaust; Phasing out of coal → death of mining communities → horrific unemployment → economic death of Wales, Scotland and other non-central areas → centralised control of energy and death of power of unions.

I met the walk at Hinckley Point: Greenham women, Welsh miners and women and local Greens forming a new mixture of people, all having the courage to defy the Tory government, all suffering for it, but not giving up.

Ann in Oxford, who had worked hard connecting women in unions and Greenham women for 24 May 1983 – Women All Out for Peace – asked me to speak at a women's rally in Oxford. It was a Mines Not Missiles March from our local Warning and Monitoring Station at Cowley Barracks, near British Leyland in Cowley, down into the centre of picturesque old University Intellectual Snobsville – Oxford. It was January 1985, freezing cold and not easy. Most of the Blue Gate turned up, having just been evicted twice after a practically sleepless night. Most of them had not washed their faces or brushed their teeth and hair. I heard a Welsh miner say, 'What sort of Greenham women are they?' in a tone of horror and contempt. I felt a rush of protective anger, but it died quickly.

Of course, we had met in a common cause, but in one sense we inhabited different worlds. We were demanding a lot of understanding and tolerance of the mining communities with our uncompromising feminism, our wild, free, perhaps insensitive sense of strength in each others' company as women, defiant and undignified by standards usually applied to women. In our turn, we need to be tolerant, listen and learn about the communities we were there to support, make real connections, person to person, woman to woman.

Speakers included two women from the Dirty Thirty in Leicestershire,* whose hideous experiences of ostracism by their community made me cry. As Greenham women we know what it is to be spat at in the street. There was a woman speaking about conditions in uranium mines in Namibia, where the nuclear chain starts, as well as a local woman Labour councillor, and Ann, filling in the gaps and connecting us all together.

At the social afterwards we seemed to form two separate groups – Greenham women and mining community women. By the time we got round to making moves towards each other it was time to go. I felt sad. We had lost an opportunity to make real contact.

I know such opportunities have not always been wasted – that real contacts have been made and are still being worked

---

* The Dirty Thirty: very few of the Leicester miners came out on strike; they had a pretty grim time in their communities, and were known as the Dirty Thirty.

on. These are the bridges which connect our parallel roads towards the future we want for ourselves and our children.

I feel now that, as women together, we've only just begun.

The Links

Vicky Smailes

Vicky Smailes lives in a mining village, Rhodesia near Worksop in Nottinghamshire, and is married to a miner. She was very active in the dispute in the local women's support group, which was strong at first, but became smaller as many men drifted back to work and their wives left the group. Some of the women from the group joined the Mines not Missiles march that went from Capenhurst on the Wirral, a uranium enrichment plant, through Winsford, Crewe, Stoke and ended up in Mansfield, with a demonstration at the pit at Sutton-in-Ashfield. It left Capenhurst on 17 August, and reached Mansfield on 20 August.

The Leicester peace movement organised the Mines not Missiles march that we went on. They sent details to us in the Rhodesia women's group. We got the invitation and as it was something that the women wanted to find out more about we decided to go. We had heard a lot about Greenham Common women, and although we believed in what they were doing, we'd always thought that it was their problem not ours. So we jumped at the invitation: we said, 'We'll do that,' plus it was a way of raising funds on the way. Other women's support groups were invited too, but in actual fact there weren't a lot of support groups that took part. I think we were the largest group. There were a couple of women from the Barnsley area, and a couple of women from the Doncaster area. But most of the women on the march were from the peace movement, a few from the Leicester women's peace movement and a lot from Greenham, about sixty in all.

It started from Capenhurst and picked up people along the way. It took four days, and finished in Mansfield. We slept on floors, hard floors, concrete floors; pub floors and floors in working men's clubs. There weren't a lot of washing facilities, but we were under cover all the time. It was in the summer and it was hot. We went to Stoke and other places.

The plan was to start off at a nuclear installation and to finish at a pit. So we started at a uranium enrichment plant, with a demonstration, and we finished up at a colliery at Sutton-in-Ashfield, in Nottinghamshire, with a demonstration.

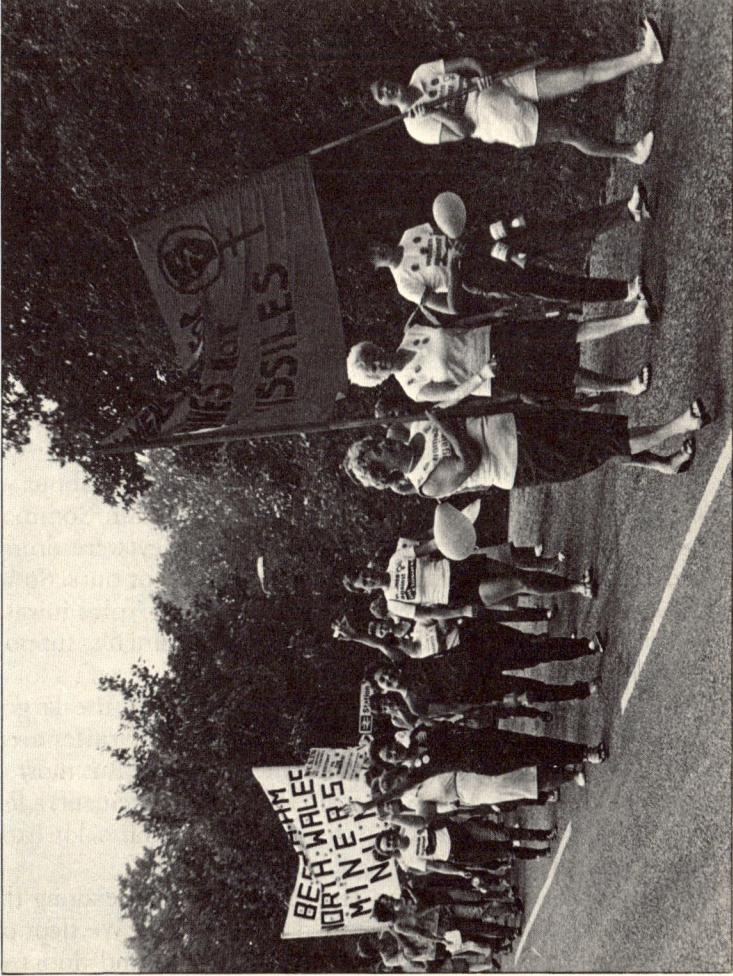

The Women's March For Mines Not Missiles, summer 1984

The way we saw the links was that Margaret Thatcher and the Tory government were interested in closing mines, and getting rid of miners' jobs, for the simple reason that when they build nuclear power stations they are not going to need the coal that they are producing. It is a good way of getting rid of miners and a good way to build up the nuclear power stations, whose waste product, plutonium, they use for nuclear weapons. So it is like killing two birds with one stone. Those were the links we saw: do away with pits and put more nuclear power stations up.

At first the peace women were a bit wary of us. They seemed to congregate together. Most of them are lesbians and I think they didn't know how we would react to them. When they found out we were alright with them, they were alright with us – in fact, we got on really well. They get a lot of abuse from a lot of people, so naturally they're wary. It's like when we have been collecting: we've got a lot of abuse from a lot of people, so you are always wary.

When you sit and listen to women from Greenham Common you find out lots of things, some things that you did know and some that you didn't know. Before that march I didn't know that waste materials from power stations went to make nuclear weapons, so that was something we found out to start with. I bet nine out of ten people, if you asked them, wouldn't know.

There were half a dozen women from Greenham that we made particular friends with, and we've kept in touch ever since. They had never been to a pit village before, and they really enjoyed it when they came to stay here. When they are not living at Greenham they're living in London, so it's entirely different. They had a right good time.

We went to stay with them down in London, because they had got a flat down there, and they were collecting in support of the miners. They collected an awful lot of money while we were down there, and we invited them back up here. They were a bit wary to start with, but we put them at their ease straight away. Now it is very rare we go to London without at some stage visiting Greenham House. It's a house not far from Kings Cross station, donated by the GLC (in fact, they won't have it for very much longer). It's used as an office, but also as a base for people who live at Greenham who haven't got a home, to come and rest before going back again.

We've been to Greenham only once. Amanda Richardson took us, the woman who made the film *Carry Greenham Home*. She did a film on all the women's groups around the area. It is going to be shown at the National Women Against Pit Closures conference in Sheffield.

There were quite a few of us from our group, and we went for the day. We visited all the different gates. I don't think I could live down there, as it's very uncomfortable. It was late summer but the weather was pretty horrible. It was cold, they were all sat round camp fires. Surprisingly enough, they said they preferred the winter, because in the summer they get a lot of insects and in winter they don't. There is a basic lack of facilities, and much as I admire them, I don't think I could do it. I might manage a weekend.

Yet *they* admire us more than they admire themselves. For what we have done in the miners' strike. They watched the NUM videos of Orgreave and the police and other things, and although they are suffering the same kind of harassment, they thought we had had it a lot worse than what they've got it down there. But I don't think there's any difference, I think we're all treated the same.

There was a blockade on when we went. They were trying to stop the Cruise missile carriers coming out. They built a great big bonfire in front of every gate, and as fast as the police were putting them out, they were building them back up again, so they couldn't get past. We were just stood there, looking amazed at it all. In the end they succeeded, and whatever it was they were going to transport, they took it out by helicopter. The police tactics there were virtually the same sort of tactics as on the picket lines; I don't think they differentiate down there from up here.

The police are very abusive to them. For example, when we were on the picket line in Mansfield with the Greenham women we mingled in with the crowd. There were a lot more of them than there were of us. Not to be disrespectful, but as soon as you see them, you know they are from Greenham Common, the way they have their hair cut, the way they dress and those big ear rings. One of the Greenham women said to the police, 'I don't know why you are wasting your time here, you ought to be doing something useful, like looking for "The Fox" ' (a man who had raped several women locally). He just said, 'I wouldn't worry if I were you, because he wouldn't touch you anyway.' We've had abuse like that on the picket line. The last lot we got was that we were Arthur Scargill's groupies.

At Greenham I couldn't believe the age of the soldiers that were stood behind the fence. Some of them didn't look old enough to have left school, let alone stand behind the fence. The women told us that if they stand round the fence, picketing or whatever, the soldiers wee on them. But we never saw that.

Two years ago I was the sort that believed everything I heard on the television. But once you've been through it, and you've seen it, it changes your opinion. I think it is the same with anybody that is in struggle. Once you have been involved, then for black people, Greenham women, you all seem to have something in common, because it is the same struggle. Before the strike you'd never been through it, so you weren't bothered. Not just Greenham Common, there are a lot of other struggles. Particularly black people. For example, the black community in London. People say, 'If they want to be accepted, why do they all live together?' You have only to go down there to know why they have to live together: for safety. You've only got to walk down Brick Lane market on a Sunday and see the National Front walking about, trying to pick off Asian stall-holders if they think the police are not looking. We met a young lad down there; he'd been cut with a Stanley knife from the top of his back, right down to the bottom of his back. You could see where they had stitched him up. There's very few black people round this area, and they are treated the same as anybody else. I couldn't believe that people would be treated like they are in London. We've seen them stopped and searched for no reason at all: we were amazed. A Transit van full of police who jump out and search them: everything out of their pockets and bags, and then they just drive off as though they hadn't done anything. It's everyday routine.

The police here weren't too bad at the beginning. It got worse as time went on. At one stage you couldn't get out of the village for police, every road was blocked in. We had very little policing on the Mines not Missiles march. Apart from the picket at Capenhurst, and when we finished at Mansfield.

At Capenhurst they didn't stop us, they escorted us down the road when we started the march. We were marching along the side of the road, and they said, but properly, 'Would you please move over to the other side of the road because there is a path there.' They were quite pleasant. As we marched, the police gradually vanished away. But when we got into Nottinghamshire and went picketing it was a different attitude altogether. We were pickets then, and treated as pickets. They arrested three of the Greenham women that day on the Mines not Missiles picket, for standing on the opposite side of the road from what they'd been told. One of the women would have got locked up if they got her to court, because she was out on bail.

We are hoping to have another trip down to Greenham but I don't know when it will be, because although the strike's over now, for most of us money is still a problem. As soon as we can get something together we shall go down and see them again. When we went down the reception we got was fantastic, they were really pleased to see us. I was pleased to be there, to be part of it for that day.

What did surprise me when we went down to Greenham was how many people there were there from different countries. We met people from New Zealand, Australia, Germany, Sweden, America. I thought when we went down that it was basically only in England. But when we got there, there were many nationalities, it must be known world-wide. In fact, on our Mines not Missiles march there was one woman from New Zealand and another one from Germany.

Some of the women stay at Greenham for months; I don't know how they do it. We went camping once in a luxury tent, and it had everything in it. As soon as it rained that was it: I wasn't going in that tent anymore, it was sold. So you can imagine what I would be like at Greenham. Some of them don't even have tents, just benders and polythene hung from trees. I don't think that would suit me. It's a good job everybody's not like me, or else there's be nobody down at Greenham. It's a good job that there's some that are willing to do it.

(*Written in collaboration with Vicky Seddon*)

Intruders Not Peacekeepers

Janet Kay and Kila Millidine

Kila Millidine and Janet Kay both work for
Sheffield City Council, Kila as a housing aid
advisor and Janet as a social worker. They are
both active members of NALGO, and both
have been involved in industrial action in their
own work-places. Janet has been a member of a
women's group, and both she and Kila have
been interested in women's politics for some
years. They joined Policewatch in the spring of
1984 and spent the next year observing and
recording police activities related to the dispute.
They attended picket lines once a week, wrote
weekly reports of Policewatch observations, and
were involved in publishing Policewatch
information through radio, television and press
reports and by speaking at public meetings.
Their involvement with the dispute brought
them into contact with women in mining
communities and they became particularly
interested in the effects of the police operation
on those women's lives.

We became involved in the strike in April 1984 when we joined
a newly-formed independent police monitoring body,
Sheffield Policewatch. Policewatch was set up by volunteers
after a public meeting, in response to disturbing tales of the
police activities which filtered back from the picket lines. The
Policewatch brief was to observe and record police operations
on picket lines in an attempt to produce an unbiased record of
events. We each went to picket lines at least once a week,
following pickets from a local pit to other locations mainly in
South Yorkshire, Nottinghamshire and Derbyshire. Our aim
was to publicise our observations as a factual account in an
attempt to offset the one-sided police and media reports. We
had direct experience of police behaviour on picket lines. We
also interviewed women in 'Women Against Pit Closures'
groups in the area, both in mining villages and in Sheffield.
Other sources were women Policewatch members' observations and personal experiences. Some information was gained
at a single interview, but with other women our contact was

176

spread out over a longer period of time, for example, when we followed women's cases through the courts.

Although the miners' confrontations with the police were news for a year, the women's involvement with them received less interest. However the majority of women we spoke to who had been in contact with the police during the dispute felt that their ideas and feelings about policing and the legal system had been radically altered by this contact. We, as Policewatch members, only encountered the police on specific occasions, but for women in the mining communities this contact was a daily occurrence.

The impact of the policing of the miners' dispute and its effect on the attitudes of women involved has to be placed in the context of the relationship between these women and the police prior to the strike. Policing in these small towns and villages had usually been in the hands of a few officers, often local people, who were considered to be integral and welcome members of the community. Women in Rhodesia (Nottinghamshire) told us of their friendly attitudes to the local 'bobbies', who they would invite into their homes for cups of tea, and in one case give home-grown vegetables. The women described the situation as policing by consent, in that there was a level of mutual co-operation between themselves and the police. Women had no reason to dislike the police, or think about them very much at all. If asked, they would probably have indicated a vague respect for the police, as something not really connected with themselves, but generally seen as protective and reassuring figures. Attitudes tended to be conservative, and as crime rates were low most women had had virtually no official contact with the police. Policing methods were low-key and uncontentious. Although some women were aware of reports of police transgressions in the media, these made little impact on their attitudes. Policing was simply not an issue that was relevant to these women's lives. The prospect of confrontation with the police therefore seemed to be a most unlikely and undesirable event.

The Communities

Although it was events on the picket lines and confrontations between pickets and the police which attracted most media coverage, for the majority of women it was the police operations in their home towns and villages which made the biggest impact. Whether women were active in the strike or not, the mass presence of police in their communities constituted a gross intrusion on their lives; during the strike, hundreds and sometimes thousands of police officers could be deployed in and around one small village. This level of police presence could last for months, with convoys of police officers moving in and out of the area with no reference to the local people. Women had to get used to the sight of fifty or sixty police Transit vans arriving in their streets, carrying a dozen officers each, often riot-equipped, and accompanied by dog and horse vans, leaving them feeling that their villages had been invaded and occupied by hostile forces.

Officers came from forces from all over the country and had little understanding of local life or people. Methods used by urban police forces to police inner-city areas were quite different from the usual methods of policing the mining communities, and the importation of heavy policing methods was bitterly resented.

We were told by women at Kiveton Park how police tactics usually confined to the picket lines could explode into the community. On one occasion several mounted police galloped up the pit lane towards the village, squashing women pickets against a wall and terrifying three old age pensioners who were sitting on a bench. This cavalry charge ended in the village with one of the police horse's heads stuck through the newsagent's door!

There was no discrimination as to who was affected by an event like this; people were caught up simply because of where they lived. One woman, who lived near a working miner, had for years walked her dog late at night. When guarding the working miner's house, the police would flash their car headlights to indicate that she should return home if the dog failed to relieve itself within two minutes. A curfew was effectively placed on this woman, simply because of where she lived.

No aspect of women's ordinary lives escaped police scrutiny, from going to the shops, taking children to school or going out in the evening. Normal events and behaviour rapidly became distorted by the police presence. One woman had a small party for her son's birthday. As her mother was standing outside the house, showing guests the way home, the police arrived and arrested her. When the daughter protested, she too was arrested, and both were put in a police van. The inspector then ordered the younger woman out of the van, saying the matter would be sorted out with her husband. As soon as she got out of the van it was driven off with her mother in it. It was driven round and round and the mother was eventually dumped in an unfamiliar place, disoriented and in tears.

For the women we spoke to, these situations were in stark contrast to their previous knowledge and understanding of policing, and they found it bewildering and shocking.

Many women pointed out to us how well organised the police operations were, and how swiftly a village could be taken over. On the day we first interviewed women in Rhodesia, men had gone back to work at the local pit for the first time since the dispute started. Until then the Rhodesia women had seen few policemen. They predicted that this situation would be changing very quickly. They had already seen two plain-clothes policemen that morning outside the house of a miner who had gone back to work. Two days later the police presence was well established in the village. One woman who was particularly active in the dispute spoke of police Transits parked outside her house, as well as large numbers of officers patrolling the village. Ancient 'besetting' laws were resurrected to bring charges against strikers and their supporters; this woman pointed out that the police were besetting *her* home. The police operations were so swift and well-organised that they seemed like military manoeuvres. Many women observed that when the police took over a village it was like the imposing of martial law.

'Normal' policing became so rare that even events unconnected with the strike which involved contact with the police became occasions for tension and conflict. The police used them to express their contempt for mining families. One woman told us what happened when the police were called to the house when her father-in-law died at home, as was legally required. Although the family was shocked and grief-stricken, the police who attended were callous and unfriendly. At one point the younger policeman said, 'I'll have to go outside for a good laugh.' None of the family could believe that they had heard him properly until the other policeman explained, 'Well, it could have been your badges.'

In Hoyland we were told how a local night-club, to which the police had occasionally been called in the past, now had a Transit van full of police parked outside it every night. The women felt that every incident in the village was blamed on the NUM. If windows were broken, it was the pickets' fault. As one woman said, 'It's a crime to be a miner.'

A common experience in many areas was the disparity between the treatment of those involved in the strike and those actively opposed to it. When a woman complained about abuse from a working miner, which included racist comments, her complaint was disbelieved and dismissed by the police. In Rhodesia working miners and their families threatened and abused Women Against Pit Closures women in front of police officers, threatening to break their windows. The police laughed and ignored the threats, though if the roles had been reversed arrests for threatening behaviour could certainly have been expected. So there was no even-handed treatment; it was blatantly obvious that the police were briefed to protect the right of the few (who opposed the strike) at the expense of the rest.

Although much of the policing affected all women or affected women arbitrarily, women active in Women Against Pit Closures and picketing were singled out as specific targets. Members of Kiveton Park Women's Action Group told us of the problems they had being singled out for police attention because of their activities. One woman was followed on her journeys to and from work, and into Sheffield. Police radios were used to keep track of her movements. On one occasion, after a women's picket of a working miner's house, she was frog-marched back to her house and sent a message from the officer in charge that she would be arrested if she was ever found in the vicinity of that house again. But she had to pass this house every time she went to the local shops. The police would play a silly game, blocking her progress along the pavement and then jeering at her if she managed to dodge them. Her whole life became subject to police controls, insults and abuse, whether she was engaged in strike activities or going about her normal tasks.

A long established soup kitchen was set on fire, despite constant checks on it. The women opened the door one morning to find the kitchen ablaze. Furniture had been moved into the middle of the floor and stuffed with newspapers. When the women reported this to the police as a case of arson, they came to look briefly at the damage, and pursued no further enquiries. The women could no longer expect police protection against criminal acts. This was not a position chosen by the women, who saw their activities as legally and morally right. But to judge from the police attitude, arson of a soup kitchen was a legitimate act.

There was no time off for the women directly involved in support work, and for many this was an incredibly stressful experience that affected them both physically and mentally. Normal events and routines could no longer be taken for granted. Even a trip to the shops could involve a frightening and humiliating confrontation with the police.

The police attempted to isolate and marginalise these women by treating their behaviour as criminal, and thereby defining them as social deviants. The women's response was twofold. Firstly, they began to treat outsiders with suspicion. Anyone who was not known to them to be clearly in sympathy with the dispute was viewed with caution, and even hostility. (Once convinced of a visitor's support, however, the welcome was warm and spontaneous.) They developed something approaching a siege mentality. Secondly, they found themselves relying on each other more and more. For many women, this was their first clearly defined experience of the strength of women collectively supporting each other, and their resistance to police harassment and determination to continue their support for the strike was based on it.

Police officers were constantly verbally abusive, using insults aimed at the women's sexuality, repeated over and over again. Although the women were initially shocked by some of the comments, they quickly learned to ignore them. They became so much a part of daily life that they ceased to register, to the extent that specific remarks and occasions were difficult to recall. They were quick to tell us that these comments did not affect them, but it is clear that they were extremely bitter at the way the police treated them. To the women, it was just another tactic to demoralise them and frighten them into returning to their 'proper role'. They had no recourse against such behaviour; their only defence was to support each other in maintaining their struggle. Their tactics in ignoring the comments were more effective and much safer than any retaliation would have been, and by expressing their feelings to one another they defused their anger and bitterness.

The women felt that the police had been briefed to break the strike by any means available to them, and this all-pervading harassment was one such means. Women were regarded as 'criminal' not just in their strike activities but in many aspects of their lives, however unconnected with the dispute.

Even women who demonstrated their support for the miners in places distant from the mining communities were not free from the long arm of the law. One woman was picked up by the police and brutally beaten after leaving a Women Against Pit Closures fund-raising disco. Horrified friends found her the next morning with black eyes, bruises on her arms and back and a perforated ear-drum. She was soaking wet after having had water thrown on her in the cell during the night. She was charged with being drunk and disorderly. Although it seems from the number of examples we were given that fund-raising events were less likely to attract police attention, we nevertheless felt that they were considered 'fair game' by the police.

It was inevitable that with the level and style of policing adopted in some of the pit villages, sometimes over a period of months, the children of the villages would be affected. The Kiveton women said that in the early days of the dispute their children were invited into police vehicles to eat sweets, drink pop and play with the controls of the Transits. The women were unwilling to put a stop to this because they were used to bringing up their children to respect the police. Only when they learnt that the police were persistently asking the children for details of their families' private lives were the children forbidden to continue this contact.

Most women that we have spoken to have taken pains to keep the worst aspects of the situation from their children. This was not easy. The behaviour of the police was obvious, overt and unremitting. It was clear that the children were going to see and hear things that were very disturbing, and this was compounded by the police behaviour towards them, for the children were not excused from the attention of the police.

Jackie's eleven-year-old son was stopped and interrogated about what both his parents did, and whether they had 'guests' staying. Jackie put in a complaint to the police and was merely told it would not happen again. Chris's eight-year-old son was playing in his front garden with a 'twizzle' stick; he was told, 'You, sonny boy, get that fucking stick in the house.' Anne's young daughter was 'flagged' (given the two fingers) by a large crowd of policemen as she was passing them on the street. On another occasion, a deaf child was thumped by a policewoman for larking around in the street with other children. The effects of these and many similar incidents showed themselves in the children's play. One four-year-old, on being reprimanded for clobbering another with a plastic spade, retorted, 'I can do that because I am a copper; coppers can do anything.' We were told of children crying at the thought of going to school because of a new game that was being played in the playgrounds called 'pickets and police'. Those whose turn it was to be the pickets could guarantee they would get hurt. As one thirteen-year-old girl said to us when asked what she thought about the police, 'I used to like them, but I've seen what they are really like now. I never knew what they did before the strike.' Having brought up their children to respect the police, women felt bitter that the police themselves were destroying it. Chris from Hoyland expressed their contradictory feelings: 'I can't say to the children, "Go on, you can trust the police," when their father comes home covered in bruises from truncheons.'

Although incensed by the treatment that their children had received, all the women we met insisted that it was important to minimise their anger in front of them, so as not to influence them further in anti-police attitudes. They did not want their children to adopt their own feelings of hostility towards the police, even if many of them felt that this was unavoidable. These efforts to protect their children from the realities seem to indicate a desire on the women's part to return to their previous opinion of policing once the strike was over. That they should do so in the face of their experience over a considerable period indicates how reluctant they were to think ill of the police. Many women told us that it took the over-policing of their communities and the hostile attitudes of the occupying forces to open their eyes to the true nature of policing and the law.

Many felt that they had seen the police clearly for the first time, and they started to recognise that they were being used as a political tool to break the strike. 'We've just found out what they're really like,' said a Hoyland woman. 'This strike's opened our eyes to a lot of things.' Another said, 'You just heard about it [police violence] – you didn't want to know. It's always happened; you just don't think about it.' Yet another woman told us, 'Until the strike, I would never have believed that the police would be allowed to act in this way. They are allowed to make their own rules as they go along.'

The women had not chosen this confrontation with the police, and although there was an underlying hope that this should not be the case, they spoke of their attitudes having been permanently and radically altered.

Many women blamed outside police forces for the majority of the problems, although we felt that local forces were equally culpable. Perhaps this was in hope that things would return to normal at some stage, which would be more difficult to achieve if local police were seen as equally to blame.

But perhaps the most significant result of the policing is the way in which women developed and used their own support systems to resist the mass criminalisation of themselves and their activities. Not one woman we spoke to accepted this definition, despite the anti-miner and pro-police bias of much of the media. They simply refused to accept that the police interpretation of their activities had any meaning whatsoever. Although they were treated as criminal and deviant they refused to accept this, and persisted in seeing themselves as law-abiding. As one woman said, 'We didn't do anything wrong before this strike, and we're not doing anything wrong now.'

Picketing

Women picketed the pits from the very beginning of the strike. A few were NUM members, but most of the women were on the picket lines because they lived in mining areas, areas which almost without exception already knew high unemployment and where nearly every job depended on the survival of the coal industry. They were defending *their* pits, *their* livelihoods and *their* communities, just as their men were. They understood that unless they stood up and fought government policies for their industry, and attacks on the NUM, their

Women and police at picket line, Thurcroft Colliery, Sheffield

whole way of life would be threatened.

The media portrayed the NUM picket lines as dangerous and violent places where angry brutish miners fought physically to prevent the strike-breakers from entering the pits, whilst the 'thin blue line' sought to preserve law and order amidst the chaos. The reality was very different indeed. The vast majority of picket lines were quiet and well-ordered. In media terms, they were quite un-newsworthy. That many remained quiet despite extreme provocation by the attendant police officers is worthy of note. At some pits the police presence was a few token officers; at others it was a full-scale military-style operation designed to break the striking miners. On occasions, thousands of highly-motivated riot-trained officers, the élite of forces up and down the country, took on the pickets. Their equipment was formidable: horses, dogs, convoys of armoured Transits, searchlights, shields and truncheons. Not only did they move with a military precision which was awesome to see, but almost without exception it was they and not the pickets who were the aggressors. The police initiated the violence.

Men and women on the picket lines were appalled, angered and intimidated by their introduction to 'public order policing'. For women especially, the aggressively policed picket lines were totally outside their experience. In such an alien, all-male environment women hung together and acted collectively for moral support. Whereas the male pickets attempted to respond to police aggression with similar aggression – open warfare at times – many of the women developed different tactics. It is possible that this was initially due to the influence of outside groups supporting the NUM (women from Greenham, women trade unionists), but women from the mining communities readily adopted the alternative methods; they sat, chanted and sang in the route of the strike-breakers and their escorts. Such tactics produced a muddled response from the police; in many cases bewilderment, but on others aggression: a clearly peaceful women's picket could lead to clearly violent policing.

One of the most brutally policed women's pickets that we heard about was at Gedling on 21 August 1984. The Sheffield Policewatch observer reported that 'The rough handling of women pickets seemed unnecessary. The women were carrying out a peaceful good-natured picket when a woman was picked out at random to be arrested … the women who were arrested behaved, so far as we could see, no differently from the rest.' The women were singing songs throughout the picket, some of which contained the word 'scab', and the treatment meted out to them by the police was particularly intimidatory and violent at each stage: before, during and after the arrests.

In the Rhodesia women's opinion, the police became angry at singing and chanting because they didn't know how to deal with it. In fact, the very presence of an all-women group of pickets could provoke a response of frustrated anger from the police which bore no apparent relation to the activities of the pickets.

Anne was arrested at Sherwood pit when women were getting up from the road where they had been sitting, singing and chanting. A policeman placed his fingers on her neck nerves and twisted with obvious expertise, leaving her bruised for weeks. Four officers dragged her into a police van. She was then ordered out because they couldn't find an arresting officer for her, but a volunteer soon materialised.

In general, when women pickets chanted, sang or sat in the road this led to arrests and rough treatment by the police, but none the less it was an effective alternative to taking on the police with physical aggression. The women from Hoyland described the confusion of the officer in charge at Silverhill on seeing a group of women pickets approaching the pit entrance: 'His face when he saw us – he didn't know what to do.'

Whereas the police can handle a degree of organised, anti-establishment action from men, it seems that working class women who abandon the kitchen sink to the extent of acting collectively and militantly for a political end are a particular threat to the police and are dealt with accordingly. They challenge the institutional sexism in the police which does not readily admit that women can act outside their male-stereotyped roles of apolitical domestics.

The sexism of male NUM members left them vulnerable to police provocation via the women pickets. On many occasions it was felt that the police deliberately abused women – verbally or physically – in order either to incite violence from, or add to the demoralisation of the men if they failed collectively to act out their traditional protective role. Either way, the pickets, women and men, lost.

Most women expected to be treated no differently from the men (or certainly no better) because they were there for the same purpose: to picket their pits. As Chris from Hoyland said, 'If you expect to be treated any differently there is no point in going.' Women *were* treated differently, but that did not mean that they were treated more leniently. Certainly, they were subject to the same violent and aggressive policing, the same arbitrary 'laws' and the same random arrests as the men. We were given many examples: 'I just said the word "scab", and was told not to say the word "scab". I said it was in the dictionary, it was a valid word, it wasn't a wrong word. I said it again and they just leant over the fence and said, "You're arrested." I asked what for, and they said, "We'll tell you what for when we decide on the charges." '

At Silverhill women from Hoyland Womens' Action Group shouted 'scab' for three-quarters of an hour without being warned not to. Police reinforcements arrived as they were leaving and four women were arrested. Describing one arrest a woman said, 'They picked her up by her arms and legs. They were walking in a zig-zag, pulling her one way and another – she was almost pulled in two. She was then handcuffed, and when she said that the handcuffs were too tight, she was told "They're not tight enough – they're not bleeding." They did bleed.'

So, clearly, being a woman was no protection against police violence, but women consistently spoke about *additional* police reactions to their presence on the picket lines. They were seen first and foremost as women, not pickets, and the police response was confused. The most common solution to the problem was to 'defeminise' the women, to strip them of their traditional and therefore acceptable status of wives, mothers, workers and so on, using verbal and sexual harassment. The aim was to see them as 'improper' women who the police then felt they could abuse with impunity.

Although both women and men were verbally abused by police officers on the picket lines, for women this inevitably involved real sexual harassment. With monotonous regularity women were called fucking slags/whores/tossers/prostitutes/ hard-faced bitches/lesbians/sluts/scrubbers and other such insults. Older women were not immune; whilst picketing at Kiveton Park an older woman was followed by two South

Yorkshire policemen past five police Transits. The officer in charge then said to his men, 'That old cow there, get her in there [a Transit van], get her trousers took off and show her what a good time is.'

For many women who picketed regularly, such behaviour became the norm to such an extent that they barely registered the insults. Some women countered such contempt by ignoring the police entirely. The women from Hoyland told us, 'We don't entertain the police at all. Whatever they say we don't answer them. They're just not worth answering.' Many women refused to speak even if the police chose to be friendly, and this inevitably produced a hostile reaction. On other occasions when women were feeling confident they answered the police back. At Brookhouse pit Audrey from Sheffield Women Against Pit Closures was walking to the picket line with another woman when the police shouted 'Greenham, Greenham' at them. Audrey replied that she took this as a compliment despite the fact that she had never been to Greenham. When asked by the police why she was at the picket line she replied, 'I've come to watch how you're spending my money.'

At a womens' picket in Scunthorpe the police followed individual women wherever they went, even to the toilet or to get chips. Eventually this situation became so ludicrous that the women began to call 'Walkies' to the police every time they wanted to move.

On the Mines not Missiles march at Sutton-in-Ashfield, women from Rhodesia suggested that the police would be better employed looking for 'The Fox', a rapist then on the loose, to which they received the reply, 'The Fox wouldn't touch you lot with a fucking barge-pole.' Later on the women said they'd rather be dead than in the police force, and were answered, 'Yes, and we can arrange for that too.'

It is easier to deal with such behaviour as a group rather than as an individual. Because the verbal abuse of women was so explicitly aimed at their sexuality, rather than the more general political abuse directed towards men, women gravitated towards each other and picketed together. They often told us with great satisfaction of the collective strength that they found on the picket lines, enabling them to return the contempt, often with scathing humour. Older women especially found it easy and very effective to belittle and castigate the policemen, most of whom were young.

Many of the women who spoke to us said that some of their worst experiences at the hands of the police were after they were arrested. Of Lynne, arrested at Silverhill, we were told, 'At the station, Lynne was wanting to go to the toilet. They wouldn't let her go and she wet herself.' The same thing happened to one of the Rhodesia women who was arrested.

The experience of the women's picket at Gedling was particularly grim. We were told: 'One of the other two ladies who were arrested on the same picket line was in a state of shock, and to be told that there were dangerous criminals outside the cells literally put the fear of god into her, plus the fact that she was badly bruised from being dragged along the floor by the police, and for doing nothing at all. In fact, her full intentions were to leave the picket line, and the police prevented her from doing so.' Another woman wrote in her report of the same picket at Gedling, after being photographed against her will, 'Still feeling extremely angry about being photographed, I made a grab for the photo, ripping it off the paper and started to crumple it up. The effect of my action was immediate and terrible: one minute I was tearing the picture, the next I was pinned painfully to the floor by four PCs. My head was twisted viciously to one side, my arms pinned and twisted, and my legs pinned and one ankle painfully twisted round. My neck was twisted so much that I could not speak and could hardly breathe. Fear just washed over me – I thought I'd had it. I then heard a male voice say, "Easy, easy," and I was rushed roughly into the next room, pinned on the floor, facing the wall. I became aware at this point that my tee-shirt was round my neck showing my tits. They eased the pressure on me and I managed to get on to my hands and knees, eventually getting to my feet.'

So although the women felt that they were treated in the same way as the men when they were arrested on the picket lines, it seems clear to us that there were certain things that happened to them that were particularly humiliating and frightening, and which either did not happen to the men, or otherwise did not have the same impact on them.

For nearly all the women involved, the strike was not only their first significant contact with the police, but also with the criminal justice system, and any belief that they may have had in British law was severely shaken. They experienced random arrests, the apparent dearth of arresting officers who possessed identification numbers and the arbitrary choice of 'offences' they were supposed to have committed. Once arrested, they were frequently rebuked for being there at all: 'You should be at home like a proper wife.'

The woman arrested at Gedling who was assaulted in the police station was then held in an exercise yard for six or seven hours, because there were no women's cells. She wrote, 'The yard was at the very centre of the building, about 12 feet by 6 feet with steel mesh at a height of about 12 feet. It had a concrete floor and a central drain grid.' She was held there for six or seven hours.

The police tried to bully the Gedling women into being fingerprinted, saying that if they refused it would delay their release, and they could get a court order to do it anyway. The women were asked the usual details about their marital status, work, education, 'and much more sinister, and the first time I'd come across it, "Have you ever been treated for mental illness?" ' They were then charged with obstructing the highway and obstructing the police, when in fact all they had done was to walk on the pavement.

Initially there was some expectation that wrongful arrests and ficticious charges would be identified when their cases were eventually brought to court. Instead many of the women found that the courts and the police had a mutual 'understanding' of the criminality of those involved with the NUM which the truth could not breach. We spent several days listening to women's cases in magistrates' courts in Nottinghamshire and South Yorkshire and we witnessed some of the blatant travesties of justice that the women complained of. On many occasions the police evidence was, to say the least, confused, and the police witnesses frequently contradicted each other. Jackie for example, was described by one police officer as 'the ringleader' and by the next as 'a puppet', and both accounts of her behaviour were not only untrue but at odds with each other. She was found guilty, as were many others, in the face of clear evidence to the contrary. After the strike was over she appealed and all the charges against her were dropped; none the less, a very active woman was effectively immobilised for most of the strike by the restrictive bail conditions placed upon her.

On other occasions individual police officers, using their allegedly independent notes made at the time or shortly after the time of the offence or arrest, each gave identical evidence in court. (Evidence given by members of Policewatch using notes made from tapes recorded at the time of the offence or arrest were disallowed by magistrates if more than one observer was involved: complicity was suspected.)

Even when the women had not been arrested themselves but were visiting their men in prison they did not escape the hostility of the police. Women visiting their husbands on remand in Armley Prison arrived wearing NUM stickers and badges. They were accosted by police officers outside the goal who shouted 'Arthur's little army' and 'Is it worth going through all this for Scargill?' and, as they waited to be let in, 'Make them wait, make them wait!'

It is clear that the 'criminalisation' of striking miners and their families, which was initiated by police activities and attitudes, was then upheld and compounded by the legal system. It is not surprising that very few of the incidents we were told about have been made the subject of official complaints, as the recipients of these police excesses have no faith at all in the complaints procedure.

Audrey was dragged by her neck off a wall and kicked by a riot policeman at Orgreave. When we asked her why she had not made a complaint about these incidents, she said it was a waste of time as the police investigated themselves.

Lesley, who was attacked at Orgreave on the same day by a mounted policeman wielding a truncheon, told us why she hoped to take criminal proceedings against the officer concerned. Lesley's case became widely known after a photo of the incident was circulated as a poster. However, although the photo clearly shows the mounted policeman about to bring the truncheon down on Lesley's head, and there were witnesses who had seen what happened, the Director of Public Prosecutions decided there was not enough evidence to prosecute. Lesley said, 'I'm not interested in damages. I'm interested in making a policeman accountable for an entirely gratuitous assault. Because one thing that enrages me most about the whole situation is that it is quite clear from my own experiences, and the experiences of multitudes of other people, that the police are not accountable for what they are doing, and that if everyone is accountable under the law then so are they.'

Many women told us that they were determined that these harshly learnt lessons would not be forgotten. The policing tactics that they had witnessed had turned their habitual respect and trust into hatred, fear and contempt – a realisation of the political nepotism of 'justice' which would remain with them and their communities long after their men had returned to work.

One woman said, 'We can be arrested for abusive language and behaviour, but the police do it all the time and get away with it.' Another commented, 'I would never have dreamt that the police could use such terrible violence and never have to answer for it.' Yet another asked, 'Who polices the police?'

Policewatch

Our experiences as Policewatch observers were broadly equivalent to those of any other women on the picket lines. We experienced the same limited police repetoire of insults regularly thrown at women (the 'defeminisation' process), the same sexual harassment and the same physical violence and intimidation. More through luck than judgement none of us was ever arrested or seriously injured by the police, but we became used to the threats and adept at avoiding their fulfillment, at times running, scaling trees and leaping into ditches a great deal more enthusiastically than we would have thought possible.

Most Policewatch members were women, and all of the most active members were, despite child-care and job commitments. It is possible that men saw the group as insufficiently active, for it was our policy not to take part in the picket or to shout. Our role was to record accurately and publicise the policing of the picket lines – a role that would have been superfluous if the media did what it purports to do.

Overall, the police response to us altered during the strike in a direct ratio to our effectiveness. At the beginning we were more likely to be tolerated and patronised. We were viewed as something of a novelty that would, they hoped, go away before too long. On the one hand the police were never happy about being watched, but on the other they were reluctant to be seen arresting or hurting us. There was a certain ambiguity.

At a rally in Sheffield Mandy went to get the number of a policeman who was arresting a picket. She was picked up bodily by another policeman with his hands and arms under her breasts, carried across the road and thrown into several more officers. She was told that this had been done '*for her own good*'.

As the strike progressed our reports received more attention from the media, politicians, the NCCL, police committees and the police themselves. Their attempts to discredit us by labelling us political extremists increased. Threats of arrest became more frequent, as did threats of violence and actual violence to ourselves and our equipment. We became well used to threats such as 'We'll stuff this camera up your fucking arse.' Overt hostility like this increasingly became the norm and was in fact directed at anyone outside the establishment media who photographed or recorded the police activities on the picket lines.

At Brodsworth pit Audrey was pushed out of the way when she was taking photographs of a number of policemen beating up a handful of pickets. They were warned, 'There's a woman with a camera!' As Audrey said, 'They don't like to think that anyone else might find out what they're doing.'

Whereas at the beginning of the strike Policewatch observers had attempted to find 'neutral space' between pickets and police, we were increasingly ordered to stand with the pickets. At the mass pickets at Orgreave, although the media were well behind police lines, we experienced the full terror of the police onslaught. When the horses and riot police charged we ran with the pickets. We saw a lot of injured men and none of them were policemen. Most of the injuries were to heads and backs as miners ran to escape injury or arrest.

Throughout the strike the police response to Policewatch women was unpredictable and inconsistent, and this remained the case even in the chaos of Orgreave. Two women were subjected to a terrifying series of events, including one woman being cornered in an alley-way by a riot policeman running amok, brandishing his truncheon and shouting 'You fucker!' Another had her camera smashed out of her hands. Later on the same two women were told by the police, 'I don't know what you women are doing here; you should be lying in your bikinis in your gardens,' and, 'Do your husbands know you're here? This is no place for ladies.' Such inconsistencies were common and, in our opinion, indicative of the confused police response to women on the picket lines. All of our experiences with women pickets reinforce this view.

We were frequently pushed and shoved by police officers. Most pickets saw it as being in their interests to protect us and our equipment, and it was frequently obvious that we were being harassed at least in part to provoke the pickets. At Treeton pit a riot-policeman snatched a Policewatch woman's tape-recorder from her. She grabbed it back but the same officer attacked her later, causing her to fall. She was only mildly concussed, bruised and grazed, but a picket who remonstrated on her behalf was very severely beaten up by several riot-policemen and arrested for a number of wholly fictitious offences. The case was eventually thrown out of court, as were many others, as the police witnesses were obviously lying.

At Kiveton Park another woman Policewatch member was harangued and dragged over a wall by the officer in command because he didn't approve of her standing where she was, despite another senior police officer having told her to stand there immediately beforehand. Most harassment experienced by Policewatch women, however, was verbal rather than physical; sexual abuse was the norm and frequently included intimidatory references to rape. For example, two Policewatch women who were stopped at a road-block were subjected to two Metropolitan policemen having a pointed and threatening conversation in their hearing about rape, with a mock-innocent reference to a locally grown crop, such comments as 'Awful lot in this area' and 'Never been in an area where there's so much.'

We were also caught up in the criminalisation process experienced by so many others at the time. Because we advertised their activities on the picket lines, the police reviled us more and more vehemently as police-bashers, communists, subversives and so on. Our photographs were taken by police cameramen in riot gear. Our backgrounds were delved into; officers let slip that they knew personal details about our marital status and past histories. Our telephones misbehaved in a multitude of ways. For example, on at least five occasions, on different phones, we got through to a police station, although the numbers dialled were entirely dissimilar. We presumed this was intimidation rather than incompetence. The house that held the Policewatch files was occupied by a single woman. It was broken into twice. On the first occasion nothing but the Policewatch telephone tree was stolen. On the second occasion a man was intercepted on his way to the Policewatch 'office' on the first floor.

As Policewatch observers from the beginning of the strike, we came to the same conclusions as everyone else who witnessed the policing of the miners. We saw that the police were used in an overtly political fashion to break the strike. It is quite clear to us that the brief of the police forces involved was to frighten and harass the miners back to work. The consequent severe breaches of civil liberties affected everyone involved. Anyone who chose to support the miners in any way could be caught up in the criminalisation process inflicted upon them by the police.

Police activities on the picket lines received totally inadequate media coverage, but there were even fewer attempts to explore the effect on the communities as a whole. The media portrayed the police role as 'the thin blue line holding back the savage hordes of mad miners'. It very rarely covered the impact of massive numbers of hostile police officers, largely from outside forces, invading villages and persecuting people whose only interest was to preserve their jobs and communities. We saw repeatedly that during confrontations between local people and the police, on or off the picket lines, it was inevitably the police who initiated the violence and intimidation. The police exerted so much control on the picket lines that it often seemed that they were doing the picketing rather than the miners. Through the use of road-blocks they decided where pickets would be allowed to congregate and how many would be allowed to attend; they decided at the picket line where the pickets would stand, what actions or words were 'legal' and whether or not, through the policing methods chosen, there would be arrests or violence. As one officer said, 'I object to the word "scab" being used on MY picket line.'

Most of us were shocked at the almost total lack of police accountability. Initially, Policewatch made a few formal complaints to and about the police because of the atrocities that we had witnessed. When these failed to accomplish anything we tried working quite closely with some of the police committees. They gave us support and goodwill but felt similarly powerless to influence the police.

A woman from Sheffield Woman Against Pit Closures commented: 'The other thing I hadn't realised was that the police were actually getting off on it, which I disliked even more. And I noticed that quite a few officers were actually revelling in this power that they have. And of all things, of all my experiences on the picket lines, the thing that I found most disagreeable was the sight of an officer with a truncheon and a shield running about, obviously revelling in the idea that he was perfectly free to clobber people and not have to suffer any come-back for it – and enjoying it.'

Police and Sexuality

The relationship between women and the police, both on the picket lines and in the communities, was marked throughout by the police's particular attitude towards the women's sexuality. The picture that emerged from all areas of activity was not one of isolated incidents but an overall pattern of verbal and physical sexual abuse. This was most evident on the picket lines, where women more clearly stepped outside traditional roles and where women most obviously gained control of some situations by using their collective strengths. The police response at picket lines often seemed confused and contradictory. They began their 'battle' against the women pickets by using male tactics of patronising and humouring them, perhaps a bit of the 'come on now, dear' attitude. When these initial tactics failed against responses like singing and chanting and the women continued to demonstrate their collective confidence, then the police swiftly resorted to savage verbal and physical abuse.

Pickets such as the one at Gedling which reflected the enormous confidence women could inspire in each other, generated an extremely violent response from the police. The police were being challenged not only as authority figures, but also as men involved in a job which upholds ludicrous sexual stereotypes. Their aim immediately became to gain control of the women in the crudest possible way – by threatened or actual physical violence. An even more common response, which has repeatedly been commented on by all the women, was the police's use of sexual imagery to 'defeminise' women pickets. By equating women pickets with socially 'reprehensible' groups such as lesbians, prostitutes and Greenham supporters, the police attempted to isolate them, to regard them as outside 'normal' patterns of femininity. The verbal abuse levelled at women pickets was invariably an attack on their sexuality, and their status as 'real women'. The police attitude clearly distinguished between acceptable and nonacceptable female behaviour. By picketing, the police view was that the women 'reduced' themselves to the same level as prostitutes.

Women rarely approached picket lines in all-male company. Although many picket line experiences were shared by men and women, the way such experiences were understood by the women was qualitatively different. The male pickets were, in general, more comfortable in an atmosphere of threatened physical aggression and more confident about their responses. To most women, these were truly alien environments. Women tended to picket with women, or stand with women on mixed pickets. Policewatch women would gravitate to stand with women rather than men on a picket line.

Off the picket lines women continued to rely on collective strengths to maintain their confidence. Many of the distressing experiences women had with the police involved being picked off individually while going about their daily business. It is quite different to be called a slag, whore or scrubber when walking alone to the shops and to receive the same insult when standing with a crowd of women psychologically prepared for abuse.

Their experiences contributed to some radical changes in mining women's attitudes, both about themselves and their environment. Contact with feminist women through fundraising and picketing opened up a large area of discussion about women's roles, within the strike and more generally. Women began to question why they were attacked through their sexuality, and to formulate their defences against this.

Although the police behaviour initially seemed confusing, women began to understand why they were attacked in particular ways, and why their natural response to this was to gravitate towards other women. For the majority of women, the police abuse failed to intimidate and failed to produce the sense of shame and inadequacy that it was intended to: the women remained proud of their efforts throughout.

Conclusion

In the space of twelve months policing in the pit villages became a major issue. Women involved with the NUM found that the police suddenly pervaded their lives. They discovered that it is not necessary to break laws to attract the wrath of the police. They learnt that the police are primarily instruments of social control. They linked the policing of the strike to other forms of state repression used against them – the judicial system as a whole, the DHSS, the collusion of the media and anti-trade union legislation. They also came to understand the links with nuclear power. They realised they were being criminalised, but they knew they were not criminals. The links developed with women outside their communities helped women directly involved in the dispute to gain confidence, both collectively and individually. We were constantly impressed by their determined optimism that their increased political awareness and collective strength would remain an effective force beyond the 1984-85 strike.

Women also realised that not only were their perceptions of policing changing but also that police priorities had changed in line with government policies: a growing emphasis was placed on public order policing, and the direct control of large sections of the working class. They were all too well aware that these changes will affect them, their children and their communities and that the public at large is as yet unmotivated to do anything to counter these developments. Women who were involved felt that 'community policing' and 'policing by consent' have become ideas of the past, to be replaced by policing through conflict. Half-way through the strike Audrey told us, 'I remember seeing the film *1984* and it made me feel really depressed. I thought about it a lot afterwards. Now we're in 1984 and it's worse, it's violent and it's real.'

These women have had first-hand experience of the way in which police powers are developing in this country with no public debate, but the vast majority of people remain ignorant of the growing threat of a police state. We believe it is important to realise that this was not a temporary change in policing tactics designed to break the miners' strike, but an irrevocable move towards the use of a national security force in a way which has never been seen outside Northern Ireland.

Their experiences in the strike have forced many women to see what has happened to them in a wider political context. Many have become politicised by their enforced appreciation of the lengths the state will go to to prevent them winning. They know all too well that the police tactics and methods are only the most overt manifestation of a system designed to rob working people of their rights and liberties, even their right to fight for their jobs. A national police force, developed to ensure that dissent can be crushed, has not emerged accidentally or in response to this one strike. It is the shape of the future for all of us who may one day not agree with government proposals. Although most women spoke of their fears for the future, and a nation that doesn't want to know, as Audrey said, 'Most people ignore what the police are doing to us, but once it starts happening to them, we'll all fight it and it will not be allowed to continue.'

Public ignorance, indifference and antipathy is consolidated by the symbiotic relationship between police and media. Women in Policewatch (and all women involved in the strike) had many personal experiences which illustrated not only media bias but the reporting of absolute lies. The police have a remarkably efficient propaganda machine which almost invariably demotes alternative accounts to mere allegations, regardless of the facts. Even on occasions when reporters were actually present we saw the police placing them sufficiently far behind the police lines to render them dependent upon police sources for their information. It was usual for the police to summon the media in time to witness retaliatory action by the NUM but too late to witness the provocation that caused it, allowing them to paint a convincing picture of violence and mob rule. Women told us constantly and bitterly of media duplicity and the anger and demoralisation that it created. Many of them linked their personal knowledge of police control of the media to events elsewhere, especially in Northern Ireland, presuming the lies and propaganda to be far worse there.

We feel strongly that the malleability of the media upheld the discretionary nature of truth in police accounts, and that it is an important part of the mutually convenient collusion of police and press. This is a dangerous and powerful marriage of interests which perpetuates the lack of public demand for an accountable police force. Many women felt that the partisan bias of the media encouraged the police to flout the law and to further increase their already considerable powers.

It is difficult to be optimistic about events at present, but we think that a lot of women gained indirectly through their conflict with the police. They have been forced to reappraise many aspects of their lives and, without exception, the police epitomise their perception of the state. Directly, they have learnt that their collective action is a force to be reckoned with, a force that can be effective in resisting unlawful police action. Mining women have linked with women outside their communities who wanted to add their support and strength. Many of the women that we spoke to told us that their attitude towards other groups of women has altered dramatically; women who they had previously seen as minority groups that they might have had nothing in common with, for example Greenham women, lesbians and black women, have been seen as comrades. These links enabled the women to provide an alternative model to combating the police with physical aggression. As one woman said, 'I don't think it's going to be a purely negative time. It will make the difference in the future. People will be more canny and less gullible. The police are bound to win if we play *their* game, and if we did beat the police, they'll get the troops in. The police will be much better prepared next time, but so will we – to undermine their authority, rather than confront it.' Perhaps this is where women can make their greatest contribution, in working out strategies that avoid a direct physical conflict that the police are bound to win.

Certainly, a lot of women have radically changed their ideas about the police. They have also changed their ideas about themselves as working class women. They realise with some bitterness that conflict has been forced upon them by present government policies and that the strike was only part of it. Four months after the end of the strike a woman told us that the South Yorkshire constabulary had had the arrogance to reintroduce a sole police officer on to the beat in a neighbouring village. 'We showed them; he was bricked out of the village.' She justified her grim satisfaction by adding, 'We didn't start the war, the government did. I was at school with that lad: if he can prostitute himself to Thatcher, he deserves all he gets.'

Women's Place in the Welsh Congress

Alex Grey

Alex is a researcher who lives in South Wales. She was closely involved with the dispute there, attending meetings, on picket lines, organising. She worked on the television programme 'Ms Rhymney Valley' about the women in that valley during the strike. She is involved in the Congress, one of the new initiatives to come out of the strike, and writes about that initiative and the necessity to take women's role in it seriously.

The Congress

The Wales Congress in Support of Mining Communities grew out of a realisation that greater unity was needed not only to feed miners and their families more efficiently but also in order to explain the case for coal. This realisation was arrived at more or less simultaneously by several political, trade union and cultural organisations.

Thus the Congress was born out of a political realisation that the miners were fighting for the future of Wales; if Thatcher and her state defeated the miners then all Welsh communities were in danger.

By the time the Congress was officially launched in Cardiff's City Hall on 21 October 1984, it had received the backing of some 300 people prominent in Welsh politics, as well as other groups. MPs such as Dafydd Elis Thomas (Plaid Cymru) and Ann Clwyd (Labour) indicated their support, as did councils, the Communist Party, local councils, trade unions, the churches, the arts, farmers, the women's movement and the peace movement.

The All Wales Conference in June 1985 was a way of developing this united front, to draw upon our experiences and then to develop a united programme of action for the future.

There is no reason why the nationalised coal industry should not work in a way that reflects the needs of miners, their families and communities, in Wales as elsewhere, and the interests of wider British society. There is no reason why the health service, schools and other welfare provisions should not be organised to meet the needs of local communities in a humane and civilised fashion. There is no reason why our communities should not be freed from the ever present threat of nuclear power and the arms it produces.

The Congress and its supporters believe these things can be attained by creating a society in which we control our own lives – in work-places, in local communities, in hospitals and health centres, in schools and colleges: in every sphere of our lives.

The aims of the Congress are to pursue these objectives, by local Congresses being set up in our communities. In this way we can co-ordinate the fight to retain our pits as a first step to demanding control over other aspects of our lives.

The Politics of the Congress and Women's Place in it

We were slaves because they were slaves to the mine owners.
                                    Esther Ronay's film, *Women of the Rhondda*

The achievements have been enormous. An alternative welfare system has been created – distributing food and clothing, providing moral and political support – which has sustained many thousands of families for almost a year in South Wales alone. The necessities of the miners' struggle have unleashed previously untapped reserves of self-confidence, organisational ability and communication skills.
                                    Wales Congress in Support of Mining Communities,
                                    October 1984.

Four months after the return to work the NUM is confronted with the problems of 25,000 redundancies, over 600 victimised or imprisoned miners and the re-emergence of Spencerism in the Nottinghamshire coalfield. In South Wales the ultra-left persist in their attacks on the role this coalfield played in the 'orderly return to work'. All of this at a time when, many would argue, the need for unity has never been greater. An analysis of what took place and why the strike ended as it did is required, but internal squabbling in the face of destruction seems pointless; as one Rhondda miner's wife said, 'whilst the NUM argues amongst itself, the NCB and the government are killing us off.'

The strike in South Wales was about unity; it brought unity to a diversity of protests. Working together with the miners cemented alliances which gave birth to a new kind of political movement: a broad-based anti-Thatcher alliance, a grouping of the left that bridged party differences and spawned the Wales Congress in Support of Mining Communities.

The formation of the Congress was a recognition that the most potent forms of mass politics had been outside the mainstream labour and trade union movement. People in Wales had participated in a whole range of issues: peace, anti-nuclear alliances, Welsh language issues. All had centred around the need to retain our communities. Once the community had been broken up then both its history and language died. Groups that had come together for peace were also involved in local protests about health or education cuts. All acted in an extra-parliamentary way to bring about a change of government policy.

By harnessing such groups and by bringing people 'out of their party political bunkers' (Dafydd Elis Thomas), it was hoped that the Congress would act not only as a co-ordinator for those groups working for and alongside the miners, but would also campaign effectively. Getting the message across had become lost in the strike as the media and the politicians centred on supposed 'picket line violence'. To stop pits closing the case for coal had to be heard and understood by everyone in the UK.

Despite the strains of political sectarianism the desire to stay together is strong. Nowhere is it stronger than in the women's groups. The rediscovery of their strength has left many women willing and determined to carry on the battle for the protection and improvement of their communities.

The All Wales Conference in Support of Mining Communities on 1 June 1985 at Maesteg was the first step in continuing the unity we had achieved as a result of the strike. By 1 June the Congress had been endorsed to carry on by the South Wales Area NUM, the Wales TUC and the Labour Party in Wales. In September the first meeting of the newly elected steering committee will take place. It is then that a new strategy based on the case for coal and fundraising will be hammered out. In June at Maesteg, Emlyn Williams, President of the South Wales Area NUM, spoke of the desire we have to stay and fight together as communities. The women's groups are the backbones of the communities Emlyn Williams spoke of. For the Congress to be effective we need those groups to be involved. The issues remain the same as the closures roll on.

Criticisms have been levelled at the NUM and the Congress for their 'tokenistic' attitudes towards women, and rightly so. Without the many hundreds of women who raised money, packed food parcels and often distributed them, the strike would have collapsed very quickly. Women organised themselves and adroitly negotiated their areas of collective responsibility. Nobody is sure of how many women were involved, but in every valley remotely connected with mining women's groups were established. Such numbers have not been reflected in any way, as yet, in the Congress.

To remedy this absence of women a process of affiliation has been established. All support groups, women's and mixed, have been contacted and asked to affiliate. Through affiliation each group can have one representative with voting rights and as many observers as they want without voting rights. All meetings of the Congress, monthly, will be open to all and it is hoped that through this method the Congress does not become 'bureaucratic', which would be a negation of the very purpose of setting it up.

Since the lock-outs of the 1920s the promise to promote equality between men and women has been talked about, but such promises are still not matched in practice. If the Congress deliberately creates a space for the women's groups and truly recognises the strength of this new movement much can be gained, and in the process the first real steps away from 'tokenism' and towards equality can occur.

For all the talk of unity it has always been the unity of the men that has been paramount. When we as women talk of unity we speak not only of the shared female experience of sustaining the strike, but also the sharing of our ideas with our men, of living our struggles together as one. The Congress and the NUM has not yet taken this on board, and until they do so the women will remain a separate organisation which will do much to weaken our collective strength.

If this notion of unity which sprang from the collective

action of the miners in South Wales is to be realised then both the NUM and the Congress must recognise what was different from previous strikes. The NUM took strike action primarily to retain the men's right to work. From that came the idea of preserving those communities which are dependent on pits for their material wealth. The women became involved when the preservation of their communities became a focus of the campaign to save pits. This was not a new idea in South Wales, for the Deep Duffryn campaign in 1979 was the first to highlight the importance of involving the community in saving a pit. However we still do not recognise the enormous shift there has been from a 'men only' dispute to an 'everyone but especially the women' campaign.

For the period of the strike in South Wales, as no doubt in many other parts of the country, solidarity reigned supreme. The differences in what motivated us were not apparent. We were in the end fighting for the same thing. Underlying this epic struggle there were differences, however, and women were prescribed traditional roles. In Gwent, for example, it was women who set up the food centre, women who packed and organised the distribution of some 6,000 food parcels every week, but it was the men who met each week to make the decisions and then relayed them to the women to be carried out. At no time during the strike were women allowed to attend one of those meetings. It was only through force of circumstances that some women managed to circumvent such male domination. Those lodges that were active picketing and therefore away 'up country' left the women to organise; most women, though, still referred any major decisions to the lodge. Some lodges made serious attempts to work with the women, while others could not bring themselves to defer to women in any way. This was most apparent over the issue of whether women should be on the picket lines. Most lodges felt there was no place for them; some women took them on but the majority did not. Feeling on the issue was so strong that one women's group in the Rhondda wouldn't allow a woman who went picketing with the men to speak on their behalf at any meetings.

Now the strike is over pragmatic considerations are taking a hold again, the old power relationships of the household are reasserting themselves and the women are finding it difficult to balance running a house, living with a man who works shifts and getting out to meetings. We must learn to understand not only the tremendous achievements of these women but also the difficulty of their lives in the valleys and mining villages, and what is important to them.

The solidarity of the women in the strike was not work-based or class-based, for against all the odds and despite the isolation of family life and the female competition ingrained in our society, women came out and stood shoulder to shoulder with other women and later on with their men. Women organised and have managed to stay organised.

In thinking about where the Congress goes from here and how it can learn from the women's movement, it is clear that a major reorientation in our thinking and in our practice is required. Merely saying 'sisters and brothers' instead of 'brothers', or 'sisters' instead of 'girls' is not sufficient. Firstly, it should be recognised that the women of the mining communities who organised themselves in the strike are part and parcel of the women's movement, and should be acknowledged as such: they are able to organise themselves and able to speak for themselves. But secondly, it is important that a narrow vision of 'sisterhood' which insists on solidarity between women to the exclusion of other solidarities, or above other solidarities, is not imposed on the women of the mining communities; for such a view fails to acknowledge the realities of the lives of women in the mining communities and their self-defined interests. Thirdly, any lapse into seeing 'working class' as synonymous with 'male manual workers' must be challenged. We cannot move forward without understanding that there is a variety of interests present in the working class, and without ensuring that a gain for one section is not at the expense of another section.

There is much of traditional working class organisation, thinking and practice which needs to be treasured and safeguarded. There is also much that is redundant and inappropriate, which should be abandoned.

We will never secure alliances between men and women, black people and white people, white collar workers and those in manual trades, or the many other minority groups, if we try to deny the conflicts that rage between us. We do not have identical interests. Unity premissed on similarity can be powerful but also restrictive. We are not all the same and the pretence that we are will not help us to create the sort of world we can all live, work and learn in.

If the Congress is to go forward alongside the NUM in South Wales, then we have to recognise that the work-based unity of the early 1970s has gone, and we have to look towards alternative sources of strength and solidarity. If the women's role in the strike has taught us anything, it has shown us that there are other forms of unity equally valid and powerful.

What brought us together in the strike were similarities not only in our working lives but also our home lives, and most importantly our vision of what we were trying to create in our opposition to Thatcher and the state she represents. This is why the Congress from its inception drew such a wide diversity of support with the recognition of our similarities of purpose. Through that emerged a powerful extra-parliamentary pressure group.

What will hold us together now is a common commitment to social and economic change, a commitment that existed throughout the strike. This should cut across the differences in the way we live or the jobs we do. We should not behave and act as if the only solidarity we have is the one that represented the miners, rather we should think of socialist unity as a complicated – often painful – construction, as it was in the strike, of many different solidarities.

From these differences, differences that many of the women recognise, we can build and go forward. By recognising our problems we can all begin to offer the much needed alternatives to Thatcher and her views on energy, peace, democracy, welfare, health, education, housing and unemployment. There are alternatives. One of the aims of the Congress is to argue the case for coal: why we don't need nuclear power and why we need a sane and rational energy policy.

I believe the Congress is working through this process. But it is a process highlighted by the sectarianism which is rampant after the strike. There is a danger that this sectarianism will destroy the very real gains of the strike. That would be a tragedy given the year of tremendous hardship that has been suffered by mining families. It is only through maintaining a unity of purpose, of the women's groups, of the Congress and of the miners that those gains can be consolidated.

June 1985

Give us a Future, Give us our Jobs!

Jean Hamilton

Many, many miners were arrested and held during the strike. So, too, were some of the women who supported them on picket lines. Restrictive bail conditions had the effect of removing many activists from the front line. If you obeyed the conditions you couldn't picket. If you disobeyed and were rearrested then it was unlikely that you would get bail again. A favourite police tactic was to pick out the union activists, arrest them on minor charges which would then carry restrictive bail conditions and rearrest if they saw the same face again. There is no doubt that magistrates helped the police to demobilise some of the activists by colluding with the standard restrictive bail conditions. Both men and women were affected.

Jean Hamilton's husband is one of the men who were caught up in this tactic. He was at Monkton Hall colliery a few miles south-east of Edinburgh; Bilston Glen is the other local pit. Feeling for the strike was never strong at Bilston Glen, and it was the first pit in Scotland to break, with large numbers of men going back quite early in the strike.

Jean told me the story of her involvement in the strike and what happened to Davie, her husband. He sat with us as we talked, and added his bit too.

My husband was the area delegate at Monkton Hall, and he represented 1,500 men at the time of the strike. At Monkton Hall and Bilston Glen they voted against strike action, but the majority of pits in Scotland voted to strike, so by the rules of the conference Monkton Hall went along with it.

People weren't really sure what to expect; we were hoping that the strike would be a short one. But when the weeks went on the women in this area got themselves together, and in May we started up a group. I was there the very first day: it was a Sunday, and it started off with about thirty women. The women from the Labour Party were talking about forming a joint group of all the area in the Lothians, but we decided to have our own group locally in Dalkeith. Then each centre round about decided to have their own group.

The first thing we did for fund raising was a sponsored walk. Sixteen miles we walked. My legs were killing me, and I had a blister on my toe this big. But we had a good day and we raised £600. Finance was important because we needed to start up a soup kitchen. We used the miners' club in Dalkeith, we used the cooking facilities there. It wasn't very big, but it did for our purposes. There are about three hundred mining families in Dalkeith. At the start very, very few were coming in. And then at one point, when the Durham men were up picketing, on four consecutive days we fed 300, on a three-ring cooker: we gave them a sit-down three-course meal, too.

We cooked for the families as well as the miners. My kids came to the club all the time. It was a main meal you got at dinner time, so at night it was just a snack I had to make: it really did save money. We were well fed; in fact I put weight on. We had jumble sales, we had a shop with a lot of clothes. The shop is still open. It is not doing wonderfully, but has some income. We still run a van, and if anyone needs to use it we have to pay for petrol. The shop pays for that, but that is about all it does pay for. The woman who runs it is due to have her baby next week, so we will have to see how long it stays open. She was dedicated to the shop when the rest of us had other things to do.

There were about twenty different support groups in Lothian, and we had a Lothian women's support group that co-ordinated them: I'm the vice-chair of that and we still get together. The Dalkeith group still meets every fortnight. Each group had its own funds, and the Lothians women had their own fund as well. But if Dalkeith was doing a fund-raising event the money went to Dalkeith, except at Christmas when all the money that came in went to the Lothians and we spread it between the twenty centres and the kids got a good Christmas.

We ran a kitchen from May until February, right to the end. We didn't have food parcels because we didn't have the income. Some places gave a meat voucher or something every second week. At the beginning there were a lot of women involved in our group, but near the end there were only about ten women left. Everybody else had scabbed.

Then we heard they were setting up a Scottish Women's Committee. At the beginning, I didn't like the idea at all, I thought we were getting more and more involved in something we couldn't understand. I thought the local support work was enough, and important. At the Lothians committee they asked if anyone was interested in joining the Scottish committee, and nobody was at first. I think the majority of women like to lead their own lives, are quite prepared to sit in the background. So Helen and I volunteered because nobody else would do it. We said we would go along and try it.

I found the Scottish committee quite interesting, because women from the six centres for Scotland met once a month, so you found out what was happening in the other areas. We had a couple of women's rallies, and they have been very successful: lots of women, people speaking, folk-singing; members of the churches, all different kinds of people.

Anyone who was willing to help was welcome to our meetings. We had a few non-mining women in the Dalkeith group at the beginning, but it dwindled off and it was only a certain few that kept doing the work.

Then there were the complaints. Margo McDonald has a talk programme on Radio Forth every Sunday, and people phoned in with complaints: that it was only the committee that got anything, that they were not allowed to go to the soup kitchens, that they were being turned away. Which was downright lies because we were open for anybody, we fed anybody from all the different areas that came. If they wanted to come they got fed. I don't understand why people were like that. They obviously didn't know because they had never been.

(Davie: You had twenty strike centres, but only eight soup kitchens, so there wasn't a soup kitchen at every strike centre.)

But the ones that didn't have a kitchen were supposed to go to the nearest one. Some people didn't attend meetings, or they didn't know the layout. So if they didn't know, it was their fault. At the beginning I never went up to the club at all, I just sat in the house. I just decided I was going up and I continued to go: nothing would put me off. I've had a few arguments as well. The men I find a wee bit chauvinist. They didn't like the women to show they could be as good as *they* were. And that is *not* excluding my husband!

(Davie: It was alright as long as you stuck to your part of the job.)

We said it a hundred times, if the women had done the

picketing, and the men had stayed in the kitchen, we'd have won this strike a long time ago. I told the women that. It was the first time I had been involved in an organisation. I had never been on a committee before. I hadn't the first idea how to go about it. Even now I'm certainly not experienced because of some of the things I don't know. But I was willing to try. The women used to argue amongst themselves, too. Each person can only cope with so much.

I think we got more support from further afield than we did locally. Dalkeith is a working class area, but most of the people would prefer it to be different. They were not for the miners; there was the odd one who was very good, but the majority of people were against us all the way, so we had to fight all the time. The majority here don't work in the pits, but in factories and other places.

(Davie: 28 per cent of the male population locally, which covers the area of about six of our strike centres, is unemployed. There is a lot of part-time work, there are bus loads of women going in to Edinburgh for part-time work.)

There's Ferranti, and a good majority of the workers there are women. There is Letts the book binders. I worked at the dental hospital in Edinburgh, and I got a job at the Provident Clothing Company in February last year and worked there right up until my husband was arrested and imprisoned. The people I worked beside were snobs, to say the least, and I got a lot of hassle at work, so I just left. I have not been at work since October '84. At the beginning of the strike I had two jobs; I used to work Fridays and Saturdays *and* five nights a week, so that helped us financially. Now I don't work at all. Neither of us do: he has lost his job. Hopefully he will get his job back, but he is a union delegate and I don't hold out much hope for the likes of him.

I was also arrested; I was the only woman in Lothian to be arrested. In October I was charged with breach of the peace and assaulting a police officer. The women's group went picketing that day; a bus-load of us were just standing on the pavement and they told us to move down. We didn't want to move down so we said 'No'. We were away from the pit gates, we weren't obstructing the traffic so we said, 'No, we are standing here.' The policemen told my husband, who was doing the organising, that if the crowd didn't move he was going to be arrested for the whole bus. I said, 'If you take him, you'll take us all.' This inspector from the back said, 'Take her.' So I was arrested. I was lifted off my feet, I was carried by the throat into the Black Maria: I was screaming like a pig.

I spent five hours in the cell. It was terrible: I was by myself, they separated me from the men. I just sat there, it was freezing. They took my shoes off me. They wanted to take my jumper off but I said, 'No way, the jumper stays on.' When I went to court, they dropped the charges. Looking back you can have some laughs, but at the time it wasn't funny.

Monkton Hall was really quite good up until October or November, with Christmas coming up. A lot of the breakdown came when David went into jail. A lot of the men at Monkton Hall stood out well, but as soon as he disappeared into jail they started to dwindle through the gates. At Bilston Glen they were bad from the very start, there were people going in from the beginning. It started with maybe only twenty going through, and it worked its way up until it was the majority that scabbed and the minority that stayed on strike.

The summer was a bad time up at Bilston Glen, when they got the Durham lads up. That was when all the windows got broke; I think it was frustration. But I don't think it was just the pickets, the police had a lot to do with the violence there because they were vicious, they were bad, there were bad men in the police force. We did have the occasional good ones, because there were some local guys we knew and they hated doing the job. But there were a lot of bad ones who took great pleasure in arresting people.

We have got a lot of video tapes of the strike. My husband was arrested at Hunterston. His face was known as he was a leader in this area. You can actually see what happened, he was standing there, not getting into any trouble. You can see the inspector pointing to him, and the horses opening up and drawing him in, and then closing in. Just him, no one else. He was charged with breach of the peace and found guilty, so he has a record now. He was fined £175 for one offence and £100 for another. But he spent two months in jail when he was charged with assaulting a scab, when in actual fact it was the scab that attacked him. He couldn't get bail, because he was on the Bilston Glen charge, for breach of the peace, and he'd broke bail. That's when they hauled him in. We went to the

High Court with an appeal, but they wouldn't budge. There were other men who got out, who had also broken bail, but he was a leader ... When it got to court, the jury unanimously found him not guilty, and you could see by the evidence that it was a set up.

Even though there are talks going on, I don't see any way that they will take him back at Monkton Hall: they fear him too much. The most serious charge, of assault, was thrown out; that will not be on his record. But the man who he is to have those meetings with, Mr Cairn, he and my husband don't get on very well. He doesn't get on with anybody: he is an arrogant man, only bumped up since the strike. He was only an under-manager, then. The manager there before was more understanding: they got rid of him.

(Davie: The manager at the time of the strike was an old miner, and he refused to allow any scab buses to go into the pit. 'The men walked out, they'll walk back, past their neighbours.' He was transferred, because he had that position. The next man in line was appointed manager: I had crossed him a number of times across the table, he had been carpeted a couple of times. So he and me had a lot of friction. The last time we sat across from a table, he pinned me up against a wall, physically. I can get under his skin like nobody else can. The only reason he is there is because he is a yes-man. The old-style managers, who came in under nationalisation, are being moved. It does nothing for our industry, because these new ones don't understand the problems. They'll do what they are told, and they will work themselves out of a job: it's stupid.)

It was the Scottish NUM Executive that decided to ask the women to picket. They came out to individual places and asked if the women would go picketing. They wanted a women's presence. A group of ours went to Ravenscraig, though I didn't go, and that was one of the worst scenes they have seen because the police were just charging in with the horses. It made the women more and more strong, more determined to go back on the picket line. At the beginning I wasn't for the women on a picket line. I thought that was the men's job, it was their place of work, not ours. But as time went by and they asked us to go, I went along with the majority. It was a few times at Monkton Hall, but mostly at Bilston Glen. I can't say I enjoyed it, because I never did. I just felt I shouldn't have been there.

We were a bit unsure of ourselves: 'Why are we here? The men should be here.' But there were a few women who enjoyed it, shouting at the scabs. That's something I just couldn't do, shout. I just used to stand and let them do the shouting. The women sang, especially 'I'd rather be a picket than a scab!' It was amazing all the things like songs that come out. There was one lady who picketed every day at Bilston Glen, and she knew the local lads and things that had happened years ago. She shouted things like, 'You're the one that used to steal stuff from the Post Office.' And on the night shift, 'Joe's gone into your wife, lad.' *And* she got the stories right!

(Davie: A lot of times the women would stand with the men on the line, and as the crush came on the men would try to protect the women instead of pushing. When we went to Ayrshire they moved the women to one side, so that the men could take the hassle and they didn't have anything to worry about. One time a car was coming in, and a wee lassie skipped in between. She dived on top of the car, she was spread eagled on the bonnet and grabbed the windscreen wipers. The police just stood there: 'What the hell are we going to do with her?' They had to wait for the WPC to come up and drive her off because they were afraid to touch any part of her.)

The women never had any serious trouble with the police here; I was the only one arrested. They were mixed pickets: I have seen the women in the majority but none that were solely women.

When David was in jail it changed at Monkton Hall. They had no spirit. As soon as the men arrived on the picket line they were being arrested. They were getting really frightened and I think him getting put in jail put the wind up them. They thought, 'We could be put in jail as well.'

(Davie: The men were terrified out of their lives; there had been 500 arrests. You could sense it. When I came out of jail I could see the change. The men were actually cowed; the biggest picket they had was about thirty men. I went round the women's sections and got the women to come out picketing to embarrass their husbands. *They* got the reaction from the men, and they started coming back picketing. We were back up to 200 and then 300 pickets, and it was the women that did that, I'm convinced.)

The women down at Bilston Glen all linked hands across the

gate one day, and the scabs just stood there frightened. We tried, but the police moved us out. I can't imagine that before the strike I would ever do anything like that. I'm very moderate, I don't like striking, but this time I felt there was no alternative and my husband stuck it out to the end. When we had the eight-week strike in '83 I kept saying, 'Have you not got anything settled yet?' But not this time. I would never, never let him go back. I wouldn't have liked him to go through the picket lines, because I think it is something you should never do, no matter what excuse you have, how bad financially you are, or under a strain. I don't think any excuse is good enough to walk through a picket line: I couldn't have lived with that. And how they can live with it, I'll never know.

(Davie: In this area, there were 50 strikers left out of 300 at the end.)

There are some people I walk by and I cringe inside at the thought of them, but I always keep my head up because I have nothing to be embarrassed about; *they* lower their heads. Some, till they move or I move, I won't speak to as long as I live here. Some of the men we have known for years. There are some I will speak to, because of different circumstances. But there are some bad ones. One particular couple used to come to the club on Sunday, wanting their dinner. We didn't open Saturday and Sunday, but we opened the cupboard up and gave them a big box of messages (shopping) because they had nothing. People like that I cannot forget, because we went out of our way to make sure they were alright. I never understood him. One day he would be shouting the odds at the scabs, the next he was scabbing himself. Just up here, five houses on the left-hand side are scabs, five houses on the right-hand side are scabs: it is called 'Scab Row'. We have to go that way to the shops but it doesn't worry me at all.

They talk about intimidation against scabs. But while he was in jail, I had terrible hassle. I got my washing burnt off the rope. My phone number was written on the wall of a public house near Leith docks where the sailors get off their boats and I used to get abusive phone calls. The police weren't interested. While he was in jail I didn't tell him because he had enough trouble without telling him about it.

(Davie: We had some of the boys go round in the van to make sure she was alright.)

I kept thinking of him being in for Christmas, that was worrying me. I thought, 'I've never had Christmas by myself.' The weeks and the days were long, it was a long two months. He was lucky enough to get out in December. I went in to see him every day, six days a week. He was in Salton, in Edinburgh, eight or nine miles away. It was a filthy place, it was mucky, it was horrible.

(Davie: It was through a glass partition, you cannot touch at all. I was on petition: in Scotland, if it is on remand, they can hold you for 40 days: if it is on petition, they can hold you for 110 days before trial.)

The people who had been found guilty have better visiting rights than the ones on remand. They sit at tables.

(Davie: But only once a month. The untried prisoners are locked up in their cells for twenty hours a day and twenty-three at weekends; the tried prisoners were out playing snooker. That is the system: they were in for years and we were in there for months, that's all.)

I did some speaking whilst he was in jail. I did a local meeting in Dalkeith, that was the first one and that was quite successful. Then I did another at Loanhead, and that seemed okay. Then they asked me to do the Usher Hall in Edinburgh, and that worried me. It was the biggest rally, an NUM rally, and Tony Benn was speaking. I wasn't very keen because I wasn't a public speaker at all, but everyone that heard it says I did well. I prepared it and I just kept rattling it off, I kept talking all the time. I never had a breather until I was finished. I was frightened to look up in case I lost my place. Everybody said it was good, and I got a standing ovation. Gavin Strang the MP had a small tape. He was going to tape me because I was going to take it to the jail to let him hear, but the tape was broken.

If it all happened again I think the women would be more than glad to get themselves together again and to get organised, and to do what we've done over the past year. I think a lot of the women who before might have sent their husbands back to work, with getting involved they understood more. I think I was luckier than most, because he's been a union rep for about ten years and I understood a wee bit more than most what was going on. I had first-hand information, too, all the time, because he was at all the big meetings, so I had a good idea what was going on.

I think it helped going to the strike centre. The ones sitting at home, not knowing what was going on, they were bound to get demented when something came on the telly and they didn't really know the ins and outs of the story.

(Davie: I was banned from the picket line for the bigger part of it: every time I walked out, I got arrested. That's why the committee grounded me.)

I hated it. I would say, 'I'm not going picketing today, you'd better not!' And somebody would come to the door and say, 'Davie's been arrested again.' I used to dread him going out in the morning. It was a relief when the committee grounded him.

(Davie comments on the role the women's groups had played: I think the decision at the National Conference against the women having associate status is a bloody disgrace. That was terrible after the role the women played.

The Coal Board strategy in Scotland was to break Bilston Glen and then to go to Ayrshire. If it hadn't been for the women in this area it would have been much worse. There was a woman in Prestonpans on the Firth of Forth whose husband was threatening to go back to work. She goes upstairs and gets all his working gear, his pit clothes, and she throws them into the sea so he couldn't go back to work! There are 300 miners down there and only 30 went back by the end of it, and it was because of the involvement of the women. They were all tied in with the Labour Party, and there was a political awareness there.

At Monkton Hall less than half the men went back early, which was no mean feat considering that nearly every miner went back at Bilston Glen, and that was brought about by the strength of the women. And that is why it is important that the women continue. If the strike had collapsed in Scotland the strike would have been finished. I know men that went back to work because of the pressure of the women, and I also know men who have stayed out because of the pressure of their wife. I'm sort of chauvinist myself, but you have to recognise the role the women played.)

At the moment there doesn't seem to be any real purpose for the local groups. But we have got this conference coming up in Sheffield, maybe something will come out of that. The

Lothians women's committee are still keeping their meetings going but the majority of women who are coming now are victimised miners' wives.

In the strike we weren't starving, so money didn't seem important. Now that he has lost his job, even now, it is not that important; what is, is the security that is not there. Every year for as long as I can remember, we've always had a holiday. This year I was lucky, I've had a lovely holiday. (Jean went with her two children to the GDR at the invitation of the miners' union there, to their holiday centre at Schmidseld.) But next year we don't know what the future is, and that frightens us. The women whose husbands have returned to work feel that maybe we're getting more than they are: 'Well, you'll be alright, you're getting looked after, and you've not got your rent to pay.' That's true, we haven't got our rent to pay at the moment. But they have a future and we haven't.

I haven't really thought out a plan for the future; if he gets his job back I'll look for a job myself, and then I'll go along my life as I did before. I have no other option, unless I get some kind of a job that involves me in union work or community work or something like that. But I cannot look at the future, because there is no future at this time. If something changes, as hopefully it will, I will change along with it.

It has been a good strike, because we have had a good time. A lot of solidarity between men and women. We met people from all over the area, we were all friends. We had tea together, we had dinner together, we enjoyed everybody. The Chileans were there. We've had meetings, we've had dances, people from every walk of life. We have had friends in Edinburgh who've been marvellous to us, always offering us things. I've never experienced that community spirit in my life, and probably never will again.

(*Written with the collaboration of Vicky Seddon*)

Warm Welcome, *Cath Cunningham;*
Sharp Realities: *Jean Miller;*
Relations with the NUM *Dorothy Phillips*

The NUM found a new ally in the 1984-85
strike, the women of the coalfields, an
unexpectedly strong ally. But it was not an
alliance without problems. How they were
resolved, or not resolved, varied from pit to pit,
area to area. Three women write about how the
new ally was received.

Fife *Cath Cunningham*

Cath is a miner's wife from Dysart in Fife, and
appears elsewhere in this book. She is a political
activist in a part of the country known for its red
politics, and was heavily involved in the
women's movement in Fife, in the strike. Her
first child was born during the strike, soon after
Orgreave, where her husband Harry had to run
to avoid being clubbed. She remains optimistic
about the future for women in the coalfields
communities.

The Fife area was more than 95 per cent solid until the end of
the strike. There are many reasons for this, one being the
traditional militancy of Scottish miners. There was also the
realisation that the Scottish coalfields would be badly hit by the
pit closures list with its intention to run down the pits in this
area. Another reason the miners were solid for so long was the
involvement of the miners' families, and in particular the role
played by women. The issue of pit closures does not affect just
miners but their families and the whole community, and so in
our area the women began to organise. It was the women who
organised themselves, but in getting off the ground they were
given a great deal of encouragement by the local NUM. They
helped us set up our organisation and, whenever we needed it,
provided transport to meet women from the ten centres
coming under the Dysart umbrella. We had many discussions
with the men as to how we could bring more women together.
    We began to realise over a short period what a tremendous

impact the women's groups were having, not just in respect of cooking meals and raising funds, which we proved we could do in most difficult circumstances, but as a morale booster for our men themselves. I believe one factor in men returning to work (scabbing) was pressure from the miner's family, or his wife. And so it really was vital to keep the women informed and to maintain their involvement. The children too were active, and many of the older ones will be able to recall and to relate to their experiences in later life. No one was untouched by the things we went through in that year, indeed many achieved things we would not have thought possible before the strike.

Soup kitchens and bingo nights soon become insufficient for many women. There was frustration at not being able to do more, as in many areas we were not encouraged to go near picket lines. We had to take a serious look at where we were going.

In March 1984 an all-women demonstration was held in Edinburgh to mark International Women's Day. All centres received invites but few were enthusiastic, as not many of the women had ever been on any kind of demo before. Still, those who did go had a great time. The theme of the demo as was 'Victorian Values' (Thatcher's favourite phrase), and was run from a working class point of view. Our women were given place of honour in the march, dressed in costumes of women coal-workers of that era. They all said how wonderful it was to see hundreds of other women who were supporting the miners, and this bucked us up a great deal. It was around this time that it began to sink in that the strike would not be a three-week wonder, and that it was going to be a difficult time for all.

The men certainly realised the importance of involving the women, at least the local committee did. It was the men's committee, around this time that began to organise an all-women conference, which was to be held at the Lochgelly Centre, in Fife. The rally took place a few weeks later. The building was packed: can you imagine over 400 women coming together from all different mining areas, and from non-mining communities showing solidarity? Ella Egan and Jane Mackay spoke to the meeting, and then the rostrum was left open to the floor. There was a constant flow of women going up to speak. To tell us what the women in their area were doing and to air their views, although in fact we were all of the same opinion – that we were prepared for a fight! My husband was there at the rally and says now that he had never experienced anything like the atmosphere in that hall! 'It was absolutely electric!'

The contacts which were made at that meeting were to be unbroken bonds for the duration of the strike. Women trade unionists from Dundee were there to give support and to find out what we needed to alleviate hardship. Other women from political parties also pledged support. It really was a turning point for the women: now we could see all the possibilities. We started visiting factories and union meetings; we were invited to speak at meetings, a skill many of us acquired quite speedily. Wherever the men went to speak the women went too. We became an inseparable partnership and this was to have a great effect on the people giving support. It brought to their attention that families were involved as well as miners and pricked the hearts of many who would not give to the miners but could not bear to see the families punished. We sent speakers to Dundee and as far north as Inverness, Aberdeen and Peterhead. Our campaign was really widespread.

The city of Dundee has always had an affinity with the coalfields, Fife in particular, and a Relief Committee was set up early on in the strike and was very active throughout the dispute. Because of the wide range of people involved we were able to find avenues to put our case across to many sections of the public. Rallies were held in Dundee also, and of course the women were always present along with our home-made banners and our chants and songs.

Again, it was the strike committee which took the initiative when it raised with the Dundee Relief Committee a very special need: that of pregnant women. There seemed to be quite a number of them in Dysart. And it was difficult enough to feed a family on the pittance we had to last us every week, but to provide for a new baby was out of the question. The strike committee raised it, and the Relief Committee took it on board. Every woman in the Dysart area who was having a baby was provided with a layette from the people of Dundee. This started in July 1984 and went on throughout the strike, catering for well over 75 babies. Our own family was the first to benefit from this scheme. It was run like an adoption agency, where a factory or work-place would sponsor a child by providing the layette for her/him, chipping in personal gifts of money or knitting shawls and mittens. In return, a photo of the baby was sent to the donors. It brought a closer contact with these people who were so desperate to help. Credit should be given to many people for this work, but in particular to Marie Vannet who dealt with the lists of pregnant women. This was a really difficult job as babies sometimes have a habit of arriving early, and she had to make up a good few emergency layettes at short notice.

The contact between the strike committee and the women was kept up during the strike: the NUM always made sure there was transport available to bring the Dundee women down on a Tuesday night for our central meetings, which was when women came from ten centres to meet in Dysart. The NUM always tried to make sure that a committee member was there to give us reports about the latest developments. This was very necessary as, although overall we had a very good relationship with the NUM and the strike committee, some centres ignored the women's groups and did not keep them informed. For many of us it was a new experience, working alongside men: a different environment from our normal. So too it was different and difficult for the men: there are no women down the pit. Indeed many men were hostile to the women's groups, perhaps for fear of us interfering, or maybe they just felt threatened by the new role women had begun to play. At first it seemed as if we could get nowhere with this line of thought. The NUM Dysart Central Committee (particularly Willie Clarke, Johnny Neilson, Sandy Sneddon and Jock Mitchell) had to try almost everyday to get the men to change their attitudes, but it could not be achieved that way. It was only over time, through our work and our support of the dispute that we gained their respect and began to be accepted.

Of course there were those whose attitudes would never change, but we turned a blind eye to this. Sometimes we were surprised when a sexist remark was made in our direction and it was the men who made the reply in our defence, even before we had the chance to reply. It also made the point very sharply when the NUM leadership emphasised the crucial role of women. Mick McGahey never failed to speak of this whenever he was present. This was more ammunition for the women to use.

So in Fife, although the picture wasn't entirely rosy, we tackled the problems together and overcame most of them. And just as we had come out on strike together, we returned together: a highly emotional week. The women with banners marched with the men as they returned to work *en masse*.

But we were determined not to drift away home and forget what we had learnt and the friends we had made. This was what everybody said at the time, but in reality there have been many women who have not come back to the women's groups. One year on strike (fourteen months in this area), takes it toll on you. Many feel they need a break, a cooling off period. Of course in the majority of homes there is pressure from the menfolk to get back to the way things were before the strike. Many of us are still going through hell to get to our meetings. I think that many women would come too, if there was not the difficulty of transport. There are also their child-care commitments: the men are back on shift-work, so the child-minding is left to the woman.

What are the women doing now? We run regular socials to aid the sacked miners. This brings in money, but also keeps the families together. We still are present whenever the Sacked Miners Committees are out leafleting and campaigning for reinstatement. We are determined not to be brushed aside or forgotten. And we are *absolutely determined* to get associate membership of the NUM, though it may take time because of decisions in South Wales and Yorkshire, much to their shame. We did nothing more than the women of South Wales and Yorkshire, so they deserve the men's gratitude no less than we do. Perhaps it is just that some NUM men are living in the past.

Here's to the future, when the issues affecting us all, and the aims of working people can be worked for not just by half the population, but by involving the other 50 per cent (women). We can achieve so much more together. And what's more, *now* we are prepared to *demand* our right to do so: here we go!

August 1985

Barnsley

Jean Miller lives in a mining village near
Barnsley and works in a community centre. Her
father was a miner, she used to be married to a
miner and her two sons are miners. She was a
founder member of the Barnsley Women
Against Pit Closures group and travelled all
over the country during the dispute, speaking at
public meetings and helping to raise cash. She
argued the case for the miners and especially the
need for material assistance for their families.
She travelled to Holland, Germany and
Belgium, speaking to trade union and political
meetings. She had a hand in setting up the
national organisation of Women Against Pit
Closures groups. She also took the greetings of
mining women to Greenham.

The women's groups sprang from the initiative of the women
themselves, particularly those intimately connected to the
dispute. It was their initiative, not the NUM's. There was a
mixed response from the NUM in different places. In Scotland,
where there is a progressive leadership, the women were
offered use of the NUM buildings in Edinburgh, use of the
board room for meetings and other facilities. But it was quite
different in other parts of the country. In Barnsley women did
not feel they could ask to use NUM buildings, nor were they
offered. Barnsley was one of the first groups to get started,
along with the Chesterfield group which emerged from the
grouping of women who had got together over Tony Benn's
election campaign to have a women's canvass. Many of the
groups which followed were started on the initiative of women
who, though members of political parties, had not been
involved in political initiatives before, certainly not as women.
They started to work in a way that they had never worked
before.

The first two groups got a lot of publicity and other women
heard about them. In the first few months of the dispute a few
of us went round to the villages talking to groups of women
about why and how we had set our groups up, and then they
formed their own groups. It was a women's initiative, with
women contacting other women, arranging the printing of

leaflets, distributing leaflets, setting groups up.

Right from the beginning we had decided in the Barnsley group that we were a campaigning group not just a support group. We believed that the dispute was as much our dispute as the men's, because we had as much suffering as the men who worked down the pit. We said as much in our first letter to the local press which generated such a response. I explained all that to one of the Barnsley NUM Panel, ie Barnsley district officials, but he didn't really understand. He came to our group in the second week of the strike and said, 'I've found you a place to run a kitchen, go tomorrow and start serving meals.' He was used, of course, to instructing his members when and where to go picketing, and expected them to do it. But that was not what those women had decided they were about, so we declined the 'offer'. And that was the way that it was: any contact with the local NUM was on their terms. That was the only offer from the Barnsley Panel to the women's group. Of course the women would have welcomed a co-operative relationship, but they were not prepared to accept that kind of direction.

Now that they had got together they moved out of the role they had always accepted, and this was clear from very early on. It took us three or four metings to decide what to call the group. We did not see ourselves as a miners' wives or women's support group. We wanted *any* woman in our area who was supporting the dispute, who was in favour of what the NUM was fighting for, to be involved, so we called it 'Barnsley Women Against Pit Closures'. Because if the pits go down, the villages go down with them, and it would become a depressed area for everyone who lived there, not just mining families. So in our group it was very clear that we were interested in campaigning, in holding rallies, in picketing: in fact, in raising political support for the dispute.

As the dispute proceeded we saw the need for the collection and distribution of food, and for kitchens to serve food communally. Of course the money given by the other unions and by individuals to the NUM Solidarity Fund went to the NUM. None of that money went directly to the women's groups, but was given to the branches to decide how to use. It went to pay for picketing, to provide transport for picketing, to print leaflets about the dispute, for general publicity and to alleviate some very severe hardship cases. If the women had not got themselves organised there would have been no systematic help for the families in terms of food and money. The NUM, as far as I can see, put all its eggs in the picketing basket, as they traditionally have, and made no particular provision for dealing with destitution amongst the families. So the women began to see that as well as campaigning there was a need to support the families. That meant going far beyond the traditional housewife role of the mining women. There has been large-scale catering, feeding five and six hundred people in a day; having to raise the money for that, learning to argue for it, to earn it in all sorts of ways, by speaking at meetings and rallies, by collecting on the streets. What they did was to set up an alternative welfare system, and an effective one at that. And these were women who had never done anything outside the home before, learning to speak on public platforms to enormous audiences. The change in those women is tremendous. Even if they do not continue to be active in a public way their attitudes will still be very different from what they used to be. They will no longer accept that their husbands know more than they do, just because they go out to work. Their opinions will be heard, even if just inside the home. They have learnt that their ideas are valuable.

The women's development has been enormous. The men's reactions to the women being involved outside the home have been mixed. On the one hand, there are many, many men who are finding out what pleasure they can gain from spending time with the kids: bath-time can now be exciting instead of a drudge, with mother shouting at them upstairs. Chores can be shared and enjoyable. Some men are learning for the first time how to cook a meal and to get the children off to school. But there are still men who don't accept it, and haven't played the role a lot of us would have liked, doing more at home to free the women to be involved. But I would say that there are a lot of men who have awakened to the pleasure they can gain from spending time at home.

In the beginning the NUM didn't react one way or the other, and because the women organised themselves they didn't go to the NUM for assistance. At one stage, when the groups were setting up, the NUM gave £120 to each group to get started, but they soon stopped when they found more and more were starting up and their finances were going down. The Regional TUC (Yorkshire and Humberside) fund had gone directly to the NUM, and that was not fed back into the women's groups. A lot of the women have complained about this because they see the union going out to collect money for food and for families, and the money not coming into the women's groups: we were having to fight for every penny we got. So the women were upset, not so much about how the money was spent, but because they were not consulted at all about its distribution. There was no real understanding of the role the women were playing and the issues the women were bringing to the public eye. And that the general public found it easier to relate to that than to some of the other issues they were being presented with.

The NUM has certainly *recognised* the existence of the women's groups and has been saying that they are an integral part of the dispute and have helped to keep the strike going. They have stood on platforms and welcomed the women's support and applauded the women's role, saying what a good job we have done. That public recognition is important, but saying things on platforms doesn't cost anything, there is no effort to it, it doesn't have to be thought out. In fact, they have had rallies where they have said how wonderful the women are – but without thinking of asking a woman to speak. So we have seen a tremendous change in a section of the working class which has been silent before, and which is now shouting from the roof-tops. The development of that section is very, very important to the working class but the NUM locally hasn't really recognised its importance yet, or really learnt to take it on board and to help it develop. I believe that the women have played a vital role in the dispute; without them, their work and support, it would have collapsed a lot earlier because the families would have been destitute. You heard stories of deprivation and poverty in mining families, but without the women's groups there would have been hundreds and hundreds more stories like that. The families could not have existed without the women's support. That is the part that the NUM, at least in this part of the country, hasn't recognised: the *essential* role the women have played.

In some parts of the country, Scotland for example, the Area NUM can see possibilities for the development of the women and will help them to continue to be organised and active, and to support the families who are in tremendous debt. But in Yorkshire, Durham and Derbyshire there will be little or no help. Kent, of course, is different, being small and with all the support from London they have been in a different situation: there has not been such sharp hardship there.

Some of the groups have used Miners' Welfares to set up kitchens, but in Yorkshire as often as not we have used municipal buildings because the Welfares are not equipped with cooking facilities. The Barnsley group used the village hall and had some of the best facilities, though to start with we had some problems. We brought in some of our own equipment, a cooker, a fridge, a water boiler, because there wasn't enough for the job we had to do, but we kept blowing the fuses. We had an electrician from North Gawber who used to come up and repair the fuses. Then they came and put in some more power lines. Of course, the women are not full members of the Welfares. The miners are deducted a penny a week to run them, and they are run by the pit branches. I have used North Gawber for years and when the secretary asked me, 'Why don't you become a member?' I said, 'When I can join on exactly the same terms as the men, then I will, but until then I won't.' Most of the women haven't thought about the implications of that yet, they haven't thought it was important.

At pit level, relations between the NUM and the women's groups have varied at different pits. Mapplewell, where I live, is a fairly typical village. There are two local pits: North Gawber with about 750 men, and Woolley, the pit with the new wash, which has about 1,700 men. North Gawber has been very supportive of the role the women have played. The branch officials have come out to us and said, 'If you want any help, come and tell us, and we will do our best to provide it.' And on a number of occasions they did that. We are in the middle of the two pits, so we fed and looked after the communities from both pits. But Woolley, from day one, refused point blank to support in any way the women's group in our area. They organised a very small number of women to run a kitchen to feed the men who go on picket duty, and no one else, not the wives and families, just the pickets. The branch raises the money for the kitchen, but it is only for the pickets. The women's group kitchen fed anyone, providing that they were striking miners or members of their families. And, of course, because of the difference in size of the two pits, this kitchen fed more people from Woolley than from North Gawber. At one stage the kitchen was desperate for money and appealed to both pits. North Gawber did everything it could to provide what we asked for. Woolley offered us £35. When the women said that they needed more to keep it running, they said that if Woolley people came we were to turn them away! Such arrogance! And such a difference between two branches! That is an extreme example of two absolutely opposite responses from pits which are side by side and is related to the differences in the leaderships.

It is like that all over the country with more progressive leaderships in some places than others. Woolley is an extreme, but not desperately unusual. Overall in Yorkshire there was support because the NUM wanted to see the kitchens continuing, but they didn't understand the development of the women or why we wanted to be autonomous, to develop ourselves and our own campaigns.

My own experience is that at panel level relations with the women's groups have been diabolical. But that is the Barnsley Panel and the problem is connected to the general political atmosphere, including the failure to include the women's groups in the decisions about how to distribute the Regional TUC money. The Panel failed to see the importance of what the women were doing. They wanted to dictate to the women, but the women didn't accept it and wanted to put in their own ideas. On various occasions we have asked for a meeting with the Panel. A lot of the women went down there and found the Panel hostile. Take just one example. The Barnsley Trades Council set up a public meeting and invited both an NUM official and the women's group to attend so that the Council could work out what more they could do in support and to build support within the area. The speech the official gave was appalling. He said that the NUM branches were themselves using the money to deal with hardships, as if the women were not doing that, and that it was wrong of the women to expect any more of them, or for any more money to come the women's way. In fact the NUM wasn't able to organise any kind of systematic back up for the families, because it didn't make that a priority. It was the women's groups which have taken that on.

We had a woman with a baby whose washing machine broke down. We took it away and one of the electricians repaired it: all these kinds of skills which the working class has and which it could use to alleviate hardship, the NUM just didn't consider organising. They have looked too much to the past strikes, of '72 and '74, and didn't work out the different political climate we are in today. Anyway, after he had made this speech I came in on behalf of the women's groups, and tried to be conciliatory. Many of the women felt I wasn't strong enough and came in to back me up in a much more aggressive way. I wanted to work out a way we could have some relation with the panel, so the next time I came into contact with this official I finally managed to pin him down, after virtually running round the room after him, and got him to listen to me. I explained to him that we were talking about a section of the working class that had been deprived of taking any action, of thinking for themselves, and that although the Panel's job was not an easy one, how much harder it was for the women who were trying to develop themselves from virtually nothing. I suggested that they invite some women to come down to the Panel meeting to try to find some understanding, between the Barnsley women and the Barnsley Panel. He suggested that I write to him and that *I* went down. 'I'm not having any of these women who fly off the handle coming down,' he said. So I took that back to the group, and it was agreed that we write and ask for a deputation to go (none of us goes anywhere alone) but we never got a reply.

The Panel kept a kitchen going, the one that the Panel had originally told the women to run; some of the women from there also came to the Barnsley women's group, and the NUM, through these women, asked the Barnsley's women's group to start financing that kitchen. We had enough problems trying to finance our own, and the women knew that the panel would still want to control it, even if the women supported it financially, so we were not too keen to comply. We finally decided that as soon as the panel replied to our letter asking for a meeting, then we would discuss it with them … So that was the Barnsley Panel.

The experience with the North Yorkshire Panel was similar. Where there was trouble between one women's group and another, it wasn't prepared to do anything to sort things out.

National march of women's support groups, Barnsley, 12 May 1984

The mines in Selby are relatively new, and mining communities just haven't built up there. You get twenty families in one village, another twenty in the next village and another little group miles away. There are five pits. One branch helped to set up a women's group in the immediate area of the pit. But when a women's group was set up in another village where all the men worked at the self-same pit, and asked for help, it wasn't given. They have even seen two women's groups setting up in the same village, and just sat and watched it happen. They have got a magnificent club at Kellingley, where the North Yorkshire Panel meets and has its offices, with a smashing dining room. There isn't another club like it in the whole of the country, but the women have had to struggle to get a foot in the door to use those facilities. Unfortunately, there has been a lot of sectarianism developing in North Yorkshire which the Panel has done nothing to alleviate. But these are only examples of difficult Panels. I think it must have been different in other places.

In Yorkshire, as far as I know, the Area did not discuss its relation with the women's groups, it was never even on the agenda. It has been seen as peripheral to the dispute. The only thing we had from them was a permit to collect, on behalf of the women's groups but sponsored by the NUM, in our own villages. And they weren't easy to get. You had to go to someone's big office and ask nicely. Each individual group had to go and ask, there was no attempt made to come to us and ask us who needed these letters, and to organise it like that. It just didn't occur to them.

The women's involvement, to the extent that it happened in this dispute, was certainly bigger than anything that happened before. The men have traditionally been in the role of leader, both in their industry and in the home. Yes, the leadership at national level has been saying how wonderful the women have been, and although they could have advised the Areas to liaise with the groups, it would have been entirely up to the Areas what they then did. Each Area has its own rule book and its own way of doing things.

As the different groups began emerging all over the country we built up a telephone network of women and groups in different places. Because there were so many groups we felt we needed to become organised nationally and to hold an event that the women could work around. Our first conference was held in Northern College, Barnsley. We had begun to think that we needed an office to organise from and we thought Sheffield, where the NUM has its national office, would be the best place, so we began looking there.

Then we heard that the NUM had made an office available in its Sheffield headquarters, and there would be some secretarial help too. The women thought that was great, an office of our own, and some resources. We could certainly use somewhere to organise our conference from! But the snags soon began to dawn on us. First of all, because of the 'security' problem, there would be limits on who could use it, and one of three women known to the NUM nationally would have to be there if it was going to be used by other women. Then there was no consultation at all about how it was going to be used, or the best way of liaising with the groups. Kath Slater, a smashing lass, was to provide the secretarial help: she was the wife of a miner who had offered her skills to the NUM for free during the dispute. But everything that was done through the office had to be verified by the three. So the offer of help – room, a secretary, and it seems, someone to look after the money for national events – seemed to have been set up by others who were party to some kind of discussion, but no discussions with the women's groups. Then we discovered that a women's rally had been called in London, for August. A conference at Northern College was set up to organise a national rally, but in fact it was all cut and dried before we got there. The week before I went to London and was given leaflets to take down with me, with all the details about the rally and how it was to be organised already printed.

The women in some of the groups were not thinking of a London rally. We thought we ought to be demonstrating in Nottinghamshire to show our support for the women there and to stand against the men who were going to work, to show what strength there was. But the decision had already been taken, somewhere, that we were going to demonstrate in London, because there was some feeling that the press only focuses on London demonstrations. Actually, there had been quite a bit of press interest in the women's organisation which was a new phenomenon and so full of energy. I think the press would have followed wherever we demonstrated.

Many of the women who went on that demonstration had never been on a demo before, and thought it was fantastic, and, indeed, there were an awful lot of women there. But in my opinion the point of a demonstration is to show the general public that something is going on, and in that respect it was disappointing. There were very few spectators. It was the longest march I have ever been on in London. It was sweltering hot; there were majorettes marching with us and dropping out because they fainted, and the children were tired out in the heat.

When the women decided to go picketing they didn't ask leave, they just said, 'We are going to have a picket at this place on this day,' and got on and did it. They weren't deterred by negative reactions of miners or the NUM. A lot of the men were saying, 'It's tough being on a picket line, and you will hear a lot of words that you haven't heard before,' (as if that were true!) 'and you won't be able to stand the pushing and shoving.' But as time has proven, the women have stood the test, and the men now accept that the women are going to be there. Certainly there were calls, like the one by Arthur at the Barnsley women's rally in May, to join the picket lines, but there was no attempt by the NUM to co-ordinate the women's picketing. Sometimes branches asked us to focus on a certain area at a certain time. In general the women organised their picketing separately from the men, apart from rare occasions when there was a big picket. Some of the NUM officials and rank and file miners were not very sure about the women on the picket lines: 'We are a bit nervous of you being there, this is our role, we are strong, and you won't be able to cope with it.' But many rank and file miners did accept that there is a role for women on the picket line, and they can do a job which the men cannot do. The women get a different reaction from the men who are going in to work than the men, who shout and bawl and have a good push. The women don't push but did peaceful things like sitting down and singing. The amount of poems and songs that have been written during the dispute, especially by women, is fantastic. And that has been a very different situation for the miners who are still going in to work to be faced with. The women's presence on the picket lines has been very significant in showing how unified the communities are in support of the dispute.

Many of the women were far from satisfied with the welcome we received from the NUM, feeling that we had been offered supportive words from public platforms, but no real consideration or say. The NUM, in fact, saw us as another weapon to be used as required. But because of the struggle that was going on and the need to be united, attempts were made to keep such criticisms within the groups. That was difficult with the women developing at such a pace and feeling cross about these things. Unless you had a developed political outlook which could put it into an overall perspective, it was not easy to keep quiet. Some women had close connections with NUM officials and structures through their husbands and would act as mouthpieces for them, expressing the 'Do this, do that' line of the NUM. At first, especially amongst women who were new to organising and to thinking things out for themselves, the women didn't see anything wrong with that and didn't see that the NUM wanted us to do things without being prepared to come and have consultations with us. They didn't understand the political arguments that I and one or two others were putting. But more and more they have started shouting louder and louder about wanting their own voice, and wanting their opinions listened to. Which is a huge step forward. You have to remember that the majority of these women didn't understand, or disagreed with because they didn't understand, Women's Liberation.

We had a lass from the Irish press come to interview us, and she asked if any of us were feminists. I said that I was, but I was the only one. Another woman said, 'I'm not, I'm not, we are equal in our household, he does what I tell him.' So such demands are quite something for those women. In fact, they are beginning to realise that Women's Liberation is not just about beating men down but about equality. The peace women did some marches round the coalfields, and that was quite an important moment. The mining women were a bit apprehensive about meeting them, but came out of it a lot surer of themselves. One of the important things about this movement has been that women have been able to sit down with other women and to discuss their problems in their own way and got a lot of relief from it. If your electricity is going to be cut off next week, and you know that so and so's was cut off last week it makes you feel better to know that there are two of you in the same boat – you are no longer isolated.

The women have certainly taken on the practice of the Women's Liberation Movement of organising themselves in whatever form was appropriate for the moment, with the women deciding for themselves what and where and how. Our group took a conscious decision right from the word go to be autonomous, and to do our own thing. There has been no question at all about the validity of the group being women only. It was natural. We did it without thinking about it, or without realising that it was important. We didn't see how we could play the role we wanted to play if we were under instructions from the NUM, and we have kept to that. If the majority of the group disagreed with what the NUM has tried to tell us what to do we objected to it and maintained our autonomy in that way.

I don't think the NUM in Yorkshire has understood the nature of the changes that are taking place amongst the women, and at this point they certainly don't see the need for the women's organisations to continue after the strike. Their attitude has changed and changed dramatically because they have accepted the role that the women have played in the dispute. But it is a case of how long it will take them to change sufficiently to understand the value of the work the women could do once the dispute is over. Some people think it would be valuable if the women had some input into the branches. In that way the women could take into the branches some of the issues of the mining villages and communities, issues which the NUM is supportive of, but which it does not campaign for directly; to broaden the NUM's interests from being solely about wages and conditions to being about the communities. Because what happens at that pit determines what happens in that village, and it affects everybody in that village, not just the miners.

The idea of a women's section is not new. It works quite well in other countries that I know about, particularly in Holland where members of mining families are in the union. There would have to be a lot of thinking about exactly who you would involve in those sections, and I think you would be talking about women who are members of mining families or perhaps involved in mining communities, because otherwise you would broaden it out for ever.

Whether there will be enough strength in the women's groups to demand such an institutional role in the NUM is another question. In Yorkshire we would have to see at least a part of the leadership's attitude change before the autonomous nature of the women's groups could be recognised. I cannot see at the moment that there would be enough understanding at grass roots level amongst the miners of the importance of the women having a permanent voice to pressurise their area council to take it on board, nor of helping the women to develop themselves. But in other parts of the country it will be different. If changes happen in Scotland they might filter through to here.

The other thing that the women are interested in is education. The NUM has schools for miners, weekend schools. In Yorkshire there are seven schools run for miners at Wortley Hall each year, and the women ought to have some involvement in them; there should also be a women's school. They are wanting to learn, and they have discovered that they need to pick up a lot of history, and how unions work and lots of other things. When I stood up in our group in Barnsley and said something about the TUC Congress, the women said, 'What's the TUC?' They are not afraid to say they don't know, and they realise it is because they have accepted a role of not knowing, of not being involved. It is important to get started now, whilst the enthusiasm and determination are there. If you let it go at this stage those women will be more frustrated, go back to square one and never learn anything. Many women are saying that the dispute has brought the women closer to their husbands, and that now they are able to discuss the dispute and politics with them. One lass who lives near the centre of Barnsley said that her husband had never discussed anything with her, and when subjects about mining, the union or anything political were brought up, he would say, 'Oh, you don't need to know about that.' But now, he will sit down with her and talk with her. I think it was because he himself did not know as much as he wanted to know and couldn't answer her questions. Maybe now there will be the opportunity for her to learn the answers for herself. And for them both to be able to learn together.

Of course, we expect the NUM to shy away from anything that is likely to be a problem, or will cause any friction. Owt for a quiet life. But somehow, I don't think the women are going to let that happen ...

(Written with the collaboration of Vicky Seddon)

Gwent

Dorothy Phillips

In the 1972 and 1974 strikes, it was Dorothy's
husband Bert who was very active. But in
1984-85, with Bert sick, it was Dorothy who
played a major role, while Bert stayed at home
taking the phone messages. She was active in the
Labour Party before the strike began, being the
secretary of the local women's section. She told
me when I met her that she should have been at
the reselection meeting the evening before, as
she is a member of the General Management
Committee. Her husband's illness prevented
her. A cetain N. Kinnock was reselected
unopposed. She became the secretary of the
women's support group in Newbridge, Gwent,
spending two days a week in the kitchen, and
was often away speaking at meetings. She writes
here about her local experiences of relations
with the NUM, but also of the strike.

My husband has worked for 46 years in the mines, and has just
retired. He was a lodge (branch) officer, the compensation
secretary, for 15 or 16 years, dealing with accidents and claims.
Over the years he has been more active in the Labour Party
than me; it is only since the children have grown up that I have
been involved in that way. Until then I was an ordinary
member, helping in a general way with organising functions
and at elections on polling day. It was my husband who was on
committees and things. It wasn't until my children grew up
that I started going to meetings and became more involved.

We were born and bred here in the valleys and my first son
was born here, but we lived in Maltby in Yorkshire for 13 years.
My two youngest sons were born there. Even as far back as that
we felt that the work wasn't here, that there were no
opportunities or prospects. But I was homesick. We had a lot
of good friends in Maltby, but I always wanted to come home.
I would go for so long, and then I would think, 'Oh, I would
love to go home.' Then I had a serious illness and I more or
less made a decision from that.

We weren't surprised when the strike began, because there
had been signs for a long time. Bert would come home and say
that they were stock-piling coal, and that in itself was a sign
that the NCB was planning something. And then because of his

lodge position we used to go to various functions like do's for retiring miners, and you would get people like Emlyn Williams there, so there would be discussions which all led up to the strike: that was the way things were pointing. Apart from that, we knew, or felt, that there were going to be pit closures, and that if that happened it would be a very big thing for us, because in the area we live in the job losses would be tremendous. There is nothing else here. Many times during the strike people said, 'What do you want your children to go down the pit for?' But there isn't anything else; there hasn't been and there isn't.

There are two collieries here, Celynen North and Celynen South. We knew that Celynen South was coming to the end of its life. It had been threatened with closure before and had been brought back to being a viable pit several times, once as recently as two or three years ago. It was talked about again just before the strike. Celynen North they closed by knocking through into Oakdale pit and calling it a complex. They closed the top at Celynen North and all the coal goes up at Oakdale, so there aren't any surface jobs at Celynen North any more. Some of the men have transferred to Oakdale. The same has happened at Markham, and it is a devious way of closing a pit without saying so, because those jobs gradually die away. I could see there were less jobs; we had young men knocking on the door because Bert was a lodge officer, asking for him to put in a good word for them. But they weren't allowed to employ anyone, so we knew then that we were going to have to fight for our very existence.

It was early on in the strike that the lodges called the women together. It was about the second week of the strike that the two lodges asked us to meet them and asked us to do some leafleting. We leafleted the village and went back the next day to collect. It meant we were going back and forward to the Institute (there is just one Miners' Institute, both lodges use it), which the miners were using as the strike centre. You went and picked up leaflets from the Institute, and took the food and money collected there. You would hear about various cases of hardship and you would go across and see them: old age pensioners who were having trouble with their coal, for example. Then the Gwent Food Fund was set up, quite early on in the strike, and that was a tremendous success. No one could have believed that it could have got off the ground in the way that it did; we were taken by surprise by that ourselves.

There was no need for picketing at the local pits early on, but the lads were going away picketing. At one meeting one of the girls whose husband was going away picketing a week at a time said, 'What if we make them pasties to take with them?' They used to do their own catering at the Institute, so there was a kitchen and we went in one Saturday morning and made pasties. And that was the start of the catering. It was a very strong thing in holding the women together, and there were very many bonuses, being in the Institute. The boys would come in off the picket line and you would hear them and their stories of what was happening with the police. We listened to those stories and didn't believe that it could be possible for these things to happen. We thought they were exaggerating. But we saw them coming in with their shirts ripped off their backs, so we went picketing ourselves to find out what was happening. I had the shock of my life.

We went to the Port Talbot steel works where they were bringing lorries of coal down. It was early on in the strike, and the first time there was only a token picket. The girls sat in the road and stopped the lorries and the police were well behaved. But the next time things had changed. There was a load of arrests and the stories that women from other support groups told us shocked us. It was also an eye-opener to see the performance in court. The police retaliated against women who refused to have their fingerprints taken (there were women there from Greenham, and they knew their rights) by opposing bail, wanting to keep the women on remand. It was criminalising people, humiliating them, using psychological tactics.

The women did a bit of picketing, but not very much. The lodges left such decisions to us. Some women came up against the 'We don't want women on the picket line' attitude from individual miners, but our lodges never took that attitude. If they thought there was going to be trouble they warned us. I remember the lodge secretary saying to my husband and me, 'We have been picketing many times,' (because they had been involved in '72 and '74) 'but it's a young man's game today.' So they sometimes warned us to be careful, but they never tried to stop us.

The kitchen developed for miners on strike. We wanted to include families, but we found that we didn't have the resources at first. The local Labour-controlled council was supportive; they provided cooked meals for school children, on Saturdays and during the holidays too, so we knew that all the school-age children were getting a cooked meal every day. The women had a little money, Social Security and their Child Benefit. They took away first £15 and then £16, as if the men were getting strike pay. The men felt it was a deliberate ploy to make them feel they were taking food out of the mouths of their wives and children. We thought that if we gave the men a meal it would take some of the burden off the women. They came back from the picket lines and the food would be there. There was a wonderful atmosphere, a fantastic feeling, and it became part of their lives and part of ours. At a later stage we found more support, and we did say women could come with under-school-age children, but we found they wouldn't come. I think there was a feeling of the 1920s attached to it, a bit of the soup kitchen stigma.

When we had scabs go back they were bringing in miners from other areas to picket. We were very much involved by being there in the Institute, and we heard about what was happening in other areas. Throughout the whole of the strike we knew what was happening, when it was happening, how it was happening.

Our lodge was very supportive. It had called us together at the beginning of the strike because they thought we could play a part and, of course, with you involved, you would bring along a friend and so it developed. But it wasn't the same throughout South Wales. If you talk to women at other lodges you will hear a different story. In one place they had a very hard time with their lodge at Christmas time about how the money which they had collected for parties for the children should be spent. The lodge was very aggressive towards them. Here they did not interfere with us, but if we wanted any help or advice we would ring the lodge. If I had a problem I would inform them so they were aware of what we were doing and we knew what was happening to them. Not every little thing, but basically, we were part and parcel of what was happening. Every notice that went up about marches and meetings, we would go and say to the lodge, 'Is there a bus going? Some of us would like to go.' If it was possible that was arranged for us. Or they would come and inform us, 'Something is going on in Sheffield, something is happening in London. Would you like to go?' So they encouraged us, they included us, they involved us.

The attitude of the lodge here was very progressive. In other areas they seem to have problems that we didn't come up against. There was a lot of variation in how well recognised and included the women were. Even here there was the odd male chauvinist, but they were few and far between. Our lodges were grateful to us for what we were doing. Amongst ordinary miners I think the response at first was a bit wary. They didn't know which way we were going to go. They could never envisage what is initially and basically a male domain, which mining is in this country, including women. That integration happened because of the kitchen. When they came in for their dinner they would sit down and talk amongst themselves; we would listen and express our views and they would listen to us. The circumstances have never arisen before where the women and the men could get together and discuss things in public. Women and men discussed things at home. I think the miners became aware during the strike that their wives were part of the mining industry, as well as themselves, and that what happened within the industry very much involved them.

In retrospect, I think we surprised ourselves with our organisation because it just developed so gradually and grew so big. I don't think that if we had stopped and looked at the picture, and seen the end product of it, that we would have believed that it could happen. It happened because there was a very strong feeling that we were fighting for our existence and the future of our families and our children. We had a government that couldn't care two hoots about the working class, and a Prime Minister who wanted to take us back to Victorian values, the good old days. They were good days – for a certain class of people. But we had fought our way out of that and there was no way they were going to take us back. Many women within the support groups couldn't express it, but before they had finished they were expressing it. To start with it was just a feeling. But by the time they were finished they knew what they wanted and what they were fighting for, and could tell you. I think everybody recognises the changes in the women.

If it had been our decision we wouldn't have gone back when they did. We realised that it was the scabs that were losing it for us and that there were reasons for a return, but the women would have gone on fighting. I haven't spoken to one woman who didn't tell me she cried on that day. I couldn't analyse my own feelings at the end of the strike, but now I am beginning to see things more clearly, in a less emotional way: we may have lost a battle but we haven't lost the war, because we gained such a lot, and we learnt such a lot. It is not finished, not by any means.

Before the dispute I would never get up in a meeting and have my say. But there was a local Labour Party meeting with an American speaking, and my husband and I went to hear him. The lodge chairman spoke about the dispute and asked me to have a few words. I felt terrible. You can only talk about what you know, if you have no experience of talking, so that is what I did. (Bert: 'That was the first time I had ever seen her speak, and she brought the house down!') From then on, the shoe was on the other foot, compared to the strikes in '72 and '74, with me going all over the country. They would ring me up from the NUM Gwent office in Crumlin and they would say, 'We want a woman, they want to hear the women's side of the strike, will you go here, will you go there?' They arranged for someone to drive me, and sometimes I stayed overnight. Sometimes I spoke at more than one meeting, sometimes I was there and back in one day: Exeter, Portsmouth …

I was very nervous at first, and amazed at people's reactions. I still don't know why people should want to hear me speaking. What really flattened me was when I was asked to speak at universities. I thought, 'Here I am, an ordinary working class housewife, speaking to children that have been educated to university level!' But they were interested and they listened! I thought I was going to get catcalls, but I only had one young man get up in a meeting and ask me a hostile question. It was at a Labour Party meeting in Weston Super Mare. He said he had uncles who were miners in Nottinghamshire and had there been a ballot it would have been different and they would have come out. I replied, 'If they were so loyal to the NUM, why are Nottinghamshire taking the NUM to court?' So he got up and as he went I said, 'Take my regards to your uncle in Nottinghamshire.' He didn't put me off.

It was the lodge that organised those speaking trips and made sure that women were invited: we didn't have to badger them. But there were some areas where I wouldn't like to say that the role women played was recognised. I came into contact with Terry Thomas, the South Wales vice-president, quite a lot when he came to speak in our area. We never found him anything but wonderfully supportive and always ready to help. He was always there if you invited him to a meeting.

The women's group still meets, but I am having to withdraw for personal reasons. I want to stand back and take a breathing space. When it was all finished I felt physically and mentally drained. Of course, we had realised for some weeks that that was the way it was developing, but it wasn't a gradual winding down, as it had been a gradual building up. It just went 'whump' and left you feeling drained. And I think that is a general feeling in the group.

When we went to the national women's conference there was a strong feeling that the women wanted to be accepted, not as part of the national union because they couldn't be that, but to carry on as a national mining women's movement and be associated with the union, nationally and locally. I don't think they wanted a part in the decision making or anything like that, but they wanted recognition. We were told that certain Areas of the NUM threw up their hands in horror when they first heard about it, and weren't prepared to look at the details of how or whether it could work. I have heard that one of the strongest votes against it was in South Wales. I knew it would be difficult, but there are avenues of possibilities that could have been looked at. But the thought of women actually being involved or actually part of the NUM was too much. Yet we *are* part of the NUM, we are *bound* to be part of the NUM. I think with the way things are developing that before very much longer, the NUM will want our support again – unless we have a change of government – and won't find it so forthcoming. Because the women will say, 'What's the point? You only want us for tea and biscuits.'

I hope the women's movement will continue, because that sense of togetherness we had at those conferences is an experience I cannot forget, and I don't think it should ever be lost. You felt that everyone of those women belonged, the bond was there, and they were all part of one big family. They wanted to be recognised and for the links with the NUM to be made. They would have carried on in their own way, working for the benefit of their communities. We didn't want to be part of their national conference, but to be part of some forum which included the men and where the links could have gone on.

The women's groups having their own autonomy has been resented in some areas. Even here we have been up against it, with arguments once or twice about the Gwent Food Fund, the kitchen where the money was best spent. The men tended to think the money should go into the central fund, but when we were out collecting we found that people supported us *because* we were running a kitchen and they weren't willing to give their money to go towards picketing: they stated that quite specifically. You found people who were prepared to contribute to their own area but not to a wider area. Although it looks as if the NUM nationally will not accept an association with the women, locally they have made a nice gesture: the women in our group have been made life members of the Institute. That is their thanks to us.

The government has tried to weaken the union by taking away the solidarity of the working class. The sooner people start realising they depend on each other the better, because we are not going to break the government until we do. They're always going to put wedges between us – that was their basic aim. But the miners have got to weld together, and I think they will be stronger for that welding. The women have, in some ways, been less tolerant than the men of the people who have not been so solid. At any rate the activists who have understood the implications of the dispute took that view because we can see the future of our children going down the drain. And that is what we are about, caring for our future: those children are our future.

(*Written with the collaboration of Vicky Seddon*)

Proletarian Patriarchs Beatrix Campbell and the Real Radicals

Beatrix Campbell is a journalist, writer and feminist thinker with the considerable reputation of being able to make complex ideas and concepts accessible to the woman in the street. In her latest book, *Wigan Pier Revisited*, she wrote about the lives of working class women, including women in mining areas. During the dispute she made contact with many mining women, joining them and their menfolk on the picket lines. She writes here of how she understands their new-found strength.

The Pain of Defeat

At the beginning of March 1985 a million tears were shed in the coal communities and among the viewers who watched in their homes the cameras' record of the return to work. Most people will never forget the breath-taking dignity of the miners and their communities as they returned to work, symbolised by the dawn march of the people of Mardy with their banners, bands and the village bells.

Perhaps it was at this moment that victory was snatched from the victor. Margaret Thatcher's hegemony dissolved if not before, then certainly at the moment when a Mardy miner wiped a tear from his eye, comforted by one of his comrades who threw his arm around him. She had not killed their spirit.

The following weekend, 10,000 women gathered in Chesterfield football stadium for their celebration of International Women's Day. The rally began with a triumphant parade around the pitch of the women's banners and ended with a speech from the man who, the women sang, walks on water – NUM President Arthur Scargill. This was a time for reflection. The end was already over, the miners were already back at work. This was a time fully to feel the pain of defeat and to celebrate the year-long resilience of the coal communities and their supporters, both to grieve and to affirm that year as the progressive movement's 'live aid' to its combatants.

But 'defeat' seems to have been erased from some socialists' vocabulary, displaced by a more convenient culprit: 'betrayal'. A pity. 10,000 grown women in Chesterfield football stadium could take it. And in any case, underneath all the rhetoric, the coal strike was never really so much a testament to triumph as to the will, the energy and imagination of extra-'ordinary' people who refused to be victims in the drought of British politics and themselves became the makers of history.

Failure to calculate the odds stacked in opposition, and the losses, also leads to failure to affirm the truth of the life-enhancing gains. They needed to hear some recognition of why the women were special; how their movement stood in relation to Women's Liberation and the men's movement which had hijacked the labour movement. Arthur Scargill thanked the women; he said the union would commemorate their contribution with a plaque in the lobby of the union's new headquarters. But he did not endorse the women's movement as such, or that dynamic sexual revolution.

A Proletarian Patriarchy

The women had had to fight to put themselves on the agenda of a union which has historically exiled them. Their voice, wrote historian Robin Page Arnot in *The Miners: Years of Struggle*, published in 1950, had been a 'dirge' which had fallen on deaf ears. They were the dispossessed of their community. But not this time.

A measure of how far they have travelled is revealed by the attitudes of some pickets who in the early weeks of the strike were making forays into Nottinghamshire (as it happened, against the better judgement of some of their national leaders). No, they said, they'd not discussed it all with their wives, because it was *our* industry, *our* union, and *our* fight. They were wrong, and a year later that sexual sectarianism was under siege.

The chauvinism of those young miners provided a clue to something else, too, beyond residual patriarchy: a personal and political élitism which has been disastrous not only for the women but for the miners themselves.

The miners have a special place in the hearts of the British, from socialists to enlightened squires. They are often regarded as the essence of the working class, 'archetypal proletarians';

even decent folk on the right get sentimental when they talk about the miners and now their 'plucky' wives. But rather than the essence, it would be more accurate to say that mining communities demonstrate the effects of patriarchal dominance in the trade union movement. For the labour movement has been used by and for men to the almost total exclusion of women's interests; it is a movement effectively hijacked by the men's movement. As in the rest of the working class, that dominance has not gone unchallenged and never more so than during the 1970s when the socialist movement faced the challenge of the Women's Liberation Movement. That challenge could rescue it from being the representation of one sex and one race, and place the needs of poor women at the centre of socialism's renewal. Of course the new feminism established itself in the cities, for which it has never been forgiven. 'Middle class trendies' has seemed a sufficient slight to banish the new feminist socialism from the pale of working class communities whose politics are controlled by the men's movement.

The patriarchal proletarians have felt secure in their isolation, immunised from the incursions of the insurgent feminists – until now. And yet in the very moment of these working class women's self-assertion, there have been attempts to colonise their movement, to cauterise its challenge. 1984 was the year in which trendy cosmopolitan middle class feminism bit the dust and a real working class women's movement was born, sang the *Morning Star* at the beginning of 1985. Like the rally on International Women's Day, it celebrated the miners' wives and yet suppressed the full implications of their movement. There was certainly a contest over the meanings of the women's movement in the coal communities, with a strong thrust from elements of the left to use the coalfield women's movement *against* feminism, to recruit it for class fundamentalism as a longed-for exemplar of the class united. But the suggestion that the coalfield women's movement was about women 'standing by their men' falsifies the reality: it was more complex than that. In one coalfield at least, the women's support groups mobilised their own flying picket in answer to some Nottinghamshire women who were escorting their men through the picket lines. In both cases, the women were 'standing by their men'. 'Standing by your men' is not necessarily a recipe for progressive action.

Sure, the women were campaigning for men's jobs. But they were also struggling for their right to organise autonomously, generally using forms drawn not only from the trade union movement but from the culture of feminism, in order to have some say in the conduct of a strike which demanded their support and yet over which they had never been consulted. In the cauldron of Ollerton in Nottinghamshire, where some of the most ferocious picket line confrontations took place, I met many miners' wives, some of them active trade unionists themselves in the public sector or in hosiery or knitwear, who supported the strike even though their husbands by then did not, but who opposed the behaviour of the flying pickets and the refusal to hold a ballot. They found no avenue of expression within the Labour Party which was, in any case, a miners' party and was paralysed by the split within the Nottinghamshire NUM. There was nothing those women felt able to do to keep the party line open. So the position of women in the coalfields was not always of supporting their husbands: it was more complicated than that.

Whatever the limits on the movement's reach, Women Against Pit Closures was to the left fundamentalists, and to the miners, the more or less acceptable face of women's liberation, perhaps precisely because it was about *men*, not *women*: it was ostensibly about men's right to work. Here was a movement concerned with bringing the sexes together – something the men's movement had never sought to do. And here was a healthy heterosexual women's movement (heterosexual not in terms of its sexual orientation, but of its political objectives). Those socialists bewitched, bothered or bewildered by feminism could sleep soundly in their beds in the belief that in the coalfields, at least, the struggle had been heterosexualised. The women were with, or as it was more often put, *behind* their men. But that isn't the beginning and the end of the story. First of all the women had to fend off many men's opposition: they had to fight the men in order to support them. To participate at all the women had to create *their own* politics – they had nowhere else to go. They were demanding an end to their own exile. And in so far as this has been conceded, there is often a tone which infantilises women, which suggests that women are children who have finally come of age. What isn't admitted is that the men of the mining industry have finally been compelled to come of age, to join the twentieth century, and must now deal with the personal and institutional revolution which will finally bury proletarian patriarchy: that domination of the working class by men.

The implications of that patriarchal tradition, celebrated in the macho histories of the industry, extend beyond the dismissal of the interests of women as a sex: they define the industry's relationship to the working class in general and the political arena in particular. When those young miners thought there was no need to take their case to their wives, and thus to their own communities as a whole, they also failed to see the need to secure a mass base for their extraordinary objectives within the body politic. It was that egocentric insularity that proved to be their undoing, and which found an echo in that sectarianism on the left which didn't notice that the mass support for the strike never materialised. It has become conventional wisdom that the miners' strike shows that a single group of workers can no longer go it alone. What seems hard to understand, and even harder to say, was why anyone ever thought that such a thing was possible, and perhaps more important, what it was in the soul of the patriarchal proletarian that produced that myopia. That's why the movement of the women, and of the men's relationship to the women, historically and now, is a cultural revolution.

Wives' Real Lives

Among the many unforgettable achievements of the strike against pit closures was the nature of the women's challenge. They challenged the closures, the National Coal Board, the police and in so doing they also challenged the masculinisation of the industry and its culture. They also challenged the politics of industrial action, both on the right and within the traditions of the labour movement.

A 'normal' miner's wife's life is one of exclusion and isolation surrounded by a culture of solidarity and support which has been immortalised in the labour movement's iconography. But that solidarity rarely extended to the women of the coal communities. Those communities have consolidated their place in history as the archetypal working class communities, places where community still means something. But women have been exiles from the political networks which exist there. It is salutory to counterpose the mythology of the miners and their community with women's position in it, as this reveals a community with a hole in the middle.

Ollerton pit village is typical of many of the newer villages where modern pits have been sunk adjacent to rural communities, where miners and their households moved after their own pit villages became redundant during earlier bouts of closure. The Miners' Welfare Institute stands out as one of its few palatial premises. 'It is the centre of community life,' says Carol Turner, a Labour councillor who moved there from a neighbouring county when the pit closed. 'But women can't be full members. You're taken, you're somebody's wife, you belong to somebody. It's not a thinking woman's place.'

Her friend Norma Wilkinson is a shop steward in the National Union of Public Employees whose husband was one of the many Nottinghamshire miners who worked during the strike, although she herself supported the strike. 'Apart from clubs and pubs, there's nothing else here,' she says, 'the Welfare is the hub of the community. It caters well for the men. But there's nothing for the women and children. Once a year there's a trip, but the last carriage is loaded up with men and drink, so by the time you get there, they're all pissed and the women have to look after the kids, as usual. Yes, they're communities – for the men.'

Politics in pit villages has been concentrated around the miners and their interests. So, far from being models of community, pit villages are models of patriarchal rela-tionships, which are summed up in the cycles of Sunday. The morning is for NUM meetings, then they fall into the bar for a pint, home for Sunday dinner and sleep it off in front of the fire with the Sunday paper. And if they're Labour Party members, it's off to another meeting after tea.

Pauline Wilkinson is a single parent who works in the colliery canteen and is herself a member of the NUM, but she never goes to meetings because they're always on Sundays, when she's busy. That's when she does her housework (unlike her male fellow-members who have someone else to do it), spends time with her children and visits her mother. Sunday symbolises the separation between men and women. It's the day when women work and live out their relationships. It's when men play or make politics with other men.

Certainly, during the strike, many miners' Welfares opened up and the women often held their meetings there, too. But by Sunday lunch-time they'd usually evacuated, because they'd got meals to make. This separation isn't neutral, it's impact is apparent in the way the NUM has produced its politics and its abstention from the concerns of the community as a whole.

'Anyway, I don't suppose there'd be anything to do with me at the metings,' says Pauline Wilkinson. 'I keep asking the union officials what's happened to our equal pay claim, but they never seem to know.'

It would be wrong to suggest that the separation is complete. Pit communities are remarkable for their commitment to the industry and it is a commitment the women share for their own reasons. It is a commitment which is rarely consulted, however, in the politics of the coalfields. The strike, while it invoked the symbol of community, revealed that symbol's dissolution in mining communities. It had been dissolved by the historic defeat of the women: their progressive exclusion from the industry and its politics.

Despite their sense of defeat, which is strongly felt amongst the women, they have retained a knowledge that they, too, have a stake in the campaign for work. Since their own economic interests were rendered entirely dependent on the fortunes of their men, pit closures involving redundancies impoverished their lives. But even if there was a job at another pit, uprooting themselves was not easy: 'I cried every day for a month,' said Carol Turner of her move to Ollerton a dozen years ago when her husband was transferred from a closed pit in Derbyshire. It's not the same for the men: 'He insisted on going down to the Welfare to get to know the other men. And there was his work, where there were other men. So he was able to make friends. But there was nowhere for the women to go to. Everything revolves round the pit and the Welfare. We were so grateful to get a house and not to be out of work,' she recalls. 'But the NCB gave you a house and that was it. I kept looking at these drab places and thinking, "What have I got to be grateful for?" I used to put the kids in the pram to go to the shops just to hear somebody speak. But when I started saying these things ten years ago, miners thought I was terrible, saying all these things about the NCB! And if I didn't like mining communities, why live in one? Mining communities – oh yes, for the men!'

How did this barren state of affairs come about?

The Purges

The mining industry and its politics retain a resonance in the minds of many, not only socialists, because of the poignancy of workers struggling for what were often not only economic rights but the right to stay human, the right to stay alive in the face of the volatile geological forces ranged against them, but also the employers' historic refusal to protect the workers from that brutality. In that visceral fight for survival the miners had their community wrapped around them. Throughout the nineteenth century the history of the industry was also the history of the communities. Initially it was an industry which employed the community directly – men, women and children. However, that history was also a microcosm of the ways in which the labour market was subject to a social scrutiny obsessed not only with the conditions of death and degradation, but a social scrutiny which sexualised the drama of coalmining, which was preoccupied with the appropriate conditions of women's femininity. The feminisation of women was equated with the purge of women from hard physical labour underground. After the 'protective' expulsion of women from underground coalmining in the middle of the nineteenth century, there were sporadic campaigns to remove women from the pit top where they worked on coal preparation, breaking up the coal and separating it from other substances. As with the underground campaign, the movement against the 'pit brow lasses' was about the regulation of women, it was about the social definition of a feminine role.

The purge found considerable support among men in the coalfields and in the Miners' Federation, and reflected the labour movement's reaction against women's economic right to employment, expressed in the concept of the family wage. The family wage supported men's economic privilege by constructing men as the bread-winners, whose wage should suffice to maintain women and children in a relation of absolute economic dependence on a man. Despite the protective gloss put on the purge, Angela John points out in her classic study of the pit brow lasses that men's relationship to women was 'on the basis of sex solidarity rather than seeing them as part of the working class'. Men's sexual solidarity with other men, in other words, was at the expense of women, it was more potent than their class solidarity with working class women. The coal communities were, therefore, a classic case of working class men's defeat of women. This defeat, according to Marx, worked against the tendency within capitalism to enrol 'under the direct sway of capital, every member of the workman's family, without distinction of age or sex'. Although mining was an industry dependent on muscularity, and therefore perhaps atypical of Marx's theory, which was concerned with the impact of mechanisation and its tendency to dissolve the 'physical strength' defence mobilised against women and children, his suggestion that the 'equalising' tendency inherent in the capitalist labour market was 'wrecked on the habits and resistance of the male labourers' is pertinent. The campaign against the women didn't arise because women *couldn't* perform heavy physical work, but on the notion that they *shouldn't*.

The differentiation of women as a sex was apparently blurred in the work of the 'pit brow lasses'. They were strong and they wore trousers; they were, therefore, unwomaned in the eyes of respectable society. The women resisted their expulsion, particularly in Wigan, which remained one of the few areas where women still worked at the pit top when the industry was nationalised.

It was a time when mechanisation was changing the nature of their work: newly constructed coal washeries removed the hard physical labour of the pit brow, but that didn't halt the women's exclusion. Mechanisation represented a new moment in the process described in Marx's *Capital*, and always tends to excite struggle on two fronts – between capital and labour *and* between men and women – for control over the new labour process. On the one hand, mechanisation contained the conditions conducive to the employment of women, conditions which created 'a new economic foundation for a higher form of the family and of the relations between the sexes'. However, the resilience of patriarchy disrupted that process. After the Second World War, the struggle to sexualise labour was renewed. The introduction of mechanised washeries, far from being the occasion of women's re-emergence into the collieries, apparently freed of the perceived problem of hard labour, was the moment of their final exclusion. Where employers had failed for 100 years, the new National Coal Board and the National Union of Mineworkers succeeded. They signed an agreement in the early 1950s to get rid of the remaining women and to hand their jobs over to men. The women were finally thrown off the work at the top of the pit, and found themselves in a severely sex-segregated society and labour market. Even where the coal industry now offers work to women, the pay is always lower than the lowest male rate. The highest-paid women, canteen supervisors, earn well below the lowest-paid men. For some reason, their case for equal pay wasn't deemed a candidate for industrial action, and was still lost in pre-tribunal wrangles in 1985, many years after the women's claim was initiated.

This history of exclusion had more than economic implications for the women of the coal communities, for it shaped the coalfields' political institutions and their priorities. The women did not separate from the industry. Instead, they were corralled into unpaid domestic work for miners, and thus indirectly for their employers. 'Nearly every convenience which the nature of the miners' occupation demanded had to be furnished and maintained by the drudgery of the womenfolk,' wrote the miners' historian Robin Page Arnot. If they were not engaged in the hard labour of the pit brow, they were buried in the hard labour of the home. Most British coalfields did not enjoy the social provision of washing facilities for the men and their clothes – that work was the private responsibility of housewives labouring alone in impoverished cottages mostly without baths or hot running water. It was indeed drudgery. The drudgery was never only a private contract between miners and women, nor between miners and their employers. The degradation of the miners and their families remained in the twentieth century a cause for concern, the object of state scrutiny. From the beginning of the century, leaders of the Miners' Federation were alert to the benefits of socialisation of this washing work. From 1911 with the enactment of the Coal Mines Act which enabled the provision of pit-head baths providing the Miners' Federation secured a two-thirds majority in a pit-head ballot, the employers could have been called upon to extend the coal communities' social wage, and in so doing mitigate the labours of the women in the community. Pit-head baths were seen by sympathetic miners' leaders as a positive benefit for the women and the community as a whole. In the face of considerable resistance from many of the male members, miners' leaders recognised that mobilis- ation of the women would be the condition for successful campaigns for the social wage, in the shape of pit-head baths. It was a 'shame and a disgrace' said the miners' leader Robert Smillie, that women's lives should be 'one long day of slavery'.

Despite the 1911 legislation, most British collieries weren't cleaned up until after nationalisation, when the muck of the pit was at last to be left at the pit. How can we explain this? Why such lack of commitment to social provisions which would have transformed the quality of life for the women of the coalfields in particular and for the coalfield communities in general? Clearly, failure to give priority to the social wage can be explained as the characteristic economism of the British labour movement. But more needs to be said. That economism manifested itself in an industrial culture characterised by the historic defeat of women, both economically and politically. Furthermore, economistic politics expressed the priorities of a labour force which was masculinised, which was able to *assume* the private labours of women and women's domestic exile from the political institutions created by the miners in their own communities. If economism is the preoccupation with the individual wage, then it is also about the pursuit of men's wages, expressed in the concept of the family wage. But we also know that it is more than that: it attaches privilege to the individual wage against social concerns, ranging from disinterest in health and safety to control over investment in resources for the community as a whole: resources for children, for education, for pleasure and above all for women. The drudgery of the women was the result of employers' resistance to the notion that they had any responsibility for life outside the colliery gates, and of the men's reluctance to relinquish patriarchal privileges. They didn't have baths but they were the centre of their women's attention.

Women's demonstration, summer 1984

1984-85: Who Are the Conservatives?

What happened in the 1984-85 strike was that women placed themselves at the centre of the struggle for the economic survival of their communities. It wasn't the first time that their support was active. It had been energetically offered in previous strikes, and certainly in the organisation of collective kitchens. But the 1984-85 strike saw women transcending the political demarcations, the sexual division of labour. In the early weeks of the strike women from a few communities piled into buses to join demonstrations in reluctant coalfields precisely to offer opposition to working miners' mobilisation of women as a conservative force in the closures campaign. That gesture of solidarity challenged two things: firstly the assumption that women were the conservatives in the coalfields, and secondly it challenged the conditions which could produce conservatism – women's exclusion from the political processes which constructed a militant consciousness. If women were excluded from the campaigns which generated consciousness of the issues among miners, then they were left only with the consequences of their isolation – poverty. If the miners did not share their concerns with their women, then the capitalist media filled the vacuum. Failure by the men to extend their own solidarity to the women would starve them of an essential political resource, the support of their community. Their patriarchal politics produced conservative class consciousness.

It was the women's movement which challenged their conservatism, by generating the community alliance which was one of the most remarkable features of the strike. And it was their intervention which exposed the political vacuum in the community. They exposed its *absence* by creating its *presence*. The very existence of the women's movement, its insistence on the right to participate, represented more than something specific about this strike – it represented a break with the historic sexual division of labour which has characterised coalfield politics.

In most of what has been written about the strike there has been an understandable tendency to be euphoric about the achievements of the women. It has seemed churlish to write about the rearguard actions against the women's movement among miners, but on reflection, to suppress that side of the story involves a suppression of history. It infantilises the women by suggesting that they're plucky little women who have grown up and come out, who have simply shed their domesticated existence for a public one. That account of the women's intervention falsifies the scale of their achievements. Furthermore it cannot explain the transformation of men's relationship to women. For the story of the women's movement in the coalfield is also about men, it's the story of the men's relationship not only to women, but to their own masculinity and to politics in general.

This book is about the women's movement in the coalfield. But its impact deserves a parallel history of its impact on the men's movement in the coalfield. The women did not simply emerge in the spring out of their own chrysalis – they took on the men. While it is certainly true that some men either encouraged the women's action, or enjoyed it once it took off, there was also a concomitant movement of resistance to the women, which has been by no means dispersed. Few have theorised their opposition, but one of them is Barnsley's David McDevitt. During the strike as secretary of the Barnsley Panel, he found himself in the unprecedented position of having to negotiate with the women. He claimed in a television interview that 'The prime importance is winning the strike, not hunting for food. People feeding people is not going to win the strike. They're saying to us "you've got money," but branches have autonomy, branches determine policy and don't want to be *told*. It's difficult, I know, they do a lot of work. But food kitchens are wearing down the strike. But if we send lads out picketing and the women say there's food at two o'clock, the pickets will be worrying about coming home. Women keep ringing me up and saying "where's the money gone?" and I say, "We're the NUM and we don't have to account to *any* women's group." We're using the money to repair cars which we need for picketing.'

McDevitt's feeling expressed two areas of tension between men and women in the strike. Firstly, the branches found themselves being supported by women organising food for the strikers and their households, who were now a force with bargaining power. The branches had to negotiate with women – and that didn't come easy. Secondly, he expresses the different priorities held by the men and the women in many instances. Particularly around the Yorkshire/Nottinghamshire area, but elsewhere too, some women had misgivings about the effectiveness of the flying pickets in view of the vast resources expended on keeping the men mobile on the one hand, and different assessments of the utility of the flying pickets on the other. As the strike wore on it became ever clearer that the food and welfare work of many women's groups kept body and soul together, particularly for the winter when the leadership's *only* strategy was sticking in and hanging on, a strategy of stamina. Their work was seen to be indispensable to the strike's survival – just as their domestic work has always been what kept everyday life going.

McDevitt's objections were not limited, however, to the issues of the men's autonomy and non-accountability and the tactical priorities of the strike. Unusually, he theorised in a novel way the impact upon men of women's independence. 'Look at where the strike was militant and where the miners were backsliding,' he said. The militant coalfields were Kent, Yorkshire, Scotland and South Wales, areas which had never provided paid employment for women and thus women's economic independence. The conservative coalfields, in the West and East Midlands, were areas with a high level of women's participation in the waged work-force. The result was obvious, he concluded: where women were economically independent the men weren't militant. His argument is arresting and audacious.

But it founders on its own economic determinism. The North-East, for example, could be likened to the clutch of militant coalfields. It has been a desert for women's employment and a fortress of male chauvinism and craft chauvinist trade unionism. But it has tended to be politically conservative. Its transformation in recent years has been a function of incipient left rank-and-file organisation which encouraged the solidity of the strike in 1984-85. It was the growth of left politics in the area which shifted the coalfield towards radicalism. The radicalism of the left coalfields should more appropriately be ascribed to the culture of working class socialism. It is salutory to recall that the old, peripheral coalfields are also the centres of a working class socialist intelligentsia – Scotland and Wales stand out precisely because they have a political culture which is rooted in their sense of nationality and in socialist ideology which has been nurtured in local institutions. At the heart of the Scottish coalfield is the 'wee red belt' of Fife, with its own 'little Moscow' and at one time its Communist MP and Communist provost. Likewise in South Wales, the Communist Party formed the bedrock of political culture in the valleys. Not surprisingly, the Kent coalfield is populated by 'immigrants' from the militant coalfields who were purged after 1926. They tramped to their southern exile, bringing with them the militancy for which they had been expelled. Yorkshire's militancy, too, has its roots not in the economic conditions so much as political energy imported by Scots, and more recently by the ambience of the Socialist Republic of South Yorkshire. Indeed, the inventor of the term had himself migrated from a mining community in the North-East. South Yorkshire's municipal socialism was not born in the men's steelyards, but in the engineering industry, with its strong Communist tradition, and in the sphere held by Labour, municipal politics. Politics, in other words, rather than simply economics, helps to explain the radical colours of these coalfields.

Although there were not a few men who shared McDevitt's view about the provision of food, there were others for whom the women's solidarity and their *work* proved to be an indispensable political and emotional fulcrum. Bill Smith, for instance, secretary of the newly militant Whittle pit in Northumbria, said of the women's work during the strike: 'It's keeping the strike solid. The women have made my job a quarter of what it would have been. 62 per cent voted to come out, but the picketing has not been very strong, the men were not really motivated before, but with the women coming out like this so many more men are coming out. It's challenging men's attitudes – the majority of men think the dispute is something for the men. But the branch officials are more involved with the women than the local lads are, and we tell them that we couldn't do it without them. The women have reacted to this as if it was a disaster, which in a way it is.'

Collections and Kitchens

The contribution of the women's movement discloses the complex material and emotional economy of a strike, especially a long one. The strike demanded offensives on many fronts: the industrial offensive by the union, the organisation of daily life – by the women, and the gathering of political support beyond the coalfield communities. By far the most successful mobilisation of support took place through local food and money collections in work-places and in the streets. It was this very practical solidarity movement which bore witness to a substantial and committed grass roots feeling for the strike which was not matched at the national institutional level by the pillars of the labour movement, the Labour Party and the trade union movement. At a national level the labour movement was never so clearly exposed as being stuck, inert, incapable of moving.

'The very fact of the food collections has unified communities and brought them into action,' says Betty Heathfield. 'We've never looked on it as just a women's thing – it's very political and very meaningful. Miners' wives are organising things that have never been done before, we've learned how the community works, who we can tap for resources. Some women lobbied our council: they'd never been in the town hall before. Sometimes it feels very chaotic, but that's in its nature. You're organising people who have never been organised before and who haven't got an organisation to belong to. What's amazed me is the number of women who want to *belong.*'

What the movement revealed was that through the collection and provision of food, the women's groups made their way into the inner life of communities: women began to find each other, reached out of their isolation, found friends among neighbours they barely knew in their 'close knit' communities. They had to lay claim to community resources, buildings and money to which they'd had little or no access before; they consolidated networks they'd already developed to find out who was in need.

In some cases it was the spontaneous combustion of the women themselves. Dunscroft is near Doncaster, a spartan mining village. There a miner's wife in her thirties, Maureen Douglass, got together with some of her friends and neighbours early in the strike and organised a women's meeting – 70 turned up. Those who couldn't or didn't want to be too much involved in organising and picketing, agreed to help with baby-sitting so that the other women could. Many of these women enjoyed shared child-care for the first time.

In Aylesham, Kent, Kay Sutcliffe recalls that a small group of women got organised during the 1974 strike, based around a local club. They came together again in 1984, but in much greater numbers, to visit coalfields opposed to the strike. The men in Kent are very proud of the women's initiative. 'I'd go so far as to say that they've got more ingenuity and imagination than we have,' said a Kent NUM veteran.

In hard-pressed Derbyshire the women's network also had a long history. Betty Heathfield went to Skegness, a resort with a miners' holiday camp, every year for the union's weekend school. 'I used to get cheesed off because the miners had their school and we were traipsing about with the kids. But we started to sort things out, we had a creche so we could do what we wanted, and then we'd have a women's thing and the men would look after the kids. We never managed to keep our group going because we came from all over Derbyshire. But a lot developed from that, we were encouraged to be something for ourselves.'

Tony Benn's Chesterfield by-election galvanised women. A Labour Club opened, which provided a base, and Caroline Benn suggested the idea of a women's canvass – by women among women – which had already been tried in London. The women involved kept their nucleus together, mobilised during the overtime ban and went on to hold afternoon meetings in villages during the strike.

In nearby Mansfield a group was organised in the first week among women: dozens soon followed, organising food at premises loaned by NUPE, welfare work and picketing. They deliberately set up separately from the NUM to appeal to people not necessarily sympathetic to the strategy of the strike.

The scale of the women's work was formidable. Two typical examples: in Barnsley a four-ringed cooker provided daily meals for 400 people; in Tyne and Wear Eppleton Wives Support Group served 300 meals a day, four days a week for pickets, wives and families.

Collecting food became part of the politics of this strike. Food convoys were despatched into the coalfields from several cities, filled with thousands of small inputs of tins and durables, and large donations from regional trade unions. The very act of collecting had been made political by a police force which appeared to be desperately improvising devices to nail any *public* mobilisation of support for the miners. Throughout the country, collectors had their funds and food boxes confiscated under some eccentric interpretation of the charity and vagrancy laws. In one absurd case in Greenwich, four people regularly stationed themselves outside the Woolwich Sainsbury's store. After a failed attempt to arrest them for obstruction, they were arrested at the end of June under the vagrancy laws – for 'begging'. Only after donors jammed the police station with complaints was the food returned to the collectors, and a day later they were told there would be no charges after all.

In Nottingham public collection has suffered a bitter twist because of the political division in the county. Collectors were stationed at Mansfield market-place, but Mansfield District Council unanimously revoked their right. Thirty-eight Labour councillors, five Tories and three SDP members voted that only registered charities could collect in the street.

Many work-places split their collections between the men and women. Half went to the strike HQ and half to women's groups as a guarantee that the 'hard currency' of food went direct to where it was needed. Women lobbied some strike HQs, demanding a fairer distribution of resources. Whether conscious or not, this gesture also respected the autonomy of the women's groups, which prized political and economic independence not yet enjoyed by many of the individual women themselves.

'Another reason we wanted to do village meetings was to get women out of their houses,' says Betty Heathfield. 'If they came for food parcels it got them out of the house and helped them realise they weren't alone and that nobody could pay their bills. We've always known about the nature of women's position, but we'd not found anything strong enough to bind them together before. The women's movement never related to them. They never felt part of it because its a bit trendy or middle class. Now it means something to them, they think it is just women standing up for themselves. We have great discussions about changing relationships with the fellas.'

Part of that change was expressed in the bargaining power the women acquired through the organisations they'd created and the success of the food campaign. But bargain they still had to do. At first we went round strike centres and we asked for a corner of the welfare,' says Betty Heathfield. 'Some really looked down their noses at us. In our centres a lot of the lads were grounded [because they could no longer go picketing without the threat of further arrests], so we gave them orders – because we're the boss – and they'd mash the tea and take the orders.'

After the initial euphoria of the strike settled down, the allocation of resources became a source of historically familiar contention between men and women. 'When money got really tight, there was great stress and quarrelling with the NUM, it strained realtionships all round,' said one activist in Women Against Pit Closures.

In South Wales, where the strike committees quickly took on responsibility for food collection and distribution with the support of the women's groups in the valleys, the women found themselves at the centre of the struggle with the men. In some villages the women's support was carefully nurtured by men whose socialist politics had already alerted them to the importance of feminism. But these men weren't necessarily the majority, and there, too, there was conflict between men and women sometimes over the forms of distribution.

'We'd argue about food,' says one woman from the Rhondda. 'We started door-to-door collections after a few weeks and we stored it ourselves because normally it was going through the central office. We decided we'd have to get it out. They said, "You can't just do that," and I said, "You wanna bet?" They said, "We'll come and get that food." We were like Ali Baba and the forty thieves, we got on the phone to each other and got rid of the food.' In some of the lodges in the central coalfield they believed that women weren't capable of organising an alternative welfare system and they wouldn't relinquish responsibility for distribution to the women. 'They were the most macho men in the coalfield and they were so macho that they wouldn't relinquish responsibility to the women. They didn't like it that the women were two steps ahead of them and we knew what we were doing.'

Collections in kind became an important way of poor people contributing something, when often the better-resourced trade union movement was unable to deliver the one thing only it can deliver – industrial solidarity. Scottish miners received collections from some of the poorest and most oppressed people in Europe – the inhabitants of Belfast's Divis flats. Printers from London sent food convoys, and so too did Northern Ireland's cleaners and school-dinner ladies who had their own 'Fill a Bag, Feed a Family' campaign organised by Northern Ireland's redoubtable division of NUPE.

Throughout the coalfields it was usually women who set up welfare rights advice services, and this, together with their food campaign, formed the basis of what has become known as their alternative welfare state.

'It was under the control of the miners' wives,' says Ann Suddick from the North-East, 'although it was initially difficult to get the men to accept that we were part of the strike. We also decided that the first people we needed to tackle were the electricity board. Nobody was briefed properly on how to deal with the board. Things had to be reorganised, because the board wasn't budging – so we organised briefing sessions. We started a petition among low-income people for a moratorium on bills, because we suddenly realised what it was like for people living with no income. We managed to build links with other trade unionists where the NUM had failed.' Through the women's advisory committee of the Northern TUC they contacted members of the public sector union NALGO, whose members worked in the electricity board offices, and secured an agreement to get early warnings on people due to be cut off, so that some money could be found for them.

Craftsmen in the General and Municipal Workers' Union were contacted to try to defer cut-offs, as were members of the electricians' union, which at a national level was implacably opposed to the miners. 'So, we were breaking into the NUM's macho image, breaking down barriers. Mind you, others were created, because they'd failed to do things and resented us for doing them,' says Ann Suddick.

Relations With the Men

The first premiss of the movement, that it was a women's movement for men's jobs, could also intrude upon the women's relationship to each other.

When Area officials in South Wales insisted that safety men working alternate weekends be docked some of their pay as a contribution to the strike fund, the men and women affected were upset. Some men on the left opposed this decision because the safety men's pay was docked from any social security they were getting for their families. In fact they were no better off for working. 'We felt any payment should be voluntary,' said Brenda Halliwell, for a time the secretary of Oakdale women's group. 'We contacted other wives and they all disagreed with us. So we resigned. It was something done on the spur of the moment – things were so fiery anyway. On the whole, most felt we'd worked hard for the union.' So something which originated as a division among the men disrupted the alliance between the women. Some of the safety men's wives felt they should separate and have their own group, but this was also felt to create difficulties in their relationship with other support groups outside the coalfield. Once again, encouraged by the men, the women tried to reunite and function together in one group, despite the difficulties.

Well into the strike, winders' wives who hadn't joined the women's support group began to come to meetings. The women had felt unable to join because safety men were working, but Brenda Halliwell commented, 'We said it makes no difference, it's the help we need.' There were big debates about whether to allow safety men in to pump out water which was endangering the life of the pit. Brenda Halliwell was among those who supported safety cover. 'I was so upset because I didn't want anything to happen to the pit. The manager pleaded with the men to go in. So they did, pending a meeting. That was quite a day. God, just imagine what would have happened if they hadn't gone back – I'd have been stoned. It would have been the winders' fault if the pit was lost, 2,000 men would have lost their jobs, I'd have died.' So, the women were divided by the divergent interests of their men. The wives of scabs elsewhere were called scabs, too. Women's political positions were thus defined largely by their support for their men.

It was the issue of picketing which seemed to cause most differences between men and women. The Yorkshire Area was opposed to women picketing. So some of them just went ahead during the early weeks when flying pickets were being barred from Nottinghamshire by the police road-blocks. Any car carrying men was stopped. A small group of women drove through the county border and reckoned that 'if the men had any sense they'd get women to drive them – that's the only way they'll get into Nottinghamshire.' But the men didn't have any sense. Their prejudice about women became most animated over picketing and distribution of resources. They rebuffed the prospect of women's Trojan horse to get past the road-blocks: another instance of their self-destructive egoism.

The Oakdale women asked the lodge chairman if they could picket. They told visitors from Hackney's Greenham network that he said 'No'. 'He doesn't agree with women on the picket line. We can do anything else, not that. He said, "You've got enough to carry on with doing the work you've been doing." In any other strike, the women have always stayed at home. But we are not satisfied with that now.'

They also had strong views about the nature of picket lines. 'We could have *talked* to the working miners instead of the pickets. This mass picketing hasn't done anything except frighten people. At Celynen pit we heard that the men were going back. So the first thing there was a mass picket. But the men got in because there were more police than pickets. The union says there is nothing to be gained by women on the picket lines, because of the danger. Myself, I think it might work if they withdrew all the men,' says Brenda Halliwell. 'We have suggested it, but they think there's other things the women can do. It has been raised since, because women felt we should do it anyway, regardless. Others feel we should stick by the lodge's policy.'

In the Dulais Valley the women didn't go picketing until one of the men went back to work. 'So we picketed his pit,' says Margaret Donovan, 'and we had a community demonstration outside his house, with children too. We were all singing. It didn't stop him, but it probably detered others.'

In the North-East a strong network of women's support groups was built around the Easington colliery. During the strike they were invited to join a picket line by the men and turned up at dawn one morning outside the Philadelphia workshops. 'We were singing and dancing, doing the hokey-cokey across the road and we stopped everybody going in, including the manager,' says Anne Suddick. When it all seemed to be over one of the male pickets arrived and 'he said we'd done really well and could go home now. We said "bugger this," and so we had two lines across the road, still singing and dancing. But around the corner we saw the grim reality and realised there was trouble. There were lines of police surrounding about thirty people. Feeling very brave, I said we'd like to talk to these people, but the superintendent said "no way" because they'd had a lot of hassle from the men. So I decided to go back, so we'd not be caught alone.' They realised that the women at the gate were unaware of the situation, and that they'd been split up, and in no time there was a tussle. 'It was too late, women were on the ground and it was a fight. I ended up with my head under a police sergeant's arm.' It was frightening; the women found themselves in the middle of an ugly fight which brought out uncontrollable feelings of violence. 'It was a humiliating and degrading experience.'

It seems that most pickets found themselves in situations in which they were either totally corralled away from strike-breakers, unable to exercise their right to peaceful persuasion, or in 'bundles' for which they were completely unprepared. As the strike wore on, it seemed to many people, participants and observers alike, that the practice of picketing itself hit a crisis during the strike. Undoubtedly, the union was not prepared, and apparently never became prepared, for the police and their well-laid plans.

The images of picket line confrontations did not pass without comment. Many women drew the conclusion that what was happening was the presentation of macho men versus macho men. Some of the women trade unionists in Ollerton went down to see the fighting for themselves on the fateful night when one picket died. Their anger was fuelled by the feeling that the refusal to call a ballot was seen to be undemocratic. 'If they'd not carried on like this, the Nottinghamshire men would be out now,' said one woman, a shop steward in her own factory, who felt she would never call a strike in this way. 'If they'd called a ballot, I think it would have gone Arthur's way, actually. But now they won't be bullied.'

Carrying Greenham Home

To many women the inspiration for their feelings about direct action, indeed any kind of action, came from Greenham

Common. The Oakdale women explained to Hackney Greenham women with whom they established close links that things had changed for them because of the women's peace movement. One said, 'I think the Greenham ladies have got a lot to do with it.' When they came to London in July for a benefit for them organised by the Greenham groups, she said she'd shown her husband – 'a fantastic man' – a Greenham newsletter. 'But he just refused to read it.' Women's politics could go just so far.

The Gwent women told the Greenham women, 'We've all said would we see violence like at Orgreave if it was all women? Get the men out, and let us women in, and see what happens. On a picket line at Port Talbot, we turned four lorries away. We used persuasion – and asked them to respect the picket line. It was lovely.'

Inescapably, the sight of the picket lines echoes the sight of blockades at Greenham Common.

To many veterans of Greenham Common it looked like little or nothing had been learned by the trade union movement of the craft of direct action which has been refined by the peace movement, and with spectacular ingenuity by the women of Greenham Common. Without a doubt, the peace movement is the only movement in Britain which has developed sophisticated tactics for direct action and direct confrontations with the police and also the military, which have not resulted in riots. The territory of Greenham Common's US air base continued to be contested by the peace women, whose strategy was never simply to aggravate the police or the military in confrontations which damaged the women more than their antagonists. Far from being soft, the peace campaigners have taken seriously the art of confrontation. The irony of the strike is that the commitment to confrontation seems not to have been matched by a commitment to planning and self-protection.

Women and men who've joined picket lines at pits and depots have received none of the training in non-violent direct action which the peace movement demands to discover its members' fears and strengths, to discover the best way of coping with violence. Sit down, comes the advice. Hold on to each other. Step back, consider how you feel, how the land lies, how the balance of forces is matching up. Make sure you can see what's going on and that you can handle what's going on. Experience shows the unnerving futility of a big crowd lurching up to the gates, pushing and shoving with the police. Today they always win. The worst thing you can do is to stay on your feet: that way you can't see anything and you are at your most unstable.

Some men have instinctively resisted speculation on the sort of tactics the miners might borrow from Greenham Common. Some are mesmerised by the idea, but interject with the proviso: 'but would miners lie down, could they?' It's as if lying down is something inherently threatening to the virility of class warriors. Is this more important than the recognition that the infantry charging the cavalry from its trench simply leads to broken heads?

Mary White is a Labour Party member and a member of the network of Greenham support groups active in Hackney. 'What was to be grindingly familiar were the tactics of confrontation leading to violence,' she wrote in the *Chartist* early in 1985. 'Could it be that in the wake of the general revulsion felt over the deaths which have taken place that the time has come for new tactics, such as those employed so creatively and peacefully at Greenham Common? Is it possible, that in addition to making alliances with each other, the miners could bring themselves to learn from women?'

'We'll Never Go Back to What We Were'

One of the mistakes made during and after the strike has been to misread the women's role as typically feminine. Weren't the women acceptable to the men because their work was the collective housework of the coalfield communities? Sure, a sexual division of labour characterised the work of the men and women, and a cynic might view it as pickets = men the hunters, food kitchens = women the housewives. But that does not do justice to the challenge those kitchens represented. Women's work was brought out from the isolation of individual homes, conducted in the service of individual men, into public view. Modern housework is, by its nature, solitary and unrewarded. All women do it, whether or not they have other waged work. And they do it alone.

Furthermore, the fruits of their work are consumed in the

privacy of the home. Outside the big city culture which has enjoyed a massive expansion in 'eating out', there is no equivalent in small communities like pit villages. Public places, or rather public houses, are where men go to drink; they are not places where households go out to eat. The privatisation of eating goes hand in hand with the continuing domestication of women.

During the strike, however, the food campaign represented a necessary break with that private economy as an aspect of women's work collectivised. The campaign also provided the only equivalent available to the women of some social focus, their organisational equivalent to the NUM. Although the women's organisation existed in solidarity with the men's movement, it also necessarily existed in tension with it. For the women were no longer taking their insubordination lying down. The Women Against Pit Closures movement collectivised the work of women and in so doing, constituted the women as a *social* force, a force the NUM had to reckon with.

That was the public consequence, but there was a private dimension, too, in the hearts and minds of the protagonists themselves. Everywhere the women were saying, 'We'll never go back to what we were.' Whatever happens in the end, this expresses a political wish that was heard during the strike, but which had hitherto been silenced.

'I've never been involved in anything like this,' says Linda King, who worked with Ollerton women's group and its kitchen. 'I was fed up at home, with my husband at my feet getting me down. If I'd stayed at home we'd have fallen out. I should think, quite honestly, that if we hadn't done this the men would be back at work. I'd have dragged mine back. I'm not saying he'd have gone, though. Because you're still doing your housework and he's sitting moping about. We'd have been falling out, now I'm too involved. I'm never in. And now we go fund-raising, we've been adopted by Norwich and they come to us every week – I went there the other week and I felt like a celebrity. They treat you like you're somebody. Before, you'd just been an ordinary miner's wife who didn't go anywhere. Before, I'd only worked in my house, I felt like a cabbage. So, I'm making the most of this.'

Mansfield's Ida Hackett, a seasoned activist in the Communist Party and the peace movement, says, 'The women are really enjoying themselves. One lass said, "Ida, I had my first child, and a second, and I never went out. The bugger's not going to get me to stay in again! I've *lived* these last weeks." And people are saying, what'll we all do when this is over?' Already mid-way through the strike women were wondering what would happen when it was all over: their work for the strike was a legitimate route out. 'Women say they're never going back to being ordinary housewives like before. They're frightened there'll be nothing to do,' said Betty Heathfield.

A Cultural Revolution?

At the end of the strike the NCB immediately began to announce closures. In South Wales, despite many difficulties, women's groups have carried on meeting as they have throughout the coalfields and the women have become central to the community campaigns against closures.

'Women are the backbone, the active ones against closures,' says Margaret Donovan, 'because the men are back at work and they're too busy. We've realised through all this that women always were in the forefront of the campaigns, but when they're over, they've gone back home and it's been forgotten.'

'One of the worst things,' says an activist in South Wales, 'is hearing women saying "If we're needed again we'll be here." It's as if they've been used for a year and then cast aside. When in actual fact the campaign against closures is very pertinent to them, because if they close pits in the valleys, their villages will just become ghettos.'

When the Welsh Congress, built up during the strike to generate *national political* solidarity with the strike, held a conference several months after the strike was over there was a workshop on the community, mostly attended by women. 'And that's because women are realising that the community isn't that wonderful, and that women mustn't lose what we've gained during the strike,' says Alex Grey, a research adviser to the South Wales miners and the women. 'And what has been gained is that women now know their neighbours. It was a complete myth that they were a community, that they were in and out of each other's homes all the time. They weren't.

Women were completely isolated. Now they've discovered each other and that they actually like each other.' The strike itself took the women into another universe as they travelled up and down Britain collecting for the strike, particularly into the world of city socialism where women's economic and social room for manoeuvre seemed to them open-ended and where sexual and domestic mores gave them space to breathe.

It's that contact, much of it maintained in friendships after the strike, that nurtured a cultural revolution that for many women in the coalfields marks a watershed in their own expectations.

A novel mobility of men and women brought coalfields into contact with a cosmopolitan culture which is a challenge to racism and sexism. I recall travelling with some Yorkshire pickets into Nottinghamshire during the early weeks of the strike. The conversation in the car was punctuated by references to 'jungle bunnies' among the police. A cuddly term, but what did it mean? 'Blacks,' said one of the pickets. There wasn't a black police constable to be seen, but the obsession ran so deep that one of their folk devils merged with another.

'We've all changed. Some of us never went out *anywhere*,' says Brenda Halliwell from Oakdale. 'It's opened my eyes to a lot of things, nuclear power and Greenham Common. It was just a name to me, I never bothered till we met the Greenham Common women from Hackney who were supporting us. They never pushed it, they just answered our questions. And then we got to thinking, what's it like, we'd love to go and see it for ourselves. I admire them, they're brave women. I went and I'd like to go again. The women I met are marvellous.'

Do they know, these women from the coalfields, that the Greenham network thinks they're marvellous, too? Brave women.

Ask anyone in the coalfields about it, and as like as not they'll always say that the lasting changes in consciousness are those contacts beyond the boundaries of their own private world.

'It improved our social life 100 per cent,' says Margaret Donovan. 'A lot of us hadn't been outside Wales much – at first the thought of London. We didn't know what we were letting ourselves in for, going out of WALES! We met all sorts of people. What amazed us was the generosity of people much worse off than ourselves. The black people in Brixton – when we went to do street collections there, everyone we asked gave us something. And lesbians and gays – they were the source of one of our biggest contributions. That was a big turning point for us.'

Nor was the political trade all one way. For many activists on the left the strike created a space for solidarity which the Labour Party or their national unions, paralysed by their own inertia, evacuated. For many a sense of connection to the coalfields brought its own pleasures. For the lesbian and gay movement, it also brought its own challenges. It was Dai Donovan from South Wales who contacted the London gay community while he was posted in the capital. The lesbian and gay solidarity movement took off after the 1984 Gay Pride march, started collecting in gay pubs and clubs and put pressure on MPs. Hundreds of pounds were sent regularly to Nottinghamshire and to the Dulais Valley. 'But we got a lot of flak initially from gay men in some of the bars,' says one of the founders of Gays and Lesbians Support The Miners, Mark Ashton. 'They'd say, "What have the miners ever done for us?" And you could understand their point of view. But we were dispelling a lot of myths on both sides.'

When a convoy of about thirty lesbians and gay men went down to Wales for a social 'we felt probably more scared than they did, because this was the first time that gay couples had danced together in a miners' Welfare. And also we felt we were putting these people in a bit of a position, confronting something they hadn't dealt with and we didn't know how to do it best, should we be closeted or up front?' Mark recalls. 'Three miners came up to me and said, "Hey, are you queer then?" "Oh God, here it comes," I thought, so I replied, "No, actually, I'm gay." He asked "Do you shove shit?" to which I answered, "Sometimes, and sometimes people shove my shit." They were nervous but intrigued; it was the only way they could ask anything; it was very aggressive and very typical. But anyway, it shook them – and we ended up shaking each others' hands. In general though, the only men we met were with women and it was the women who were in touch with us.'

Around the Dulais Valley the women drive an orange mini-bus with a pink triangle on the doors and the message that the bus had been donated by lesbians and gays. In return for the gay solidarity shown during the strike, the women brought the bus to London to join the biggest ever Gay Pride march in 1985.

It has also been revealed that in the coalfields, as in British society as a whole, it is women who make those progressive connections and seek to keep them while it is men who remain the conservative sex.

'It's too difficult for the men,' says Mark Ashton, 'because they'd have to accept something that threatened them as men. We were confronting their own fears and instabilities about their sexuality. They were powerless, too, because they were depending on us, queers and dykes, to eat!' Margaret Donovan remembers the first contact producing 'a lot of giggles and nudges, but actually we had no trouble finding them accommodation. To come out here to the macho miners – it was tremendous! They gave us a van saying on the side of it that it had been donated by lesbians and gays, and it had the pink triangle, and that got a few comments at first, but then it was accepted.'

'Some of us in the women's group went down to London to stay with the lesbians,' says Margaret Donovan. 'I could never have visualised that happening before, and going to a gay disco. It was great. One of the best things that's come out of the strike is that we've kept up that contact. I think the men have had more difficulty. A lot of people said what nice boys the gays were, but the men were more defensive. It's the women who've been doing the exchange visits, and when the women went to London to see the lesbians, some didn't go. The men resented it and reacted against their wives hanging around with lesbians.' The connection with feminism has brought a challenge to the culture of respectability in the coalfields. 'You never knew who was married and who wasn't down in London,' says Brenda Halliwell. 'And if I'd had people coming to stay with me I'd be thinking I'd have to get the place decorated. But they don't. They seem to bother more about people than possessions. And they'd just give us the keys and let us have the run of their homes.'

The women's groups are finding in many places that they're just as busy with politics as they were during the strike. Now many are bringing women's politics to their own communities, for themselves and for their communities.

'We've discovered that infant mortality is twice as high in South Wales as it is nationally,' says Alex Grey. 'Women have discovered that their communities aren't that wonderful and are doing something about it.' 'We've continued meeting,' says Margaret Donovan 'and we're discussing all sorts of things. Some of us joined the demonstration against the Powell Bill on embryo experiments and we've affiliated to the National Abortion Campaign. We've never had discussions like this up here. We're trying to open our eyes to everything. We've had someone up to speak about abortion, for instance. And we go out together – I'd never have gone out for a night with the girls before. But it's great, we're so much more relaxed among women.'

Her women's group has taken over the production of the *Valleys' Star*, a bulletin brought out during the strike, 'and we're selling it at pit-heads.' For many of the women, there is terrific resentment at the way the strike was ended. 'It's because we were never consulted,' says one South Wales woman.

Life After the Strike

Earlier, I rejected the inference that Women Against Pit Closures, and the vocabulary of their solidarity – 'we're behind our men' – was the revitalisation of the stalwart working class family. I think that the movement represented no simple reunification of men and women, because it challenged women's role within the family, it challenged men's seizure of all the public, political space within the community, and it insisted on the autonomy of the women's own movement.

The irony is, of course, that the challenge was only possible because of its contradiction. It had presented the men with a dilemma: here was a women's movement in support of men's jobs *and* in support of women's political autonomy, however delicately that may have had to be negotiated. The latter was contingent on the former. Men's opposition was stymied because, after all, the women of the pit villages were fighting for men. But they had to fight against them in order to fight for them. It was an insubordinate movement.

The relationships of subordination and power have not been washed away in the euphoria of the strike; the dynamic of power remains. It was, however, manifestly challenged. The challenge nevertheless remains constrained by the political conditions in which the men and women operate. The women's ability to continue the challenge depends, as it did in the strike, on their own fragile political resources, and the men's willingness to co-operate.

'The women's movement in the coalfield operated with the men's permission. So far, women have caved in when the men withdrew that permission,' says one of the activists in South Wales. It is a measure of the ways in which the labour movement is affected by the cultural revolution that permission has not been withdrawn everywhere, and that the women have found not only each other in their own communities but a women's movement 'out there' to support their resilience.

The links between these profoundly and chauvinistically heterosexual communities and the lesbian and gay movement is a symbol of the cultural revolution born of the strike. Over the last ten or twenty years sexual politics has been forced onto the left's agenda, largely because of the pressure of Women's Liberation, which not only placed women's demands on the political stage, but challenged the heterosexism of class politics, both in its culture and in its consequences. Just as many socialists have romanticised the notion of community as the reservoir of working class continuities and culture, so the chauvinisms of coalfield communities have often been sentimentalised as these things and more, as a pristine working class culture spared the degradation of the inner cities. That has led the left to an uncritical embrace of the political poverty and prejudice in the community's backyard. The imperative to *produce* politics, and to challenge the status quo, has positively waned in the coalfields since the establishment and consolidation of the Labour Party, and certainly since the post-war reconstruction.

Labourism, besieged in the cities by feminism, black consciousness and sexual politics on the one hand and the corporate might of capital on the other, has slept soundly in its bed in the outposts of supposedly pure working class socialism. The defenders of Labourist chauvinisms have always been able to turn to these outposts, the cradle of the authentic working class, and mobilise them against the queers, the blacks, the 'middle class feminists' and the miscellany of modernisers. Not any more.

Ann Suddick from Durham believes these contacts are 'about the new socialism. This is the emergence of a new socialism. We've been working with lesbians and gays and black people. The Indians in the Midlands were powerful! It's the only way forward, this.'

In the North-East a petition to the European Parliament has been drawn up over the EEC's withdrawal of subsidy. 'It's a women's initiative, a women's coalfield petition. We took the initiative, we'll do the lobbying, because we can mobilise. Don't underestimate these women. The government did. The union did and they nearly got trampled on. Now every event has a creche. Yes, the men can wish they could have their wives back. But they can't. These are women who've never used creches before, and thought their kids wouldn't go. Now the kids know that if they're going with their mother to a conference they'll have a good time. We've made independent women, much to the horror of the independent man!' says Ann Suddick.

Already there is a new joke culture about life after the strike. One Kent miner said, half-joking, half-earnest, at a meeting, 'Please, Mr Chair, when this strike is over, can I have my wife back? Not this one, the one I had before.' Women expected the men to revert, and inspired though they are by their own efforts and ingenuity, many still feel that politics is no place for them. 'I'm still hoping to carry on after this,' says Linda King, 'but I'm not clever enough to get politically involved.' The quality of the women's involvement has not made the national world of politics any less alien.

But the future of this women's movement lies in its commitment to women and to changing the relationship between women and men. In decades to come, when we come to write and reflect upon the history of this strike as a watershed in working class politics, the real test of change to come will be whether this women's movement is allowed to survive – for the women themselves.

Index